KENSINGTON AND CHELSEA

1   *Beaufort House, Chelsea* (c. 1707). *Engraved by J. Kip, after L. Knyff*

WILLIAM GAUNT

KENSINGTON AND CHELSEA

B.T.Batsford Ltd

London & Sydney

By the same author:

The Pre-Raphaelite Tragedy, The Aesthetic Adventure and other works on art and artists

Books on topography include *London* (1961) and *Oxford* (1965), both published by Batsford

First published as separate volumes
Kensington 1958
Chelsea 1954, reprinted 1958

New and revised edition in one volume published 1975

Printed in Great Britain by
Richard Clay (The Chaucer Press) Limited Bungay Suffolk
for the publishers B.T.Batsford Ltd 4 Fitzhardinge Street
London W1H 0AH and 23 Cross Street,
Brookvale, NSW 2100, Australia

CONTENTS

CONTENTS

THE ILLUSTRATIONS

ACKNOWLEDGMENT

The author and publishers would like to thank the following for permission to reproduce photographs:

> Kensington Public Library, Pl. 17
> A. F. Kersting FRPS, Pls 2, 22, 23
> London Museum, Pl. 31
> Eric de Maré, Pls 7, 26, 27
> The National Gallery, Pl. 10
> The National Monuments Record, Pls 4, 6, 24
> The Victoria and Albert Museum, Pl. 20

Pl. 29 is reproduced by gracious permission of H.M. The Queen

Pls 1, 3, 11, 12, 15, 21, 25, 28 and 30 are from the publishers' collection

The map of the Royal Borough of Kensington and Chelsea and the drawing of the coat of arms are by Patrick Leeson

FOREWORD

This reissue in one volume of the author's books on Kensington and Chelsea calls for a brief prefatory note. They were first published separately by Messrs Batsford, *Chelsea* in 1954 and *Kensington* in 1958, but both have been out of print for some time. An interest in these historical surveys, coinciding with the lively present-day interest in the regions they describe, has since been often enough expressed to suggest that republication would be welcome. There was an added reason in the fact that since 1964, when London's government was reorganized, the two metropolitan boroughs have been united as The Royal Borough of Kensington and Chelsea.

From an administrative point of view there was an obvious advantage in the union of adjoining territories. In some respects the boundary was always ambiguous, the Brompton Ward of Kensington, for instance, forming part of the constituency of Chelsea for parliamentary purposes. But in spite of such a close geographical relation there is no mistaking the difference of ways in which the two regions have evolved. Each has acquired in the course of its history a strong individual tradition. They are rich in associations with the arts and sciences though these on the whole have been differently oriented.

Many famous men and women whose names are intimately linked with the regional histories have left their impress on local character and memory. Whistler and Walter Greaves among the painters 'belong' to Chelsea, just as Lord Leighton and the Victorian Academicians who were his neighbours 'belong' to Kensington. Institutions, buildings, street names, personal recollections, weave their distinctive patterns. Crosby Hall, moved to its present site in Chelsea, makes one think of Sir Thomas More, just as the Albert Memorial gives its reminder of the Prince Consort. The Botanic Garden in Chelsea is a fruit of Sir Hans Sloane's interest in botany as the Victoria and Albert Museum in South Kensington of Prince Albert's interest in design.

The historical chapters in the present volume are substantially as they originally appeared with such amendments as the later disappearance of old landmarks and the progress of redevelopment called for. Set side by side, they give a comparative view of two

Foreword

remarkable and distinct phases of town life and structure. A new last
chapter combines the account of change in both components of what
is now the single Royal Borough, inevitably noting the many ways in
which, as elsewhere, the familiar scene and the localised community
are eroded by the dominant and impersonal forces of the twentieth
century since the Second World War.

Some may be deplored as a progressive erasure of local character
but in the present mingling of intentions and plans the thread of
continuity is not altogether lost. The future of the Royal Borough
has its foundations in the past. The good of progress has to be set
against its destructive aspect. This it is the endeavour of the last
chapter to suggest. The number of studies of both Kensington and
Chelsea that have been produced in recent years are noted in a
revised bibliography.

W.G.
21 April 1974

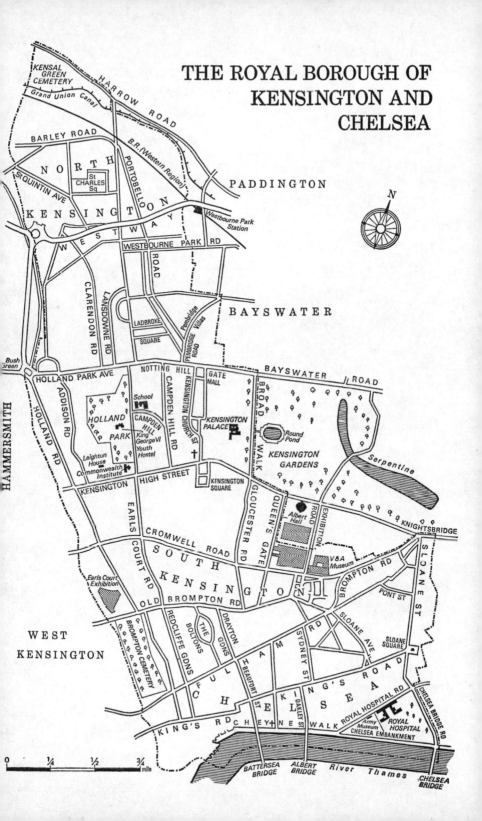

THE ROYAL BOROUGH OF KENSINGTON AND CHELSEA

KENSAL GREEN CEMETERY
Grand Union Canal
HARROW ROAD
BARLEY ROAD
B.R. (Western Region)
PORTOBELLO
NORTH
KENSINGTON
St QUINTIN AVE
St CHARLES Sq
PADDINGTON
WESTWAY
WESTBOURNE
ROAD
Westbourne Park Station
WESTBOURNE PARK RD
CLARENDON RD
LANSDOWNE RD
LADBROKE SQUARE
Pembridge Villas
PEMBRIDGE ROAD
BAYSWATER
N

Bush Green
HOLLAND PARK AVE
ADDISON RD
HOLLAND RD
HAMMERSMITH
HOLLAND PARK
School
CAMPDEN HILL
King George VI Youth Hostel
Leighton House
Commonwealth Institute
NOTTING HILL
CAMPDEN HILL RD
KENSINGTON CHURCH ST
GATE MALL
KENSINGTON PALACE
BAYSWATER ROAD
BROAD WALK
Round Pond
KENSINGTON GARDENS
Serpentine
KENSINGTON HIGH STREET
KENSINGTON SQUARE
GLOUCESTER RD
QUEEN'S GATE
Albert Hall
EXHIBITION ROAD
KNIGHTSBRIDGE
EARLS COURT RD
CROMWELL ROAD
SOUTH KENSINGTON
V&A Museum
BROMPTON RD
SLOANE ST
PONT ST
Earls Court Exhibition
OLD BROMPTON RD
REDCLIFFE GDNS
THE BOLTONS
DRAYTON GDNS
H BEAUFORT ST
FULHAM RD
SLOANE AVE
SLOANE SQUARE
SLOANE
WEST KENSINGTON
BROMPTON CEMETERY
C H E L S E A
SYDNEY ST
OAKLEY ST
ROYAL HOSPITAL RD
KING'S ROAD
CHELSEA BRIDGE RD
KING'S RD
CHEYNE WALK
Army Museum
ROYAL HOSPITAL
CHELSEA EMBANKMENT
BATTERSEA BRIDGE
ALBERT BRIDGE
River Thames
CHELSEA BRIDGE

0   ¼   ½   ¾ mile

BIBLIOGRAPHY

Books on Chelsea include; John Bowack, *The Antiquities of Middlesex*, 1706 (with reference to both Chelsea and Kensington); Thomas Faulkner, *An Historical and Topographical Description of Chelsea and Its Environs* (2nd ed. 1829); Alfred Beaver, *Memorials of Old Chelsea*, 1892, reprinted 1971; Reginald Blunt, *Handbook to Chelsea*, 1900; Randall Davies, *Chelsea Old Church* 1904; C. G. T. Dean, *The Royal Hospital, Chelsea*, 1950; Tom Pocock, *Chelsea Reach*, 1970; Thea Holme, *Chelsea*, 1972; Mary Cathcart Borer, *Two Villages, The Story of Chelsea and Kensington*, 1973. Architectural surveys are the four volumes in the L.C.C. Survey of London, *The Parish of Chelsea*, I and II; *The Old Church*, III; *The Royal Hospital*, IV; Nikolaus Pevsner, *London (excluding the City of Westminster)*, 1952, chapters on Chelsea and Kensington; B. Curle and P. Meara (Ed.) *An Historical Atlas of Kensington and Chelsea*. Incidental reference is made in the text to biographies, memoirs, diaries or letters of Chelsea's many historical personalities, this also applying to the celebrities referred to in the chapters on Kensington.

Books on Kensington include : Thomas Faulkner, *History of Kensington*, 1820; Leigh Hunt, *The Old Court Suburb*, 1855; W. J. Loftie, *Kensington, Picturesque and Historical*, 1888; R. Ridgway, *A Short History of Kensington and Past Notabilities of Kensington*, 1936; Earl of Ilchester, *The Home of the Hollands 1605–1820* and *Chronicles of Holland House 1820–1900*, 1937; T. Crofton Croker, *A Walk from London to Fulham*, 1860 (chapters on Knightsbridge to Brompton and Brompton to Little Chelsea); Florence M. Gladstone, *Notting Hill in Bygone Days*, 1924, new edition with added material by Ashley Barker, 1969. Architectural surveys are; The Royal Commission on Historical Monuments Vol. II, *West London*, 1925 (with detailed accounts of Kensington Palace and Holland House) and The Survey of London, Vol. XXXVII, *Northern Kensington*, 1973 (Ed. F. H. W. Sheppard, the first of three volumes to be devoted to Kensington); *Country Life*, articles by Mark Girouard on extant Victorian mansions in Kensington, 1971–2. Local historical papers issued by the Kensington and Chelsea Public Libraries include notes on Portobello Market, the Hippodrome Race-Course, Notting Hill and The Potteries, Notting Dale.

COAT OF ARMS OF THE ROYAL BOROUGH
OF KENSINGTON AND CHELSEA

'Royal Borough' the present appellation of Kensington and Chelsea was first assigned to Kensington. The distinction conferred by Royal Charter in 1901 carried out Queen Victoria's wish that Kensington, her birthplace, of which she had happy memories, should receive a special mark of her regard. The use of the royal title was made applicable by Letters Patent to the two united boroughs in 1964 and a new Coat of Arms marking their union was designed by Sir Anthony Wagner, Garter Principal King of Arms, heraldically symbolic of the history of both. 'A Broom Bush Flowered Proper' aptly stands for the fields of gorse or broom of the old 'Broom Town' (Brompton) linking the two regions. The Blue Boar of the De Vere family, once Lords of the Manor of Kensington is a Supporter balanced by the Winged Bull associated with St Luke, the Patron Saint of the ancient Parish of Chelsea. The three crowns of the Shield symbolise royal status. The Abbot's Mitre refers ambivalently to the old connection of Kensington with the Abbey of Abingdon and of Chelsea with the Abbey of Westminster. The Latin version of the 133rd Psalm, *'Quam Bonum in Unum Habitare'* provides an appropriate motto. 'What a good thing it is to dwell together in unity' is equally unexceptionable in a general and specifically local sense.

2   *The Royal Hospital, Chelsea: the South Front* (1691)

3 *Sir Thomas More's chapel in Chelsea Old Church*

I CHELSEA

CHAPTER ONE

Village and Manor

Of the many villages that London has absorbed, and to some extent preserved, within its extending framework, Chelsea is perhaps the most remarkable for strong local traditions and associations that have quite surprisingly outlasted or accompanied material change.

It has been so intimately linked with the lives of a number of famous people that one might say its story is theirs—the story of Sir Thomas More, Sir Hans Sloane, Thomas Carlyle, Dante Gabriel Rossetti, James McNeill Whistler. . . . The personal legend, in this comparatively self-contained 'village', has been more powerful than elsewhere in London; painters and writers who have lived in other districts here seem more distinctly and definitely at home. The great Turner, mysterious in his Queen Anne Street mansion, ceases to be remote when he comes to Chelsea: exists for us vividly as a character of the neighbourhood. To understand his celebrated seclusion in Cheyne Walk one needs only to visit the delightful cottage in which he lodged (very trim in these days with its well-cared-for brick and its prettily painted door): one can almost see him on the roof with its balcony, that commands such an excellent view of the river in its chromatic mist.

Or Rossetti—there was a man of many addresses, interesting always wherever he happened to be, yet more easily separable from Red Lion Square or Blackfriars than from Queens House, 16 Cheyne Walk, the stronghold of his mature years. Even the student of architecture will be compelled to think of the tenant as well as the architect of certain notable houses. It is true enough to say that the present No 24 Cheyne Row, built by Lord Cheyne in 1708, is a good specimen of the Queen Anne domestic style; yet it is intensely permeated by the personalities of its nineteenth-century occupants, Thomas and Jane Welsh Carlyle; and the pilgrim goes to the first floor drawing-room less to study a period interior than to stand where *The French*

Revolution was written and to experience whatever may linger of the mental atmosphere of an extraordinary household.

'Carlyle Studios', 'Rossetti Mansions'—Chelsea conserved its associations in several forms : a Chelsea chemist was known to advertise the 'Carlyle Bouquet', the description, 'though powerful, it is not heavy, for the odour is as refreshing as that brought by a summer breeze from a garden full of bloom', accompanied by a wood-engraving of the great man. Tradition is persistent in other ways. Variants on its late seventeenth- and early eighteenth-century architecture, though not exclusive to Chelsea, are so much in evidence there as almost to constitute a local revival. 'Chelsea Arts'—the words go naturally together, and applied to modern institutions continually remind us how it has been a resort of artists in general. 'Chelsea' figurines are still made by artist-craftsmen though the original porcelain manufactory ceased to operate in Lawrence Street about the year 1768. The Chelsea Flower Show perpetuates the historic celebrity of its gardens, already established in the days of Evelyn and Pepys.

The search for the historical origins of this well-defined place-personality need go no further back than the sixteenth century, though one may dubiously and briefly refer to speculations as to its ancient existence and name. The historian of London, Maitland, argued that Chelsea was the point at which Julius Caesar forded the Thames in pursuit of the retreating Britons. Greatly to his satisfaction Maitland discovered a ford, in the year 1738, 'about ninety feet west of the south-west angle of Chelsea College Gardens', which at least suggests that the theory was tenable. The name indicates a settlement of Anglo-Saxons, though in its numerous early spellings it is one of the mysterious grotesques of etymology—Chelchaya, Cealchyde, Cealchythe, Cealchyll, Cercehede. . . . . What are we to make of its 30 different spellings? Possibly it was a 'Chesil-sey', or shelf of sand by the water, to be compared with the Chesil Bank outside Weymouth Harbour or Selsey on the Sussex Coast : kindred with its neighbour across the Thames, Battersea—Peters-ey or Patricks-ey, piece of land near water belonging to the Abbey of St Peter at Westminster. On the other hand, the persistent 'd' or 'th' of the termination, may signify 'hythe' or wharf as in the reference to a synod at 'Cealchythe' in the Anglo-Saxon Chronicle, A.D. 785. Assuming (which is not beyond all doubt) that Cealchythe was Chelsea, it may well have been a 'chalk wharf', not because it is a district of chalk but because chalk may have been landed there—and was certainly a material used in the older parts of the old church. But for all practical purposes it seems enough to remark that the simplified form, Chelsey, was in use in Tudor times and that Dean Swift, referring to his sojourn in 'Church Lane', already spells Chelsea in the modern way.

In the roughly triangular figure of the metropolitan borough that Chelsea became in 1900, with its base on the Thames, between Chelsea Bridge and the industrial terminus of Lots Road, its apex at Knightsbridge, the ancient manorial plan can be discerned. Towards the western end of the river frontage was the village nucleus of small houses clustering near the church. Tributary streams bounded it on either side. A creek flowing from Wormwood Scrubbs into the Thames defined its western corner. To the east the meanderings of the West Bourne can be traced in the boundary that zigzags its way through the streets on the eastern side of Sloane Street. The opposite and more regular side of the triangle follows the course of the old road to the next riverside village of Fulham. Fields, park and common land filled in the area into which London in the nineteenth century was to pour its buildings and increasing population. As a pleasant rural spot, not too far from London by road or river, Chelsea emerges from obscurity with the advent of Sir Thomas More who built his house there about the year 1520 and became the first of the famous residents whose affection for it may be called a creative influence on its history.

Sir Thomas More was not a country gentleman or lord of the manor in any except a cultural sense (though sharing the manorial privilege of a chapel in Chelsea Church) but the prototype of the Londoner seeking retreat. Born in Milk Street, sent to school at St Anthony's, Threadneedle Street, trained in the law in the Inns of Court, drawn somewhat reluctantly into a political career, he had, save for his years at Oxford and until middle-age, spent most of his life in the city. When he came to Chelsea he was a man of forty or a little more, Master of Requests and high in favour with King Henry VIII, the friend of the great scholars of his time and author of that classic, sociological romance, *Utopia*, precursor of many ideal 'nowheres'.

Utopia, it has been acutely remarked 'was but the author's home writ large' (Maurice Adams). There was a delightful view across the river of the woods and pastures on the Surrey side. Waterfowl flew among the reeds and where now the chimneys of industrial undertakings smoke. The pure waters of the Thames teemed with fish: salmon, trout, pike, carp, roach, dace, perch, chub, barbel, eels, lampreys, flounders, gudgeon. No doubt they fished then, opposite the church, in six or seven feet of water (as Thomas Faulkner, historian of Chelsea, was later to advise). The peace and quiet of the country enfolded the area of what is now the King's Road, to which the gardens of More's house extended.

For several reasons his life in these Utopian surroundings remains curiously vivid. His own personality so distinct, though subtle enough to be inconsistent and in some respects, to the modern mind, puzzling, moved those who knew him to make the intimate records that have been often quoted. Holbein has made him and his domestic circle in the Chelsea house visible to us. Finally, his execution throws its own lurid gleam on the idyllic retirement he stoically gave up. Nothing remains of Tudor Chelsea save a few mellow fragments of brick wall. We must in imagination reconstruct the house that Erasmus described, at second hand, as 'not mean nor invidiously grand but comfortable' and the Jesuit, Ellis Heywood (in estate-agent terms) as a 'beautiful and commodious residence'. Imagination is supported by the excellent view of Beaufort House drawn by Leonard Knyff and engraved by Kip, dated 1699. It is now generally accepted that Beaufort House stood on the site of More's, Kip's print representing the mansion as rebuilt by Sir Robert Cecil, afterwards Lord Salisbury, who took possession in 1597.

The original house, then, stood where Beaufort Street was later built: and set back some distance from the river: being approached by two garden courts, the inner guarded by two gate-houses. It is to be assumed they had flat roofs from which More enjoyed the view. One of them was the scene of his adventure with a lunatic who threatened to throw him over and was baffled by More who threw a little dog to the ground and persuaded the lunatic to go down after it, meanwhile bolting the door and calling for help. At the tree-lined river-front was a quay where More's barge waited to take him to the offices of state business at Westminster. Behind the house stretched the gardens where the guests, as Heywood relates, surveyed 'almost all the noble city of London' from a green hillock and admired the 'lovely flowers and sprays of fruit trees, admirably placed and interwoven'—less formal in arrangement, the description suggests, than in 1699.

Two plans, found by Walter H. Godfrey in the Salisbury archives, and described in the L.C.C. Survey of London, *Chelsea* (Part II) seem to represent the original ground and first floor before the rebuilding: from which we visualise the Tudor porch flanked by projecting bays, and note the little chapel with a room above, having an open floor so that those in it could share in the service. The inner stair near it led to a door opening on a long eastern terrace, appearing also in Kip's view but probably built by More.

It was on this property that he spent some fourteen years, until his attainder in 1535: returning home with relief, from the public life that led him to the uncomfortable eminence of Lord Chancellor. All chroniclers agree that the Chelsea household, depicted from the life by Holbein in a celebrated drawing, was a happy one. We see Sir Thomas with his father, Sir John More, at left, Alice, his second wife, with a pet monkey beside her, in front of her, Margaret Roper and Cecily Heron, his eldest and youngest daughters, to his right, the second daughter, Elizabeth Dancy, behind him, his son John and his wife Anne Cresacre. There were eleven grandchildren and a poor relation, Margaret Giggs, also living under his benevolent eye.

Erasmus, practised eulogist, found this family circle perfect. 'There is not a man living,' he said of his friend, 'so affectionate to his children as he' ... 'he loveth his old wife as well as if she was a young maid.' As to the daughters 'if you should hear them playing skilfully on various instruments of music or watch them poring over every kind of Latin or Greek author like little busy bees ... you would say that they were muses toying sweetly in the loveliest paths of Ionia. ...' The chronicle of More's son-in-law, William Roper (who lived in the house for many years as its head), subsequently amplified by More's grandson, Cresacre More, even more authentically pays tribute to the gentle conduct of this Utopia and the piety of Sir Thomas himself. We picture him withdrawn in quiet contemplation in the 'New Buildings' (chapel, library and gallery); or in the church (where his chapel survived the air raids of twentieth-century war) singing in the choir 'with a surplice on his back', and shocking the Duke of Norfolk on this account ('God's body, my Lord Chancellor, a parish clerk ...')

Utopias being perfectly disciplined are never free and More's régime was not without its severity. That he suffered none of his servants to play games; strictly segregated the sexes, so that the men and women lived on opposite sides of the house and seldom spoke to each other; and rigidly enforced every religious observance, allowing no absentees from domestic prayer; all this suggests the iron hand. He was charitable to the poor but not to dissenters; and if the story that he bound heretics to the 'Jesus Tree' in his Chelsea garden and had them mercilessly flogged is the invention of a protestant martyrology there is evidence enough of a strangely mingled strain in his character of merriment and sternness, kindliness and bigotry.

Even Erasmus became critical on this score and the slab (that still survives) with its epitaph composed by More to hang over his tomb in the church bears its dramatic witness. There is a gap at one point. The Latin reads 'FURIBUS AUTEM ET HOMICIDIS   MOLESTUS'. More described himself as the scourge of thieves, murderers—and, in the draft he showed to Erasmus, of (the missing word) 'heretics'. Erasmus, the humanist, protested against this declaration of intolerance. It is typical of More that he could make the declaration—and also, with a certain humour, defer to his more tolerant friend by leaving the significant blank, for posterity to read into it what they would.

More's last days at Chelsea are most vivid of all. He seems to have had a premonition that in the end his rigid principles would clash with Henry VIII's ruthless absence of principle. One can feel him wince on the day that Roper describes when the King walking in great good humour with More, in the Chelsea garden after dinner flung his arm affectionately round his neck. When Roper commented on this mark of favour, More gave his famous answer. 'I find his Grace my very good Lord indeed . . . Howbeit (sonne Roper) I may tell thee I have no cause to be prowde thereof. For yf my head would winne him a Castle in Fraunce (for then there was war between us) yt should not fayle to go.'

To resign the Lord Chancellorship, as he did in 1532 was to accept poverty and obscurity. He gave his barge, with its eight watermen, to his successor in office, Lord Audley : his 'fool' (he was mediaeval enough to keep one) to the Lord Mayor of London. He spoke of economies in housekeeping with gaiety—they would begin with Lincoln's Inn diet and if that proved too expensive, come down next year to Oxford fare. Yet even in humble retirement, he was forced to commit himself on the issue between Pope and King.

He goes to confession and to hear mass in the church one morning in 1535, determined not to take the 'Oath of Supremacy and Matrimony' for which purpose he has been summoned to Lambeth. Sadly he shuts the gate in the courtyard so that this time his children shall not see him off from the water's edge. The boat bears him away along Chelsea Reach, determined on the refusal for which he will shortly be beheaded. . . .

He was not, as he had wished, buried in Chelsea. His body, it is supposed, remained in the chapel of St Peter's-within-the-Tower; his head after being impaled on London Bridge was removed to the Roper vault in St Dunstan's, Canterbury. Yet he is still a presence, not only in national and political but in local history. He enables us to see Tudor Chelsea and in many respects is the prototype of later famous inhabitants. A lover of art, a collector of antiques and curiosities, the patron of Holbein who stayed with him, probably designed the Renaissance capitals in the More chapel (and may be called the first of Chelsea artists). Like Rossetti at No 16 Cheyne Walk, he had his private menagerie—some rare birds, an ape, a weasel, a ferret. In wit and humour More seems in advance of his time and was capable of witticisms that sometimes have an even Whistlerian ring. Quite worthy of that later Chelsea celebrity is Sir Thomas's answer to the Tower official who hoped he was not too uncomfortable, 'You can always turn me out of doors'.

The More connection with Chelsea was not quite at an end. After the confiscation of Sir Thomas's estate, poor Lady More, bewildered by what seemed to her the wanton foolishness of her late husband's behaviour and reduced to extreme poverty, was comforted to some extent by the grant of one of his smaller houses in Chelsea. William Roper is mentioned in 1543 as a freeholder of the manor. The King's affection for the district (and perhaps for the memory of More himself) was undiminished. He acquired the manor from Lord Sandys in exchange for Mottisfont Priory in Hampshire and built (1536–7) a new manor house, standing somewhat to the east of Oakley Street, on Cheyne Walk. Its appearance can scarcely be judged from the engraving in Faulkner's history (taken from an old 'roll') but its accommodation when it comprised the adjoining Winchester House is given in the deed of sale by the Parliamentary commissioners in 1653 as 'three cellars in the first [ground] floor, three halls, three parlours, three kitchens, two parlours, larders and nine other rooms with a large staircase, in the first story; three drawing rooms, seventeen chambers and four closets [in the second] with garrets over part of them, and summer rooms with a bedroom'. Gardens, orchards, stables and coach-house extended the property to five acres. Fragments of garden wall remain, Tudor brickwork is to be found in the lower course of the walls between Nos 19 and 26 Cheyne Walk : the Survey of London, *Chelsea* (Part 1) detected in their gardens an 'air' of the palace grounds.

Here Henry stayed at intervals and Princess Elizabeth was lodged as a girl, being subjected to the unpleasant advances of Lord Admiral Seymour, who was married to Queen Katherine soon after Henry's death. The unfortunate Lady Jane Grey lived in the Manor House : Anne of Cleves, Henry's fourth wife, died there in 1557 : Lord

Howard of Effingham, victor of the Spanish Armada, became its tenant in 1585 and was visited there by Queen Elizabeth. The interesting personal histories of these Tudor residents are not, however, so directly relevant to Chelsea as those of later lords of the manor, whose names have become a permanent part of its topography; Cheyne Walk, Cheyne Row ... they take us back to the year 1657 when Charles Cheyne purchased the manor and settled in Chelsea with his wife, Lady Jane, daughter of the Duke of Newcastle, who brought him a large fortune. She died in 1669 and Dr Adam Littleton, Rector of Chelsea, gave a funeral sermon paying tribute to her piety, fortitude during the Civil War, and good works. 'Of her charity to this place I question but one shall see in a short time some fair testimonies noted.' Cheyne Walk was so named in her honour. Her husband, who was made Viscount Newhaven and Lord Cheyne by Charles II in 1681, and married a second time—the widow of the Earl of Radnor—continued to take a great interest in Chelsea. On 20 June 1696, John Evelyn records, 'I made my Lord Cheyney a visit at Chelsea and saw those ingenious waterworks invented by Mr Winstanley wherein were some things very surprising and extraordinary.' (Winstanley, engineer and builder of the Eddystone Lighthouse, was noted for his 'mechanic tricks' so much to seventeenth-century taste.) Lord Cheyne's concern for the welfare of the parish appears in a letter to the rector (1698), 'The Church doth indeed want a gallery, even for ye inhabitants you have and I shall be ready to help you to more, if I could myselfe or gett others to build more houses. I would be glad to lett land for that purpose, and particularly put down a tavern and bowling-green, for your designs of better and more sober purposes ...' Lord Cheyne's will expressed the desire that his body should be laid by that of his first wife 'in the vault where there is a place prepared in the chancel of the parish church of Chelsea under the communion table'. He left his properties to his second wife and his son William: among the bequests to the latter being 'all my lands in Chelsea commonly called Blacklands' (the present Sloane Street area).

Sloane Street, Sloane Square, Hans Place ... another set of street names commemorates the most famous of the manor's later lords, Sir Hans Sloane, who bought it in 1712 from William, Lord Cheyne, second and last Viscount Newhaven. He was then fifty-two, a famous physician and naturalist, for many years Secretary of the Royal Society of which he became President, full of its spirit of scientific enquiry. In many respects he was a notable pioneer: a first advocate of a national health service for the poor and one of the early propagandists of vaccination. He was noted for his study of medicinal and exotic plants: a visit to Jamaica as physician to the Governor having produced a catalogue of Jamaican plants (1696) and a profusely illustrated account of his travels (1707). He had married the rich widow of a Jamaica planter, but acquired considerable wealth by his own professional efforts, devoting large sums to a collection of books, manuscripts, antiquities, curiosities, gems, minerals and botanical specimens which grew to surprising dimensions.

This temperate, wealthy, learned, able and genial man became in the long latter part of his life (he lived to be 93) the same sort of tutelary spirit in Chelsea that More had been. He came to own a large part of the parish, including Beaufort House that had once been More's (though this he pulled down). He transported his collection from Bloomsbury and among the illustrious visitors who went to Chelsea to see it were the Prince and Princess of Wales. Naturally, he took a great interest in the Botanic Garden, where he remains a distinguished presence in the statue by Rysbrack (erected during his lifetime).

Chelsea Place, in his later years when he was confined to a wheelchair and had long given up his duties as Royal Physician, was in effect a museum. Long tables in the three front rooms carried cases of precious stones. The gallery, 110 feet long, was lined with geological and insect specimens. There were rooms filled with books and volumes of dried plants: 'below stairs some rooms were filled with curious remains of antiquities from Egypt, Greece, Etruria, Rome, Britain and even America'.

'Sir Hans Sloane is dead,' wrote Horace Walpole in 1753, 'and has made me one of the trustees to his museum, which is to be offered for 20,000l. to the King, the Parliament, the Royal Academies of Petersburgh, Berlin, Paris and Madrid. He valued it at four score thousand: and so would anybody who loves hippopotamuses, sharks with one ear and spiders big as geese!' 'You may think,' he added, 'that those who think money the most valuable of all curiosities will not be purchasers.' Fortunately for the nation, the official view was more enlightened. The collection was bought by the Government (from the proceeds of a lottery) though the Chelsea house was not, as Sir Hans had wished, made its permanent home. Combined with the Harleian and Cottonian libraries it became the splendid nucleus of the British Museum.

In the manorial pattern of names, that of Cadogan comes next, Sir Hans Sloane having divided his Chelsea estate between his married daughters, Mrs Stanley and Elizabeth, Lady Cadogan, with a reversion to the Cadogan family. The building programme of the late eighteenth and nineteenth centuries divided the honour of nomenclature. The doctor's Christian name gave 'Hans Town'—the ancient 'Blacklands' —developed by Henry Holland, architect of the original Brighton Pavilion. The development began (1777) with Holland's house, 'The Pavilion', a project for the Brighton scheme, with Doric portico and in the grounds an arrangement of Gothic ruins for which Cardinal Wolsey's house at Esher provided material. It stood in 20 of the 100 acres Holland leased from the Earl of Cadogan but vanished in the wave of subsequent building. There are late Georgian houses still in Hans Place but Hans Town in late Victorian times was a memory erased by the affluence of Cadogan Square.

The centre of Chelsea individualism and personal memory was the Old Church, the parish church of St Luke until 1819 when the new St Luke's was built. It then became a Chapel of Ease and reverted to its original dedication, All Saints. This ancient foundation (mentioned in Papal letters of 1290 and 1299 as the Church of 'Thelchurche' and 'Chelchuthe') like the rest of Chelsea scarcely begins to exist for us, before the sixteenth century. Traces of mediaeval work, few enough, were further reduced by the air raid of 17 April 1941 which destroyed the greater part of the fabric, including that most homely and un-pretentious of landmarks, the seventeenth-century brick tower and the Lawrence Chapel, once the freehold of the lords of the manor. Fortunately the More Chapel survived almost intact, together with the famous Renaissance capitals, dated 1528, which it is almost certain (from the evidence of style as well as date) were designed by Holbein when staying with More. Rebuilt in 1958, the church approximates to the landmark of the past.

The monuments, clustered together in a small space, were to become the main ancient feature. There is the plain Gothic altar tomb (1532) of Sir Thomas More (restored by J. Faulkner, 'statuary' of Chelsea in 1833) with its celebrated inscription slab, and the appended epigrammatic lines in Latin verse in which his unconventional humour came out. Praising the devotion of his second wife to the children of his first wife, he scarcely knew which was dearer to him:

> O! Simul, O! Iuncti poteramus vivere nos tres
> Quam bene, si Fatum, Religioq Sinant
> At societ tumulus, societ nos obsecro coelum
> Sic Mors, non potuit quod dare, Vita, dabit.

'Ah! how well could we three have lived together, did fate and religion permit. But the tomb shall unite us, I pray, and Death give us what Life could not.'

More referred in his own epitaph to resigning the Lord Chancellorship. 'He therefore,' he wrote of himself, 'irked and weary of worldly business, giving up his promotions, attained at last by the incomparable benefit of his most gentle Prince (if it please God to favour his enterprise) that thing, which in a manner from a child he always wished and desired; that he might have some years of his life free, in which he, little and little withdrawing himself from the business of this life, might continually remember the immortality of the life to come.' It was the sentiment he put succinctly on the day when he went to his wife's pew in the church, after his retirement, and in parody of the phrase used, during his Chancellorship, by one of his gentlemen at the end of the service, himself announced 'Madam, my lord is gone'.

Other memorials tells us of various lords of the manor, of the inhabitants of More's house in its later form, and the division of his estates on which further mansions were built; some also meriting separate appraisal as interesting examples of sculpture and ornament in the late sixteenth- and seventeenth-century styles.

The tomb-chest of Sir Reginald Bray is that of the owner of the manor in the time of Henry VII. Sir Reginald, a statesman of some note, and an architect who perhaps designed the Henry VII chapel at Westminster, left a disputable will which resulted in the manor's passing, by agreement, not to his nephew Edmund, as he first planned, but to his niece Margery and so also to her husband, Sir William Sandys, later Baron Sandys, from whom King Henry VIII purchased the property.

The remains of the once magnificent monument (1555) to the Duchess of Northumberland, with Gothic niche and diapered shafts supporting a canopy, with a representation of fan tracery in the soffit, are a reminder of the later Tudor history of the manor. Edward VI granted it in 1553 to John Dudley, Duke of Northumberland, who was executed in the same year for his plot to put Lady Jane Grey and his son, Guildford, on the throne. The Duchess was allowed to stay on at the manor house until her death, two or three years later. A remaining brass shows the Duchess with her five daughters, of whom Mary became the mother of Sir Philip Sidney and Catherine, who married the Earl of Huntingdon, died and was buried in the church in 1620. The Richard Jervoise monument (1563), a free-standing arch with heavy strap-work ornament and fluting is, architecturally, an early example of the classic revival and, in human terms, brings us to another phase of the Chelsea family story. The elder Richard Jervoise, apparently a 'self-made' man of wealth, lived in the old manor-house after Henry VIII bought it from Lord Sandys. He married Winifred, daughter of a London mercer, John Barnard, whose son, James Barnard, married Ursula, Lord Sandy's daughter. The monument seems to have been erected by Winifred Jervoise on the death of her son, Richard. There are no Barnard monuments; but Ursula reappears with her second husband, Thomas Hungerford, in the tablet of alabaster and marble (1581) where Hungerford and his two sons face his wife and daughter in conventional kneeling posture.

A similar memorial is that of Thomas Lawrence (1598). The Lawrences, who gave their name to the Lawrence Chapel in the church and also to Lawrence Street, were a family whose obscure but not uninteresting history has been patiently examined by Randall Davies in his *Chelsea Old Church*. They acquired the old manor house between 1557 and 1587 and were great people in Chelsea for some 150 years until the death (1725) of Margaret, daughter of Sir Thomas Lawrence (appointed Secretary of Maryland, 1691, buried at Chelsea, 1714). The wall tablet with its kneeling figures commemorates Thomas Lawrence, goldsmith. The monument (dated 1631—it should be 1632) to his eldest daughter, Sarah, who married Richard Colvile of Newton in the Isle of Ely, is the most striking in the church. Shroud-clad, the alabaster half-length figure rises from a coffin of black marble. The combination of the physical and the ecstatic echoes in another medium the metaphysical poetry of the age and resembles that in certain other early seventeenth-century English funerary sculptures (like Nicholas Stone's John Donne in St Paul's).

The monument to Gregory, Lord Dacre (1594) and his wife, Anne (1595) draws attention to the fate of More's house. After his execution, it passed to William Pawlet, subsequently Marquis of Winchester, who died there in 1572. His son, John, married (a second time) Winifred, daughter of Sir John Burgess and widow of Sir Robert Sackville. Winifred's daughter, Anne Sackville, married Gregory, Lord Dacre, and obtained the Chelsea estates, to the annoyance of the third Marquis of Winchester, by a sharp piece of bargaining. (She contrived, according to a document found by Randall Davies among the State Papers, to buy the house and land for a fraction of their value.) The recumbent figures of their tomb, he in armour, she in ruff, mantle and bonnet, lie in a recess beneath a structure that is cumbrous and topheavy, with its 'pyramids of freckied marble', heraldic emblems and its crowning allegory of Time, Death and Judgment, but impressive in its Elizabethan ornateness.

The More estates later belonged to Sir Arthur Gorges. Lady Dacre left her Chelsea property to Lord Burleigh : from him it went to his son, Sir Robert Cecil, who rebuilt the house in 1597 but sold it, after two years, to Henry, Earl of Lincoln. Gorges, third son of Sir William Gorges, Vice-Admiral of the Fleet, and one of the Elizabethan seamen who volunteered for service against the Armada, married Lincoln's daughter and thus acquired the whole estate, including the More chapel and the satellite mansion perhaps already built by Lincoln, but known as Gorges House. In the church a brass (1625) shows him kneeling in prayer with his wife and family. Gorges House later became Milman House, after Sir William Milman, (commemorated by a tablet, 1713) who gave his name to Milman Street. Sir Arthur Gorge's daughter, Elizabeth, married Sir Robert Stanley, son of the sixth Earl of Derby. They occupied a house called Brickhills on the site of Stanley Grove, later residence of the Principal of St Mark's College.

Sir Robert Stanley provides the most grandiose of the church's monuments, splendid in its way, though the alabaster figures of Justice and Fortitude may have been an afterthought and a little confusing to the spacious composition. The central urn surmounted by the eagle of the Stanley crest is fine, so are the medallion busts of Sir Robert, and (on either side) his infant children, Ferdinando and Henrietta. The eagle motif comes into their epitaph :

> The Eagle Death greedie of some good prey
> With nimble Eyes found where these Infants laye
> He truste them in his Tallents and conveyde
> There Soles to Heaven & here theire ashes layde.

Matching in impressiveness the Dacre, Colvile and Stanley monuments is that (1672) of Charles Cheyne, Viscount Newhaven and his first wife, Lady Jane, who owned the manor after the Civil War, the lady's benefactions permitting the completion of the new church fabric and tower some years after her death in 1669. The monument was made in Rome, letters discovered by Randall Davies in the Bridgewater MS indicating that the architect was the great Bernini's son, Paolo and the sculptor of the reclining figure of the lady, Antonio Raggi, who worked from drawings sent him. The collaboration was not aesthetically perfect. The architectural frame tends to obscure the figure : the recess is too equally divided by sarcophagus and sculpture, but the result has suitable dignity.

The manorial record ends with the surviving monument in the churchyard (1753) to Sir Hans Sloane, erected by his two daughters, Eliza Cadogan and Sarah Stanley, and designed by Joseph Wilton (1722–1803), who was also responsible for the tablet in the church (1781) to Lucy Smith and Anne Wilton, apparently his daughters. We advance then from the period of close-knit relationships and family pomp to the simpler memorials of artist and writer, noting in particular the calligraphic tablet dedicated to William Frend De Morgan (1917):

ARTIST—POTTER—INVENTOR—NOVELIST
BORN 16TH NOVEMBER 1839   DIED 15TH JANUARY 1917

who did much of his best work in Cheyne Row, the Vale and Church Street, Chelsea—where he died.

Recreating in Ceramic work upon his own vigorous designs the colour of the Persian & the lustre of the great Umbrian craftsmen Enriching literature by his faithful & sympathetic presentment of homely and very homely character And beloved by all who knew his breadth of intellectual interest, his catholic sympathy, genial humour & lambent wit.

And the tablet (1916)

IN MEMORY OF
HENRY JAMES O : M :
NOVELIST
BORN IN NEW YORK 1843 : DIED IN
CHELSEA 1916 : LOVER AND INTER-
PRETER OF THE FINE AMENITIES
OF BRAVE DECISIONS & GENEROUS
LOYALTIES : A RESIDENT OF THIS
PARISH WHO RENOUNCED A
CHERISHED CITIZENSHIP TO GIVE
HIS ALLEGIANCE TO ENGLAND IN
THE 1ST YEAR OF THE GREAT WAR

In his Chelsea novel, *The Hillyars and the Burtons*, Henry Kingsley, who spent his childhood in the rectory, fittingly describes the church

Village and Manor

as a combination of historic personalities. ' "Four hundred years of memory," says Joe Burton, "are crowded into that old church, and the great flood of change beats round the walls, and shakes the door in vain but never enters. The dead stand thick together there, as if to make a brave resistance to the moving world outside, which jars upon their slumber. It is a church of the dead." '

31

CHAPTER TWO

Town of Palaces

Writers on Chelsea have had a fondness for the title 'Village of Palaces', though 'Town of Palaces' was the phrase originally coined by Defoe in his *Tour through England and Wales* (1724–6) in which he reflected on the narrowing space between Chelsea and London. 'A town of palaces, and which by its new extended buildings seems to promise itself to be made one time or other a part of London, I mean London in its new extended capacity, which if it should happen what a monster must London be, extending (to take it in a line) from the farther end of Chelsea, west, to Deptford Bridge east, which I venture to say, is at least eleven miles.'

In his time its popularity among the great and wealthy was assured and increasing. It had received Stuart no less than Tudor approval. Charles II favoured it as Henry VIII had done. He swam gaily in the Thames 'over against Chelsea', careless of the Irish adventurer, Colonel Blood, who lurked with a gun in the reeds on the Battersea side, waiting to take a shot at him. According to tradition he visited Nell Gwynn at Sandford Manor just over the Fulham border. This seventeenth-century manor house, long decaying, still survives as a possible part of modern projects for development. A rough track across the fields was converted into the King's private road—it officially became the King's Road in 1713. The court followed him; so fashionable was Chelsea that it was known as 'Hyde Park on Thames': and this fashionable phase lasted well into the eighteenth century. The series of great houses gave Chelsea a distinguished profile. Greatest of them was that which had been More's, Beaufort House, where Beaufort Street now is. Its 'Kitchen yard or garden' on the west extended to the backyard and buildings of Gorges House (the clustered Elizabethan gables of which can be seen in Kip's engraving). Adjoining, on the west, the forecourt of Beaufort House, was Lindsey

4   *Crosby Hall (built c. 1470: moved to Chelsea, 1910)*

5 *The Physic Garden, Chelsea*

House, the one seventeenth-century mansion that has survived until the present day. Originally More's principal farmhouse, rebuilt, according to Chelsea's earliest historian, Bowack (1705), by Sir Theodore Mayerne, physician to Charles I, 'after the modern manner', probably rebuilt again by the third Earl of Lindsey in 1674, it still looks, in spite of subsequent changes, very like the plain three-storied house depicted with such admirable precision in the Kip engraving of 1699. Danvers House flanked Beaufort House on the east. Possibly the 'New Buildings' with chapel and library to which More had retired for meditation, reconstructed in 1623 by Sir John Danvers, it is part of the insubstantial pageant of vanished architecture on which, with the help of Aubrey's description, it is pleasant to linger. A quaint old house in his time 'not according to the staid perfection of Roman architecture now in vogue': but certainly—a house of culture. In the days before the Civil War, the King's Musick performed for Sir John in the 'stately Roome' above the Hall, with Dr Gibbons at the 'excellent organ of stoppes of cedar'. Danvers laid out the 'great gravelled walks of the Garden' in Italian style. One imagines him there, pointing out the merits of Nicholas Stone's sculptures of Cain and Abel, or brushing his beaver hat on the borders of hyssop and thyme to 'perfume it with their natural essence'.

Among other architectural phantoms of Chelsea are: the Lawrence House to the north of Lordship Yard, possibly on the site of the old manor house; known in its later days as Monmouth House, having been leased by the widow of Sir Thomas Lawrence (*d.* 1712) to Ann, Duchess of Monmouth: Shrewsbury House (west of Oakley Street) which took its name from George, Earl of Shrewsbury (henchman of Henry VIII), dated back to Henry's reign and was long confused with More's house: Winchester House, adjoining Henry VIII's manor house, built about the middle of the seventeenth century by James, Duke of Hamilton, the palace of the Bishops of Winchester until the end of the eighteenth century, two-storied, of plain red brick, but with an entrance hall 40 feet long and a grand staircase leading to three drawing-rooms extending the whole length of the south front: Gough House, in Tite Street, built (*c.* 1707) by the third Earl of Carberry (who made a fortune in the slave trade) but taking its name from its subsequent owner, Sir Richard Gough, a wealthy merchant, and now merged into the Victoria Hospital for Children: adjoining Gough House with beautiful gardens to the river, Walpole House, built about 1690, improved for Sir Robert Walpole by Sir John Vanbrugh, whose additions were almost certainly the part of the house incorporated in Sir John Soane's Infirmary (1810) for the Royal Hospital, though of the Infirmary, bombed out during the Second World War, fragments only remain.

Seen from the Thames, gay and lively then with any number of small craft (as no doubt Defoe saw it) the line of stately brick mansions with their lawns and flowered walks reaching riverwards, must have been unique in effect. Eastward, and completing its harmony, was what Defoe well called, 'the noblest building and the best foundation of its kind in the world', the Royal Hospital. And, as a palatial outpost on the London side of the Hospital, there was the house built (about 1690) by Charles II's favourite, Richard Jones, Earl of Ranelagh, with gardens and land totalling 23 acres, the 'little palace, I had almost called it paradise', said Defoe, 'of the late Earl of Ranelagh' (*d.* 1712).

Away from the river, the mansions were fewer and smaller. They included the (existing) Argyll House (No 211 King's Road), built 1723 by the Venetian architect Giacomo Leoni for John Perrin (or Pierene), though taking its name from John, fourth Duke of Argyll who lived there in his last years, 1769–70. Grand, though small, is what Leoni called 'this little House of my Invention', with its delightful wrought-iron gate, its stone doorway comprising Tuscan three-quarter columns, Doric entablature, urns and balustrade, and within a beautifully spacious staircase. The architect congratulated himself on the, to him, novel harmony he obtained between grey brick and white stone.

Also in the King's Road is Stanley House, the property being in the possession of the Stanleys until the death of the last of the line, William, in 1691. The new house, built some years after and perhaps not completed until the beginning of the eighteenth century, is a good, sensible building, with an interior doorway, supported by Ionic columns and having a broken pediment, that achieves magnificence.

No trace remains of the famous seventeenth-century houses in the region of the Fulham Road, at the then hamlet known as 'Little Chelsea': of Shaftesbury House, originally built by Sir James Smith in 1635, altered about 1700, by Anthony Ashley Cooper, third Earl of Shaftesbury and author of *The Characteristics of Men, Manners, Opinions and Times*. It was occupied by him until, suffering from asthma, he was driven by the 'great smoake' of Chelsea northwards to Hampstead. Or of the house with its fine laboratory where Robert Boyle the physicist lived and was visited by Evelyn in 1661; where 'glasses, potts, chymical and mathematical instruments, books and bundles of papers did so fill and crowd his bed-chamber, that there was but just room for a few chairs'.

A corollary of the 'palace' was a form of palace life and it is needful to imagine the routine of courtly humanity, especially after the Restoration, of which the catalogue of mansions is a projection. The exquisite rooms were full of courtiers and court ladies, posing, gossiping, intriguing. There was a constant round of receptions, festivals and entertainments; like the 'very sumptuous treat' given by the Duke of Monmouth in the summer of 1673 for 'Madame Carwell' (Louise de Quérouaille), Charles II's mistress, then lately made Duchess of Portsmouth, the treat being accompanied by fireworks and illuminations. The flow of life through the vanished (smaller) houses of Paradise Row (now Royal Hospital Road) has been admirably described in his *Paradise Row* by Reginald Blunt; whose pen sketched its characters with so much appreciation, sadly for whom the camera recorded in 1906 the last of the beautiful doorways, at Nos 5, 6 and 7, remaining from the end of the seventeenth century and due for demolition.

The person and the household of Mazarin's niece (Hortense Mancini) have all that vividness which belongs to this village of long memories: the self-styled Duchesse de Mazarin was certainly the most spectacular inhabitant of Paradise Row. She had a stormy past, had fled to Italy in man's clothes to escape from her obnoxious husband, Duc de la Meilleraye. An intimate of Charles II in the days of his exile she remained so after her arrival in England in 1675 (aged 28), receiving a 'Secret Service' allowance of £4,000 a year, but spending so recklessly on gambling and display that she was always in arrear with the poor rate, and it was a well understood thing that guests at dinner might leave money under their plates. A foil to the personality of this wild, black-haired, dark-blue-eyed beauty was that of the Seigneur de Saint-Evremond, another refugee in Chelsea, barred from France for political sarcasms on the Peace of the Pyrenees but welcomed by Charles and esteemed as much in London as in literary Paris for his satirical and elegant prose, though he never learnt to speak the language of his adopted country and, unlike Voltaire, did not attempt to read Shakespeare. Thirty-seven years older than the Duchesse (though he long outlived her, reaching the age of 93) he lodged in her house, not quite a lover—or a father—but a philosopher deeply attached to the object of his study, regarding with indulgent interest her losses at basset, her pets—the parrot 'Pretty', the dog 'Chop' and the cat 'Monsieur Poussy'—the course of her relations with the King, and with that unfortunate Swedish baron whom her nephew killed in a duel. Their joint salon has been described not only by Faulkner but by Sainte-Beuve also. In the words of our Chelsea historian it was 'daily frequented by the principal nobility and persons of wit and genius'. There, says Faulkner, 'in the style of free conversation, were discussed subjects of the deepest speculation, such as philosophy, and religion, history, poetry, criticism, on dramatic and other compositions, and the niceties of the French language'. Variety was provided by the card-table where 'an obscure man named Morin' acted as banker, and by elaborate musical and dramatic performances which seem to have encouraged the introduction of Italian Opera into England.

Another dweller in Paradise Row was Betty Becke, whose attraction for Lord Sandwich was considered so regrettable by Samuel Pepys, that in 1663 he wrote the nobleman a tremendous letter of reproof. Sandwich, according to Pepys in his fit of morality, did 'grossly play the fool'. 'His daughters do perceive all and do hate the place and the young woman', though Pepys, on meeting her in the following year, wondered 'the less at my Lord's favour to her', finding that while 'she hath not one good feature in her face', yet she was 'a fine lady, of a fine taille' and 'I dare warrant she hath brains enough to entangle him'. Did Nell Gwynn live in Paradise Row? is a question that Chelsea historians have asked—with all that tenderness that the most puritanical of Britons display towards 'frailty' at a distance of a century or two, but her link with the region is vague. It is not certain that she lived at Sandford Manor; nor is there any evidence that she urged on Charles the foundation of a hospital for the poor soldiers; but her son by him, made first Duke of St Albans, lived in the Row and her reputed presence in Stuart Chelsea invests local tradition with a cheerful warmth, such as a star of the music-hall might leave behind. By way of contrast, Paradise Row had its militant bluestocking in a younger contemporary and neighbour of the Duchesse de Marazin, Mary Astell (buried in the old church), daughter of a Newcastle merchant and auther of a *Serious Proposal to the Ladies*, advocating a lay religious retreat for Church of England women.

The hospitality and entertainments of the town of palaces were lavish; lights, music and the river made its hospitable occasions splendid. A memorable banquet was that given for George I one August evening in 1715 by Lady Catherine Jones, unmarried daughter of Lord Ranelagh, who inherited Ranelagh House, when a fanciful flotilla brought the Royal party in decorative barges, accompanied by hundreds of small boats sparkling with coloured lights in the blue dusk. Handel himself conducted his water music, played by an orchestra of 50, from one of the City barges; and music and banqueting went on in the house until two in the morning.

Equally splendid were the entertainments at Walpole House, where Sir Robert Walpole spent a good deal of time between about 1722 and 1746, appearing there as cultivated and charming host rather than cynical statesman. Pope described this 'happier hour' when he had

> Seen him uncumbered by the venal tribe,
> Smile without art, and win without a bribe.

Here he received Queen Caroline and members of the Royal Family in August, 1729. A temporary kitchen was built in the stable-yards with 20 fireplaces to prepare the dinner, set out in the greenhouse or orangery designed by Vanbrugh. After it, the royal visitors took tea in the octagon summer-house overlooking the Thames, while musicians stationed in barges played for them; no doubt admired the gardens and the grotto devised by Lady Walpole in emulation of Pope's grotto at Twickenham, and looked at the paintings in the house (later to form part of the Imperial Gallery at St Petersburg); returning finally to the greenhouse for the Ball and the supper that accompanied it.

> Go with old Thames, view Chelsea's glorious pile,
> And ask the shattered hero whence his smile.
>
> Rogers, *The Pleasures of Memory*

If a palace be defined as a spacious building for entertainment (not necessarily of an ostentatious kind), the incomparably greatest palace of Chelsea was, and is, the Royal Hospital designed by Sir Christopher Wren. In examining its origin we must revert for a moment to Nell Gwynn, whose name is a quite modern addition to the List of Benefactors in the Great Hall. A portrait 'after Lely' hung there for a long time, though the original (National Portrait Gallery) is now adjudged to be neither of her nor by Lely. Legend has it that Charles ii, when the site was discussed, recalled he had promised the land to her; that she, generously, offered it back again. Documentary evidence is against it and John Evelyn, certainly one of the scheme's main promoters, makes no mention of any such interchange: but whether or not it took place, the Hospital was historically inevitable.

In the Middle Ages, the old and infirm, including superannuated and disabled soldiers, were accommodated in the hostels or hospitals largely supported by the monasteries. The dissolution of the monasteries threw the onus of support on private charity which was bound to be inadequate. Since Tudor times there had been many complaints of the neglect of 'maymed souldieres'. The beginning of a regular army in Charles II's reign demanded state planning; a hospital for soldiers to which that for sailors at Greenwich was a later complement.

At Chelsea there was a suitable site, the ground on which stood the remnants of an unlucky enterprise, the Theological College, founded in 1618 with the sanction of James I. It was intended to house 20 learned doctors warring on the 'pedantry, sophistries and novelties of the jesuits and others', likewise 'the treachery of pelagians and arminians'. Archbishop Laud aptly filed correspondence concerning it under the heading 'Controversy College'. As a building, it was curiously planned and never completed; as an idea, it did not come off. The Puritans suspected it; the Commonwealth turned it into a military prison : 'a cage for unclean birds' as the Rev. J. Darley complained. Scottish prisoners of the Civil War were first housed there; then prisoners taken in the wars with Holland. It was Evelyn's job to supervise the place : hence the entry in his diary, 8 January 1665 : 'I visited our prisoners at Chelsey College and to examine how the marshal and sutlers behaved. These were prisoners taken in the war; they only complained their bread was too fine.' Conditions later worsened. The prisoners went hungry; plague broke out among them; as the Dutch ambassador, van Gogh, feared, a number found a way out by volunteering to fight under the English. In 1667, no longer used as a prison, what was left of the College was turned over to the Royal Society as a gift from the King.

For many years it stayed derelict while the Royal Society wondered what to do with it : being much relieved in 1682 when the King bought it back for £1,300. What Nell Gwynn would have done with the 'roofless ruin' is speculative—though a heavy charge on the Secret Service funds might have been foreseen; but meanwhile Evelyn and Sir Stephen Fox, first Army Paymaster-General, had concerted the hospital plan.

It had a recent precedent; the foundation stone of the Hospital for the army in Ireland, at Kilmainham, near Dublin, was already (1680) laid. Fox 'who had', says Evelyn, 'gotten so vast an estate by the soldiers' (by paying them out of his own pocket and charging interest

of a shilling in the pound), was anxious to assume the role of bene-
factor. He and Evelyn drew up a list of officials and salaries (the
official continuance of Fox's system of deductions largely financed
the Hospital until Victorian times). Evelyn 'would needs have a
library and mentioned several books, since some soldiers might
possibly be studious when they were at leisure to recollect' (1682).
With Sir Christopher Wren as architect, from that date the scheme
went forward with great speed, though the buildings were not completed until 1691, and not until 1693 did Wren who, as Surveyor-
General (and President of the Royal Society), had given his services
gratis, receive from William III a grant for his 'Paines' of £1,000. By
that time 476 non-commissioned officers and men (the number of in-
pensioners has remained fairly constant) were installed under a
modified form of military organisation. Wren was one of the Board
of Commissioners, which has always remained a civil authority. There
have been no major changes in the building as a whole, which is
generally acknowledged to be one of Wren's most masterly achieve-
ments, though the approach and general aspect from a distance were
probably rather more impressive in the seventeenth century than
they are today. The northern approach is complicated by the inter-
position of two roads, Royal Hospital Road and St Leonard's Terrace
between the north façade and Royal Avenue, laid out by Wren,
though its date and axial direction discredit the theory that it was
intended as a stately boulevard leading to Kensington Palace. The
original forecourt, now Burton's Court, thus became a separate piece
of ground, though it still belongs to the Hospital and is used for recreation.

The south aspect from the river, also, was evidently much more
impressive when the formal gardens, laid out between 1687 and 1692,
extended to the river; and from the river-steps, along the broad
avenue, bordered by 'Kanalls with fish and fowles' there was an un-
impeded vista to the great quadrangle and the south front of Chapel
and Hall.

That a certain reticence accompanies the majesty of design has
often been noted and is not an adverse criticism. Thomas Carlyle, in
his unusual venture into aesthetic judgment, well remarked: 'I had
passed it almost daily for many years without thinking much about
it, and one day I began to reflect that it had always been a pleasure to
me to see it, and I looked at it more attentively and saw that it was
quiet and dignified and the work of a gentleman.' With New England's
suspicion of splendour, and possibly some national prejudice against

a building that contained flags taken at Bladensburg and Fort Niagara, Nathaniel Hawthorne (in *Our Old Home*) conceded that 'the effect is by no means that of grandeur, which is somewhat disagreeably an attribute of Greenwich Hospital, but a quiet and venerable neatness'. It was entirely Wren's own conception, unlike Greenwich where he had to reconcile his work with existing buildings and the design of other architects. It took little from the slightly earlier and similar foundation, the Hôtel des Invalides in Paris (though Charles II may have wished to rival it). In comparison with Mansart's dome, Wren's central cupola seems almost too modest. If one looks for some part of its inspiration outside England, it may more obviously be traced to the sober brick buildings of the Dutch: though Wren never went to Holland, Evelyn did, bringing back architectural books and prints, and it is not at all unlikely that in their discussions these came under review.

Yet the gentlemanliness on which Carlyle commented may otherwise be defined as a beautiful appropriateness or 'fitness to purpose'. The simplicity of the plan derives from the monastic infirmary with its connecting hall and chapel and adjoining quadrangular almshouses (it was to indicate the size of the proposed building that Evelyn referred to the quadrangle of Christ Church, Oxford). The Hall (115 feet by 38 feet) and Chapel (113 feet by 38½ feet) are separated only by the domed vestibule; the Hall, formerly used as recreation and reading-room being now re-equipped as a refectory (as it is depicted by Pugin and Rowlandson). The two wings at either end four storeys high, divided into corridors lined with wooden cubicles and terminating in the houses of Governor and Lieutenant-Governor, nicely solved the problem of accommodation, and made, with the northern block and its loggia, a dignified enclosure, the main or 'Figure' court where the bronze statue of Charles II in Roman dress, by Grinling Gibbons, stands. The four pavilions, added 1688-9, absorbed the residential overflow, without disturbing the architectural composition, creating subsidiary courts on either side with pleasant effect.

Wren's attention to 'fitness' may be seen in such a detail as the pitch of the staircases, made easy for old limbs (treads, 15 inches wide, risers, 5 inches high): while the oaken cubicles have their privacy ensured by a panel that can be opened or obscured at will. It is all very homely—but that is as it was intended to be. There is nothing of the museum or 'gallery' about the Hospital, though the beauty of functional detail is amply present—in the wrought-iron gates at the main north entrance, the lamp standards in the shape of Ionic columns (east and west courts), the altar rails with their carved foliage in the Chapel, the silver-gilt altar-plate (by Ralph Leete, 1687–8), the appointments of the Council Chamber (with additions by Robert Adam when Clerk of Works). Paintings, however, are few. The huge, dusky picture, at one end of the Hall, of Charles II on horseback, with the Hospital in the background, begun by Verrio and finished by an English follower of Salvator Rosa, Henry Cooke, has never aroused enthusiasm. Nor until recent times has the painting of the Resurrection, in the half-dome of the apse in the Chapel, by the able Venetian artists Sebastiano and Marco Ricci. Hawthorne, with a typical aversion from the baroque, could not 'trouble himself to make out the subject'. What Dr Pevsner has called 'a splendid piece of Venetian *brio*' is a rediscovery of the twentieth century. There is no collection of military pictures to match the naval pictures of Greenwich—sea warfare undeniably has the advantage of the land in art, though the Army Museum now supplies the want to some extent. The standards hanging in Chapel and Hall (described and illustrated in the MS book compiled in 1841 by Captain J. Ford, Captain of Invalids, of which one copy belongs to the Hospital and another is in the Chelsea Public Library) were long a stirring enough reminder of historic campaigns.

The history of the Hospital since Wren's time has been fairly uneventful, architectural changes minor. Robert Adam, 1783–6, replaced the mullioned windows of the wings, with their transoms and small panes, by sash windows. Walpole's house, the entrance to which was through the Hospital stable-yard, was assimilated and the Infirmary designed by Sir John Sloane in 1810: the obelisk by Cockerell, commemorating the desperate Battle of Chillianwallah was added in 1849. Scars have been left by war; the north-east pavilion, bombed by a Zeppelin in 1918 and rebuilt, was again destroyed by a rocket in 1945: the east wing was damaged in 1940, the Infirmary, in which there were many casualties, bombed out in 1941. Otherwise the buildings have mellowed with age, the green slates of the roofs, the warm red brick of the walls and the Portland stone and wood of the porticoes combining in rich harmony. A new Infirmary was completed in 1961 and since then a new library and Roman Catholic chapel have been added.

Among famous names, apart from those of its architect and sponsors, associated with the Hospital, is that of Dr Charles Burney, its organist for many years. He, as his daughter, Fanny, records, in

1791 'resided entirely at Chelsea College ['the College' has remained its traditional description]; and he found his sojourn so perfectly to his taste, that though obliged some years afterwards, to remove from the ground-floor to nearly the highest range of rooms in that lofty edifice, he never wished to change the place of his abode'. Here 'completely to his satisfaction ... he placed his learned, classical, scientific and miscellaneous library'; when he died, in 1814, he was interred in the Hospital burial ground.

Few unusual happenings, save those of wartime, have disturbed the even tenor of the Hospital's life, though the Hall, in 1808, saw the trial of General Whitelock for bad generalship and in 1852 the lying-in-state of the Duke of Wellington. The veterans, in their uniform that takes us back to the time of Marlborough's campaigns, have lived out their days in peace : and with a dignity that Herkomer's once celebrated, sentimental painting, *The Last Muster*, depicting them assembled in the chapel, somewhat misrepresents.

The replacement of one architectural profile by another, the decline and disappearance of most of the palaces, the contemporaneous, and subsequent, rise of smaller, domestic buildings; is a phase of Chelsea's story that requires to be traced in detail.

The great houses passed through a succession of noble hands and then, one by one, were pulled down, Danvers House, scene of brilliant entertainments in the reign of Charles II, which Pepys considered 'the prettiest contrived house I ever saw in my life', was the first to go. Occupied 1660–85 by John, Lord Robarts, who became Earl of Radnor and, according to Anthony Hamilton, 'an old dog, snarling and peevish' with the beautiful young (second) wife, Laetitia, who later married Lord Cheyne, it passed after his death to the Marquis of Wharton and his wife (who wrote a poetical paraphrase of the Lamentations of Jeremiah). Their marriage was childless and unhappy. The house was demolished in 1720, the lands that went with it were sold to Benjamin Stallwood, builder, who began to build Danvers Street as early as 1696. Part of the Danvers estate, in the early eighteenth century, saw the incursion of industry; in 1721 a silk manufactory, in 1723 the tapestry works of Christopher Le Blon.

The More house, rebuilt 1597 by Sir Robert Cecil, was successively occupied by the Earl of Lincoln, Sir Arthur Gorges and his wife, Lionel Cranfield, Earl of Middlesex, who lost favour with Charles I and was forced to give up the house to the first Duke of Buckingham.

The Duchess lived there after his assassination; the Parliamentary Commissioners, Sir Bulstrode Whitelocke and John Lisle followed, during the Commonwealth period; the second Duke of Buckingham recovered the property after the Restoration, when it was known as Buckingham House, though in 1664 he had to part with it to his creditors. It was then sold to the Earl of Bristol, whose widow sold it in 1682 to the Marquis of Worcester, later Duke of Beaufort, after John Evelyn had unsuccessfully tried to sell it for her. It was, he noted privately, 'large but ill-contrived' : but in writing to the Earl of Ossory he termed it 'magnificent . . . capable of being made (with small expense) perfectly modish . . . The fruits of the garden are exquisite; there is a snow-house—in a word I know of no place more capable of being made the envie of all the noble retreats of the greatest persons neere this court and citty.' And a bargain at £3,500. As Beaufort House, it was occasionally occupied by the family until about 1720. Then the Beauforts lost interest; for years it stood empty until in 1737 it was bought by Sir Hans Sloane.

Sloane, who bought Beaufort House for £2,500, seems to have had no intention of living in it, but merely, on principle of extending his estate; and his posthumous praises are tempered by disapproval of his ruthless destruction of the place. Beaufort Row, later Beaufort Street, was laid out on the site in 1766. Only a wall in the Moravian Burial Ground (the stable-yard of Beaufort House) and a wall midway between Beaufort Street and Danvers Street, once dividing the two houses' gardens, have been left to the twentieth century on the site; though Inigo Jones's gateway (1621), perhaps that facing towards King's Road in Kip's engraving, is now at Chiswick as Pope's lines explain :

> Oh gate, how com'st thou here?
> I was brought from Chelsea last year, [1737]
> Battered with wind and weather;
> Inigo Jones put me together,
> Sir Hans Sloane
> Let me alone,
> Burlington brought me hither.

It is tempting to linger over the personal history of the Gorges (outlined by Randall Davies in his *Chelsea Old Church*): of Sir Arthur, the typical Elizabethan in his combination of poetry and adventure by sea, the translator of Lucan's *Pharsalia*, the friend of

Spenser;* of Timoleon Gorges, his son (whom Spenser might have named), the Fellow of All Souls who met his death in a duel; of the sadly short-lived daughter, Ambrosia, of other descendants—but here it must be enough to say that the house was sold about 1664 and became a school. Josias Priest, 'Dancing Master, who kept a Boarding-School of Gentlewomen in Leicester Fields', removed to what was already 'the great School-House at Chelsey' in 1680: and the young ladies took part in the first performance of Purcell's opera *Dido and Aeneas*, given there, with words by Nahum Tate and an epilogue by Tom D'Urfey. The house reverted to domestic use when Sir William Milman bought it about 1697 and remained with this family until pulled down to make way for 'a new row of buildings intended to be called Milman's Row' in 1726. The old manor house, long the home of the Lawrences, was pulled down in the early years of the eighteenth century; between 1704 and 1750 Lawrence Street came into being. The sites of Henry VIII's manor house, Winchester House and Shrewsbury House gave us Cheyne Walk and Cheyne Row. Shrewsbury House (1543) was not pulled down until 1813. A school at the beginning of the eighteenth century, and later a wall-paper manufactory it is still 'Shrewsbury House' (modern flats). Part of its garden wall still remains at the back of Cheyne Row: 'Nothing I know of,' said Carlyle in 1867, 'is more lasting than a well-made brick—we have them here, at the head of this garden (wall once of a manor park) which are in their third or fourth century (Henry VIII's time I am told), and still perfect in every particular.' Winchester House disappeared in the early nineteenth century (1828) and its site is occupied by modern houses and by Oakley Street. The manor house survived until the death in 1753 of Sir Hans Sloane who took up permanent residence in 1742, though he had bought the house and land in 1712 and as early as 1717 had leased part of the eastern end of what is now Cheyne Walk for building. After Sloane's death, a row of mid-eighteenth century houses (Nos 19–26 Cheyne Walk) replaced the manor. Cheyne Row dates back to 1708 when William, Lord Cheyne, sold the land for building. Cheyne Walk was a later name, eventually given to the whole length of the old main thoroughfare of Chelsea (which had comprised 'Lombard Street' and 'Duke Street').

Some curious changes were involved in the decline from courtly life. Where the Duchesse de Mazarin had lived in Paradise Row, Miss Elizabeth Fry established in 1825 her reformatory for girls (which

* His collected poems, the 'sweet layes of love', perhaps, of which Colin Clout speaks, edited by Professor Helen Sandison, were published early in 1954.

remained there until 1890). Ormond House, at the east end of Paradise Row, home of the Duchess of Ormond, became a Naval Academy in 1779. Shaftesbury House at Little Chelsea became a workhouse, though it remained in its original condition until pulled down in 1856. In 1860 T. C. Croker (*Walk from London to Fulham*) wrote, with a keen sense of incongruity, of 'the trim gardens of Queen Anne's time ... the antique summer houses ... the little leaden infant Hercules which spouted water to cool the air from a serpent's throat ... all this too in the garden of a London Parish Workhouse! Not less surprising was the interior. The grotesque workshop of the pauper artisans, said to have been Lord Shaftesbury's doing, and over which was his famous library, was then an apartment appropriated to a girl's school ... nor should the apartment then occupied by the intelligent master of the workhouse be overlooked. The panelling of the room, its chimney-piece and the painting and framework above it placed so completely as in a chamber of the time of William III. ...'

Nor would one have expected a Chelsea mansion to become the headquarters of a Czech religious brotherhood, yet this was the fate of Lindsey House between 1751 and 1770, when occupied by Count Zinzendorf, the 'Bishop' of the Moravians (who were not without their influence on the English Methodists). It is probable that this early seventeenth-century house was rebuilt or refronted by the Earl of Lindsey in 1674 and came, in this condition, to the Count who planned it as the centre of a utopian colony to be called 'Sharon'. 'The Count's house at Chelsey is a palace for a prince,' wrote John Wesley in 1769, adding, somewhat cryptically, 'Truly are they wise in their generation.' All that remains of 'Sharon' is the austere little area of the Moravian Burial Ground at the end of Milman's Street: nor did the Count make any drastic alterations to the house. These came later when it was divided (1775) into separate dwellings (now Nos 96–100 Cheyne Walk). The cupolas, the balustrade to the roof, the pediment with its coats of arms, the iron gates and piers then disappeared. Front doors were inserted: yet here, in an excellent state of preservation the framework of a seventeenth-century mansion remains visible. The conclusions of the tale of demolition is that 'Old Chelsea', so rich in earlier memories, is, as far as it still exists, an architectural product of the eighteenth century, though it has seemed to retain a certain Dutch flavour which belonged to the reign of William and Mary and to the Hospital of Wren. In the middle of the seventeenth century it had only some 40 houses, in 1717 about 350, in 1780 more than 700. Cheyne Row has its beautiful houses of the time of Queen Anne intact: and the eighteenth-century cottages, like that in which Turner lived and those in Milman's Street (Nos 55, 57 and 59), which may be earlier, specially remarked in the Survey of London, *Chelsea* (Part II), now seem typical of Chelsea in its village rather than palatial aspect. Into that tantalising early history, so exact in many particulars, so scanty in visible remains, there is left an underground avenue of research. At various times, subterranean passages have been excavated, in Beaufort Street, Limerston Street, Paulton's Square, Lower Church Street, Justice Walk, Trafalgar Square, Manresa Road, Oakley Street and Cheyne Walk: though no attempt has apparently ever been made to map out their possible connection. Were they subways leading to the lead conduit which, tradition states, supplied the manor house with water from Kensington? or themselves channels for water pipes? It is an incidental question why it should have been necessary to bring water from Kensington; but in any case these subways in which it is said a man could walk upright seem too elaborate for their supposed purpose. A fascinating account of one of them is that given by Miss Eliza Gulston (*d.* 1859) the amateur artist who helped Faulkner with material for his *History of Chelsea*. An old man who had worked as a boy in the 'paper manufactory' (i.e. Shrewsbury House) told her of finding a winding stair under a trapdoor in the paper-stainers' room, leading to a passage below. Miss Gulston herself (or the artist who made the drawings, with appended description, now in the Chelsea Public Library) explored and arrived at what was believed to be a Roman guard-house, fronting the river. 'The Roman arch prevales all through, which is eliptic.' The 'further elucidation' for which authorities on Chelsea have hoped has not been forthcoming: though a twentieth-century find was in 1952 when a lorry sank through the roadway on the bombed area north of the site of Petyt House (school of Queen Anne's time). Beneath was a brick vault, 30 feet long, 8 feet wide, 8 feet high, parallel with the river, the debris on the floor including fragments of eighteenth-century wine bottles and clay pipes. There were signs of a continuation to the west under Old Church Street and north. The bricks, notes the Report of the Chelsea Society, 1952, resembled the seventeenth-century brickwork of the Church. Again, an interesting discovery, though perhaps no more than the foundations of part of old Church Street.

CHAPTER THREE

Gardens and Pleasures of Old Chelsea

The prestige of its healthy air and fertile soil, as well as of its famous early inhabitants, drew people to Chelsea. There is an impressive historical list of invalids and convalescents who went there for health's sake. In 1599 'the gallant Earle of Essex' was reported (by Rowland Whyte) to have 'gone to Chelsey where he purposed to be sicke'. In 1639 the Earl of Danby came to stay at Danver's House 'on account of the malady which assaulted him in old age'. Pepy's errant friend, Lord Sandwich, ostensibly at least, came 'to take the ayre'. Dean Swift, in 1711, wrote to Stella 'I design in two days, if possible, to go to lodge at Chelsea for the air, and put myself under the necessity of walking to and from London every day.' Dr John King, who became Rector of Chelsea in 1694 and compiled, between that date and 1712, a MS 'account of the Parish and Rectory' remarked in it that 'No village in the vicinity of London contributes more to the ease and recovery of asthmatical and consumptive persons.' Shaftesbury gave Chelsea a trial for his asthma.

Not even Chelsea escaped the Plague. Pepys, in April 1666, was put out by finding the White Swan Inn closed because of it. Yet Fanny Burney (or Mme D'Arblay as she was in 1832) then justly said that 'Chelsea air is even proverbially salubrious', and on this point the eminent doctors Arbuthnot, Sloane, Mead and others agreed by settling there.

Air and soil by their own happy agreement gave, it seems, a special luxuriance to Chelsea gardens, though a race of keen and able horticulturists must share the credit. The fragrance of herbs drifts to us from the seventeenth century. Evelyn had orange trees from the garden of Beaufort House. Narcissus Luttrell, the bibliographer and

49

book-collector, who bought the Earl of Shaftesbury's house at Little Chelsea, between 1712 and 1717, cultivated 25 varieties of pears in its garden. Faulkner (1810) computed that half the vegetables sold at Covent Garden were raised in Chelsea and the adjoining parishes.

It was natural enough, then, that Chelsea should be the site of what is now the oldest Botanic Garden in the country, left to the Society of Apothecaries in 1673 by Charles Cheyne.

The 'Physick', 'Botanick' or 'Apothecaries'' Garden, still existing, may have lost that peculiar fertility that once was Chelsea's. 'The growth of London,' lamented Reginald Blunt in 1900 (though even after that date—in 1902—new buildings, including laboratory and lecture-room were put up), 'has now encircled it in its grimy toils, and the herbs and exotic plants which it was established to cultivate and study, either will not grow at all, or vegetate reluctantly and without developing their medicinal qualities.' The visitor peers through locked gates at the walks, the distant glimmer—sculptural phantom—of Rysbrack's statue of Sir Hans Sloane, yet three-quarters of the world's cotton crop are descended from its cotton seeds and it is still a centre of active research.

In its time it has been of great practical use: and in the seventeenth and eighteenth centuries became famous under a series of able men. The botanist John Watts was appointed curator in 1680; a greenhouse was built; an exchange of plants arranged with Dr Hermann of Leyden in 1682; in 1683 its long celebrated four cedars of Lebanon were planted. Of these two died in 1771, a third in 1878, the last in 1903, their lasting memorial is the set of four chairs in the Hall of the Society of Apothecaries made from a branch blown down in 1848.

Evelyn approved in 1685, 'August 7, I went to see Mr Watts, Keeper of the Apothecaries' Garden of simples at Chelsea, where there is a collection of innumerable varieties of that sort; particularly, besides many rare annuals, the tree bearing Jesuit's bark, which had done such wonders in quartan agues. What was very ingenious was the subterraneous heat, conveyed by a stove under the conservatory, all vaulted with brick, so as he has the doores and windowes open in the hardest frosts, secluding only the snow.' In 1691 the 'banks set with shades of herbs in the Irish stitch-way' were much admired; but the Garden gained its highest prestige with the support and interest of Sir Hans Sloane, who bestowed it (1722) on the Apothecaries at a nominal rent, on the sole condition that they should supply 50 dried specimens of plants to the Royal Society yearly. The great Linnaeus,

6 *Cheyne Row* (c. 1708)

7 *Cheyne Walk: Rossetti's House*

who visited Chelsea in 1736 and collected plants in the garden, highly praised its demonstrators and curators, who remain distinguished in botanical history: Philip Miller, 'Prince of Gardeners', author of the *Gardener's Dictionary* (appointed curator, 1722), his successor (in 1771), William Forsyth, William Curtis, author of *Flora Londinensis* (1776)—an account of all plants within ten miles of London—are among them. The names of botanical genera—Milleria, Hudsonia, Forsythia, Randia, Petiveria, Sherardia, preserve the names of those associated with the Physick Garden; the tree 'from which the Hottentots and Caffres make their Javelins' was called Curtisia. The organised growth of Kew Gardens from 1795 may be traced back to the experience gained by its manager William Aiton, as assistant to Miller at Chelsea.

The blooms of Chelsea inspired the artist. Elizabeth Blackwell, wife of the wild adventurer Alexander Blackwell (who was eventually executed for political conspiracy in Sweden), raised money to rescue her husband from a debtor's prison by drawing plants in the Physick Garden. With the encouragement of William Rand and Sir Hans Sloane, the lady (who lived in neighbouring Swan Walk—she was buried in the old church in 1758) made engravings of 500 of the rarest and medically most useful of the plants, coloured them by hand and had them successfully published in 1737 as *A Curious Herbal*. It seems in accord with Chelsea's character that the Dutch flower painter Van Huysum should have lived there two years, in Sir Robert Walpole's house, and that Horace Walpole should mention, in his collection, 'a pot of carnations drawn at Chelsea from the life by Van Huysum'.

Valetudinarians found a renewed or novel attraction in eighteenth-century Chelsea when an aristocratic Venetian, Dr Bartholomew Dominiceti, installed his medicated baths at his house in Cheyne Walk (No 6), which he took in 1765. As an annexe to the house he built what Faulkner describes as an 'elegant' brick and wooden building (100 feet by 16 feet) containing the baths and 'fumigatory stoves', and 'four sweating bed-chambers, to be directed to any degree of heat', the water and vapour being 'impregnated with the properties of such herbs and plants as might be supposed most efficacious to the case'. Dominiceti claimed to have spent £37,000 on these devices and extensions, of which the Survey of London, *Chelsea* (Part 1) notes in 1909 two remaining rooms, one with 'a curious metal-lined recess, the shape of which suggests the reception of a large medicinal bottle of some kind'.

It was estimated (by the doctor) that some 16,000 people, including Edward, Duke of York, perspired at Cheyne Walk under Dominiceti's care. Sir John Fielding, the blind magistrate and half-brother of the novelist, was all in favour of the treatment and vouched for a number of cures, including that of Miss A—— S——, sister of Lady W—— W——, who suffered from general debility and swelling of the knees but after a course of vapour baths and 'saponaceous frictions' was able to get to her coach 'with only a thin lady's cane in her hand' and soon 'often walked a mile'.

Somewhat unfairly Dominiceti has been the object of ridicule. It was his misfortune to be discussed at the table of Dr Johnson, who observed 'there is nothing in all his boasted system'. Reasoned argument from one of the company provoked that most famous and unreasonable of his retorts, 'Well, sir, go to Dominiceti and get thyself fumigated, but be sure that the steam be directed to the *head* for *that* is the *peccant* part.' The great man's antagonist and the Venetian doctor seem equally the butt of the 'triumphant roar of laughter' that followed. A species of Turkish bath and a variety of bath salts scarcely deserved it; yet Chelsea historians once spoke with contempt of the 'Italian quack' and 'charlatan', and implacably chronicle his bankruptcy and disappearance in 1782.

A 'quack', however, they may have felt, was part of the 'fun of the fair' and Chelsea in Dominiceti's time was quite a fair—or pleasure-ground. The pleasant air and rural setting were attractive to many besides invalids. Lovers came out to Chelsea Fields—to quote Gay, early in the century, in his *Epistle to Pulteney* :

> Chelsea's meads o'erhear perfidious vows
> And the press'd grass defrauds the grazing cows.

Places of refreshment were many : the vista of vanished inns as long as that of the palaces; Chelsea, Hawthorne remarked with an accent of disapproval was 'endowed with a prodigious number of pot-houses'; though these, in his time, were the Victorian counterparts of older resorts, the names tenaciously remaining.

The 'Queen's Elm', at the Fulham Road end of Church Street, recalls that here Queen Elizabeth was supposed to have sheltered under an elm in the company of Lord Burleigh whom she was visiting at Chelsea : the Queen's tree being mentioned in the Parish Books in 1586, when loyal Chelsea planted a commemorative 'arbour' or ring of nine elms, the spot being referred to by Swift in 1711 as the 'Nine

Elms'. The 'Cow and Calf (or Calves)', later the 'Admiral Keppel', was the old drovers' house, at the eastern corner of Chelsea Common, on the Fulham Road between Keppel Street and Marlborough Road (now Draycott Avenue), adjoining the Pound. Rebuilt as the 'Admiral Keppel' in 1790 (according to Alfred Beaver) it stood on the boundary between Chelsea and Kensington, 'older inhabitants' Beaver says, in 1892, remembering the custom by which boys, beating the bounds on Ascension Day, went in at the front door and out through a window at the back : while T. C. Croker recalls the legend beneath the sign, before the house was again rebuilt in 1856 :

> Stop, brave boys and quench your thirst
> If you won't drink your horses murst.

The 'Goat and Boots' at the east corner of Park Walk and Fulham Road preserves the memory of the original, seventeenth-century 'Goat' (which had common rights for '2 cows and 1 heifer'). Its sign, an emblem ingeniously and doubtfully explained as a corruption of the Dutch 'der Goden Boode' (or Messenger of the Gods) denoting a 'Mercury' post-house, was supposed to have been painted by George Morland (to pay his bill), and repainted by the tapestry designer Le Blon.

The taverns indeed make a prodigious catalogue of picturesque titles : in the King's Road were the 'Man in the Moon', the 'Globe', the 'World's End' (dubious rendezvous which Mrs Foresight and Mrs Frail in Congreve's *Love for Love* detect each other's having visited), the 'Six Bells' with its bowling alley : in Church Street, the old 'White Horse' (destroyed by fire and rebuilt, 1840) a sixteenth-century timber-framed house, with much carved ornament and projecting brackets in the shape of human figures, and the old 'Black Lion' (c. 1690); in Lawrence Street, the 'Cross Keys', convenient for the pottery workers at the near-by manufactory. In Cheyne Walk, a little west of Oakley Street, was the 'Magpye and Stump', a Tudor house (burnt down, 1886) where the Courts Leet and Baron met to fine those who failed to repair the river wall, or let their cattle stray; and a parish feast for the poor was held from Stuart until Victorian times. Here, in a room with a painted ceiling, Colonel Despard hatched his plot to assassinate the King and seize the Tower and Bank of England, for which he was hanged and beheaded in 1803. Most famous of all was the 'Old Swan' (demolished after being turned into a brewery, in 1873, to make way for the Chelsea Embankment), on the river's edge with projecting wooden balconies and a terrace and steps to the water. Here Pepys and Mrs Knipp made merry, while Mrs Pepys sulked, and gay companies in the eighteenth century watched the finish of the annual waterman's race for Doggett's coat and badge. This institution, founded in 1716 to commemorate the anniversary of George 1's accession, by Thomas Doggett (comedian, playwright, theatre manager and Whig), the prize being a coat of the Whig colour, orange, and badge bearing the White Horse of Hanover, remained part of Chelsea's pageantry. It incited Thomas Dibdin, when visiting the 'Swan' to nautical opera: and the genial pathos of Tom Tug's lines in *The Waterman* has its local interest :

> Then farewell my trim-built wherry
> Oars and coat and badge farewell,
> Never more at Chelsea ferry
> Shall your Thomas take a spell.

Finally, at the eastern boundary of Chelsea, in the Five Fields, now Pimlico, extending east beyond Chelsea Barracks and the Buckingham Palace Road, were the neighbouring 'Star and Garter' and 'Dwarf's' taverns. Faulkner locates the 'Dwarf's Tavern' on the spot in Chelsea Fields which was afterwards called Spring Gardens between Ebury Street and Belgrave Terrace. In the eighteenth century, the district was, normally, a lonely marsh, its silence disturbed only by the shots of the duellist, the sportsman after snipe, and, perhaps, of the prowling highwayman. But at holiday times the influx of Londoners created a more cheerful atmosphere. They came to see the famous John Coan, the Norfolk Dwarf, known also as the 'Jovial Pigmy', hailed, from the Haymarket stage, as 'thou wonder of a Chelsea Field'. They devoured the ham, collared eels, potted beef and drank the 'sound old bright Wine and Punch like Nectar' which the Dwarf provided for 'those that love to live well'; and admired the fireworks at the 'Star and Garter' devised by Carlo Genovini, 'the Italian artificer from Rome'. In 1762 the visiting 'Cherokee King and his Two Chiefs' were 'greatly pleased' with the curiosities of the 'Dwarf's Tavern'; the Guillochees, Tourbilions and Gerbes of the Fire-Work confected by Genovini 'in Honour of the last victory gained by the Forces of His Majesty over the French Army in Germany'; and the horsemanship of Mr Johnson who, 'to the great Surprise of the Spectators leaps over the horse when at his greatest Rate'. The Cherokee King and his chiefs drank tea with the Jovial Pigmy and most Chelsea taverns were provided with tea gardens, with rustic arbours and benches (the 'World's End' gardens look quite delightful in the old—early nineteenth-century—water-colour in the Chelsea Public Library); also with skittle or bowling alleys, the local game at the old 'Swan' being called 'Four Corners' and the skittles arranged in diamond formation.

Whatever its potations, the eighteenth century could be very lively on tea and buns: and the old Bunn House was an immensely popular resort. It would be a quibble to say that this early eighteenth-century establishment (pulled down in 1839) which stood at the end of Jew's Row (Pimlico Road) not far from Grosvenor Row, was over the Chelsea border. The bun belonged to Chelsea. Swift, in the *Journal to Stella*, 1712, renders the street-cry 'r-r-r-r-rare Chelsea Buns', remarks on the crowd of 'boys and wenches buzzing about the cake-shops like fairs'; on the 'great cakes frothed with sugar and decorated with streamers of tinsel'. Beneath the colonnade of the Bunn House, even Royalty nibbled the 'flour of the ovens! a zephyr in paste' (in the words of a local versifier whom Alfred Beaver quotes but does not name). George II was a customer, and George III and his Queen and all the Princes and Princesses. The populace followed. In the early nineteenth century, according to George Bryan (author of *Chelsea in the Olden and Present Times*), at least 240,000 buns were sold on Good Friday, and some 200,000 people collected, in what was 'a fair to all intents and purposes'. It was quite in accord with the Chelsea sense of tradition that the Bunn House should have been revived, in Sloane Square, in the Festival summer of 1951, when it was once more a great attraction.

It was, perhaps, the fame of Sir Hans Sloane's collection, that caused such places of entertainment to collect and exhibit curious objects—among which even the proprietors could be numbered. At the Bunn House, the visitor would examine; the half-gallon silver mug, given by George III; the lead soldiers, British Grenadiers of 1745, presenting arms, four feet high; the portrait of 'Aurungzabe, Emperor of Persia'; the paper model of St Mary Redcliffe; the model of the Bunn House itself, with moving figures; find also a curious interest in the last proprietor, Mr Hand (the Bunn House had sup-ported four generations of Hands)—once an officer in the Stafford-shire Militia and known as 'Captain Bun'—in his long dressing-gown and Turkish fez.

A like curious interest attaches to James Salter ('Don Saltero') and his tavern-cum-museum known as Don Saltero's Coffee House. Salter, an Irishman, who had been a servant of Sir Hans Sloane and accompanied him on his travels, was decidedly a character, one of those with a gift for attracting facetious praise. Steele in No 34 of *The Tatler*, 1708, set the style in his well-known description of this 'Sage of thin and meagre countenance . . . of that sect which the ancients called Gingivistae—in our language tooth-drawers. . . . My love of mankind made one very benevolent to Mr Salter; for such is the name of this eminent barber and antiquary . . .'

It was one of his patriots, Vice-Admiral Munden, who with a flash of humorous invention, christened him 'Don Saltero', suggesting at once a Chelsea Quixote—and buccaneer. The flavour tinges Salter's own doggerel verse in the *Weekly Journal*, 23 June 1723:

> Sir, fifty years since to Chelsea great,
> From Rodman on the Irish main,
> I strolled . . .

He was in Chelsea in 1685, for he was fined £6 in that year by the Court Leet, for allowing the adjacent section of river wall to decay. Moving from 'Lombard Street', he can be traced as a 'coffee-man' in Church Row and Danvers Street (and to this period Steele's description refers), but his palmy days came when he moved in 1718 to one of the new houses (No 18) just built in Cheyne Walk. The house has been so much altered that little of its original character now remains, though a neatly lettered plate at the front gate, 'Don Saltero's', bears its own witness to the persistence of Chelsea legend.

It was the meeting-place of local celebrities, and of visitors from London and elsewhere—Benjamin Franklin came to see Don Saltero's curiosities as well as 'the College'. The proprietor judiciously joined in the laughter excited by his collection, complacently describing it as a 'Knackatory' and himself a 'gimcrack-whim' collector. It consisted, no doubt, in part of throw-outs from Sir Hans Sloane's museum; like the 'lignified hog'—a tree-root of curious shape—Benjamin Franklin's asbestos purse; and many 'corals, chrystals, ores, shells . . . stuffed animals . . . idols . . . missals . . . butterflies, medals, models, firearms, fishes . . .', but such items (if Steele did not make them up) as 'Pontius Pilate's wife's chambermaid's sister's hat', would seem to have made it a caricature of Sir Hans's serious passion.

Yet so poetic or imaginative is the list of Don Saltero's curiosities that it deserves a somewhat extended enumeration. It includes; the heads of the four Evangelists carved on cherry-stones; a rose of Jericho and an Israelitish shekel; a large worm that eats into the keel of ships in the West Indies; the bark of a tree which when drawn out appears like fine lace; a fairy's or elf's arrow; a piece of Solomon's temple; Job's tears that grow on a tree, wherewith they make ano-dyne necklaces; the caul of an elephant; a Muscovy snuff-box made of an elk's hoof; a set of beads made of the bones of St Anthony of Padua; a curious piece of metal found in the ruins of Troy; a starved cat found between the walls of Westminster Abbey when the east end was repaired; a frog, fifteen inches long, found in the Isle of Dogs; the Staffordshire almanack used when the Danes were in England; the lance of Captain Tow-How-Sham, King of the Darien Indians, with which he killed six Spaniards; a cockatrice; Mary, Queen of Scots' pin-cushion; a purse made of a spider from Antigua; and among other animal oddities the 'wild man of the woods'. There were some who considered Sir Hans Sloane's collection to be no less fantastic and Young, in his *Love of Fame* remarks:

> How his eyes languish! how his thoughts adore
> That painted coat which Joseph *never* wore!
> He shows on holidays, a sacred pin,
> That touch'd the ruff that touch'd Queen Bess's chin.

The famous Coffee House lingered on after the 'Don's' death, until 1799 when the collection was sold for £50 and then as a public house until 1867—an old photograph showing it in this latter phase with charming, small paned, ground-floor windows and two massive lanterns flanking the entrance. Yet the bun and coffee house, the taverns and tea-gardens, were minor attractions when compared with the Rotunda and pleasure grounds of Ranelagh.

It was a vulgarisation of the private splendour of Ranelagh House and Gardens. The means by which Richard Jones, third Vis-count and first Earl of Ranelagh, attained his fortune were dubious enough to cause his expulsion from the office of Paymaster-General to the Forces, yet before this happened he had been able to build his handsome house adjoining the Hospital and, on the plea of hav-ing suffered heavy losses, to secure 23 acres with the house for an annual rent to the Hospital of £5. The gardens 'curiously kept and elegantly designed' were, in 1705, esteemed the best in England. The great party given for George I by the Earl's daughter in 1715, showed how well gardens and river combined to make a splendid occasion.

In 1733 the property was sold to the lessee of Drury Lane, Lacy, who proposed to make it a place of public entertainment. The scheme, costly, and objected to by the Hospital authorities, languished, until a new company, encouraged by the success of Vauxhall Gardens, pushed it through. The Rotunda, in the Ranelagh grounds, built by William Jones, architect to the East India Company, after the style of the Pantheon in Rome, was opened with a public breakfast in 1742.

Externally, this round building with its 60 windows must have had a faint resemblance to the Albert Hall and internally, as much to the Reading Room of the British Museum as the Pantheon, but its size (internal diameter, 150 feet), its circle of 52 boxes (each with its 'droll painting' and bell-lamp with candles), its chandeliers suspended from the olive-green ceiling, its grand central fire-place with four black pillars, long provoked wonder rather than architectural comparison. The painting by Canaletto in 1754 for his patron Thomas Hollis (National Gallery) shows the fashionable strollers dwarfed by its large proportions.

The splendour, of this 'illustrious monument', as one writer termed it, of Mr Jones's 'genius and fancy' was illusionary; an element of burlesque, and perhaps of what is known as *l'ironie anglaise*, tempered the grandiose with the homely and the nondescript. The fact could not be disguised that the core of its magnificence was a series of kitchen ranges. 'The enchanted palace of a genie', as Miss Lydia Melford calls it in *Humphry Clinker*, dispensed tea, coffee and bread-and-butter at half a crown a head. 'The pomp and splendour of a Roman amphitheatre,' remarked a visitor in 1742, 'are devoted to no better use than a twelvepenny entertainment of cold ham and chicken.' The subsidiary buildings, the Temple of Pan at the bottom of the garden, the pavilion in the ornamental 'canal', sometimes referred to as the 'Chinese House' and sometimes as the 'Venetian Temple', were pinchbeck. In its off-moments, at various times in its history, it caused disappointment. 'I was there last night,' says Horace Walpole, shortly after the opening, 'but did not find the joy of it. Vauxhall is a little better ...' A French visitor coldly criticised it as 'the most insipid place of amusement one could imagine'. Samuel Rogers (1786) describes a grimly frozen moment when it was 'so orderly and still you could hear the swishing sound of the ladies' trains'. Yet the hypnotic influence of size, fashionable crowds and fireworks, regatta and masquerade, produced, in the main, extravagant superlatives of praise. Walpole changed his tune. 'Nobody goes anywhere else—everybody goes there. My lord Chesterfield is so fond of it that he says he has ordered all his letters to be directed thither.' 'The floor,' he said, ecstatically, 'is of beaten princes.' To Dr Johnson, who was fond of these 'innocent places of recreation' and went to Ranelagh, as to Vauxhall, with Boswell and company, the *coup d'œil* was the finest thing he had ever seen.

It is interesting to observe the conquest of a not very impressionable German traveller, Carl Philipp Moritz (*Travels in England*, 1782). He paid his entrance and found himself in 'a poor, mean-looking and ill-lighted garden': had some difficulty in getting rid of a familiar young woman who took his arm; and then . . . 'suddenly entered a round building, illuminated by many hundred lamps the splendour and beauty of which surpassed anything of the kind I had ever seen before'. In this 'magic rotondo', the *beau monde* of London 'moved perpetually around'.

Special performances contributed to its 60 years of success. In 1763 the company was diverted by Bonnell Thornton's burlesque *Ode on St Cecilia's Day* with 'antient British music'—salt box, Jew's Harp, marrow bones and cleavers and 'humstrum' or hurdy-gurdy. In the following year Mozart, aged eight, played on harpsichord and organ. 1769 saw the performance of Dibdin's *Ephesian Matron*. The masquerades were already in the spirit of the Chelsea Arts Ball. Walpole describes in sprightly style, the Jubilee Masquerade of 1749 'after the Venetian manner', with its masked peasants dancing round the Maypole to the sound of tabour and pipe; huntsmen with French horns; troups of harlequins and scaramouches; masked shopkeepers with stalls of china; festoons of flowers hanging from tree to tree . . . Shortly after, the 'Subscription Masquerade'; the King disguised in 'an old fashioned English habit', the corpulent Duke of Cumberland, in similar dress, looking 'like *Cacafoco*, the drunken captain, in *Rule a Wife and Have a Wife*', Miss Pitt with a red veil 'which made her look gloriously handsome'. Miss Chudleigh was Iphigenia 'and so lightly clad that you would have taken her for Andromeda . . . The maids of honour were so offended they would not speak to her . . .' Lady Betty Smithson 'had such a pyramid of baubles on her head that she was exactly the Princess of Babylon in Grammont'.

A certain licence accompanied what the eighteenth-century memoirist, Mrs Carter, described as 'these revels of Comus'. The masquerades were eventually suppressed by the Justices of Middlesex, though the entertainments went on. At the Regatta and Ball of 1775 (the ticket for which was designed by Cipriani and Bartolozzi) the Thames was 'a floating town', the guests landing at the stairs at 9 p.m., were met by dazzling clusters of lamps, an orchestra of 240 musical masters; danced, among imported palm-trees, and in the Temple of Pan. In 1789 Mr Callot's fireworks coruscated while the fire-music composed by Mr Handel was played. In 1792 the view of Mount Etna 'painted by Signor Marinari', erupted with a resounding explosion. In 1802 M. Garnerin and Captain Snowden soared up from the gardens in their balloon, landing at Colchester an hour later. In 1803, at a gala given by the Spanish Ambassador, the boxes of the Rotunda became 'a Spanish camp', each tent guarded by a boy in Spanish uniform, the gallery was a Temple of Flora, women wreathed with flowers made tea, a Spanish dance was performed by children, 'a hundred valets in scarlet and gold, and as many footmen, in sky-blue and silver, waited on the company'.

The decline of Ranelagh was swift. By 1805 it had had its day. The decoys sent out, to mingle in fashionable assemblies for the purpose of being overheard remarking 'What charming weather for Ranelagh' had lost their power of suggestion. Robert Bloomfield, the 'peasant poet' bleakly described the disillusion of the promenade.

> First we trac'd the gay circle all round
> Ay—and then we went round it again.

A new Marius among the ruins of Carthage, Sir Richard Phillips (*Walk from London to Kew*) mourned the demolition (1805) of the Rotunda. He walked along the avenue of trees he had often seen blocked with carriages. 'On a spot covered with nettles, thistles and other rank weeds' he met a working man who told him this was the site. Sadly he looked at the broken arches of the cellars 'once filled with the choicest wines', traced the position of the orchestra. The Byfield organ had gone to Tetbury Church. The melodious falsetto of Tenducci was but a memory. 'All was death-like stillness! Is such, I exclaimed, the end of human splendour?'

Yet Ranelagh amply remains in the literature of fact and fiction; especially in the descriptions of Walpole and Smollet, and Dr Johnson's remark is classic that there was 'half-a-guinea's worth of inferiority to other people in not having seen it'. A second Ranelagh sprang up in the suburbs of Paris, survived the Revolution, and lingered until the fortifications of Paris cut through its gardens in 1840. In Chelsea itself it had its successor in Cremorne.

The beautiful name conjures up a golden rocket in the blue twilight of a Whistler canvas. The gardens of Cremorne flourished in the latter half of the nineteenth century, though never so fashionable as Ranelagh had been. They stood on the site of the house known as 'Chelsea Farm', built by Theophilus, Earl of Huntingdon, in 1745, the White House, Chelsea, of Girtin's water-colour, acquired in 1778 by Thomas Dawson, Baron Dartrey (created Viscount Cremorne in 1785). He employed James Wyatt to enlarge and improve it. It is described as a brick house, on the architecture of which nineteenth-century comment is slighting: but it overlooked the river from which it was separated by a lawn, with noble elms, ash and oaks. Philadelphia Hannah, Lady Cremorne, great-grand-daughter of William Penn, and born in Philadelphia, lived in the house (her husband died in 1813) until 1825. She left it to her cousin, Granville Penn, who after several unsuccessful attempts to sell it, found a buyer in 1831, Charles Random de Bérenger, Baron de Beaufain. The Baron turned it into a 'National Club' for 'various skilful and manly exercises'—they included swimming, rowing, shooting, fencing, archery, riding, driving, skating, coursing, hunting and racing— called 'The Stadium'.

The Stadium (which gave its name to Stadium Street) lasted until 1841, but did not, apparently, pay its way and was re-opened as Cremorne Gardens in 1845. Its programme included the concerts, fireworks, balloon ascents and galas that had made Ranelagh's success; but, 1845 was not 1745. The cocked hat and French wig were replaced not only by the top hat but by the proletarian cap. The neighbouring public-house was enlarged for the benefit of the rougher element, not content to promenade and drink tea. Beaver speaks of 'some years of disreputable existence' before Cremorne was closed as a nuisance to the neighbourhood in 1875. Yet the more garish glitter of its coloured lamps, its theatre and its grottoes, its fountain with the plaster figure of the 'Stooping Venus', still have a glamour of their own in retrospect; partly, no doubt, because, in its later days Cremorne was frequented by Whistler and his boatman-artist follower, Walter Greaves, and both have left us romantic pictures of it. The balloon ascent here and in 'the Lots' and adjoining grounds of the old Ashburnham House (built for Dr Benjamin Hoadley in 1745), was a popular item in the 1860s of which the 'Balloon Tavern', at the angle of Lots Road preserved the memory. There being as yet no gas in Chelsea, the Cremorne Balloon was taken to the Gas Works at Vauxhall—Greaves has drawn its journey back in tow of one of the Citizen Steamboats. A 'Space Ship' was a modern successor to be seen from Chelsea in the pleasure gardens of a later age. Though they are across the water in Battersea it is appropriate that the same stretch of river as of old should border the modern pleasure ground.

CHAPTER FOUR

The Writer's Chelsea

The Chelsea of the fashionable and pleasure-seeking, became also, in the eighteenth century, the resort of an increasing number of people of ideas and talent. Politically it might be called Whig, in view of the presence of such recipients of Whig patronage as Addison and Steele, and in the early Hanoverian days of Sir Robert Walpole himself. In science, it could claim (over a longer period) by residence or association, six Presidents of the Royal Society, the Earl of Carberry, Robert Boyle, Sir Joseph Banks, Sir Isaac Newton, Sir Christopher Wren, Sir Hans Sloane. It had its distinguished doctors and botanists, and already a certain number of artists. Men of letters, to whom the attractions of local good company and easy access to town were as obvious as to others, above all found it a quiet and pleasant place to write in.

'We dined,' says Swift, in the *Journal to Stella* (September, 1710), 'at a country-house near Chelsea where Mr Addison often retires.' The country house has been identified with Sandford Manor, Sandy End, Fulham, the reputed home of Nell Gwynn (surviving into the twentieth century but marooned among gas works). It seems likely that Addison occupied it at intervals until 1716, when he married Sarah, Countess of Warwick; that some, at least, of his essays for the *Tatler* (1709–11) and *Spectator* (1711–14) were written there, that he would find it an agreeable diversion to walk across the fields to see his Countess at Holland House, Kensington (where he died in 1719). That he mused on the history of Chelsea's first great man is shown by references in the *Spectator* to Sir Thomas More. 'I shall only observe,' said Addison, 'that what was philosophy in this extraordinary man would be phrenzy in anyone who does not resemble him, as well in the cheerfulness of his temper, as in the sanctity of his life and manners.' The urbanity of the Humanist appealed to the Augustan. If More had been simply a martyr, Addison would have been colder.

While Addison was at Sandy End, his collaborator, the original Tatler, Richard Steele who 'fared [with Addison] like a distressed prince who calls in a powerful neighbour ... I could not subsist without dependence on him', was living at Cheyne Walk, i.e. renting a house at the water-side, rated at £14 a year. The sociability of the easy-going Anglo-Irishman, which caused him to delight in all places of public resort, led him to describe Don Saltero's as zestfully as White's Chocolate House, Will's Coffee House, the 'Grecian' or St James's. One guesses at a convivial occasion in the letter he wrote from Chelsea, in 1716, to his wife: 'Mr Fuller and I came hither to dine in the air, but the maid has been so slow that we are benighted, and chuse to lie here than go this road in the dark. I lie at our own house, and my friend at a relation's in the town.'

Steele was then in expansive mood; in favour, as a Whig stalwart, with George I, who had knighted him the year before; the manager of Drury Lane with a handsome share of the profits, but the prospect was soon to darken. His 'dear Prue' died in 1718, a breach with Addison remained open, until the latter's death in 1719. Debts mounted up; Drury Lane passed into other hands; after a few years he vanished into Wales, and London and Chelsea knew him no more.

Neither Addison nor Steele ever seems so alertly and vividly present in Chelsea as Jonathan Swift. A middle-aged Irish parson, with a mission from the Irish Archbishops to secure concessions for the Church in Ireland, he had no specific attachment to place—or party —in London. He came to Chelsea in 1711, perhaps because it was the resort of his Whig friends, Addison and Steele; though by then, in his efforts to gain remittance of the tax ('First Fruits') on Irish benefices, he was veering to the Tory side temporarily in the ascendant: and Chelsea comes frequently into his famous journal—letters to his 'star', Esther Johnson.

He lodged in Church Lane (Church Street). 'I got here in the stage-coach with Patrick and my portmanteau [sic] for sixpence, and pay six shilling a week for one silly room with confounded coarse sheets.' It may not have been without its political significance that the lodging was 'over against Dr Atterbury's house'. 'And yet, perhaps,' Swift remarks in his sharp and casual style, 'I shall not like

the place the better for that.' But the Jacobite Dr Atterbury's Tory-
ism was in accord with Swift's change of political front, and the
Doctor no doubt saw him as a possible ally. Mrs Atterbury sent over
veal, small beer and ale : and subsequently Swift's dinners with her
husband are often mentioned.

His view of Chelsea was vivid rather than affectionate. It was the
critical foreigner who remarked on the 'r-r-r-r-r-rare Chelsea Buns'. 'I
bought one to-day in my walk; it cost me a penny; it was stale and
I did not like it' : who called Chelsea's 'haymaking nymphs' 'perfect
drabs' : who, on a rainy day found 'the cunning natives of Chelsea
have outwitted me, and taken up all the three stage-coaches' : it was
the merciless man of intellect who called the Earl of Ranelagh 'the
vainest old fool that ever I saw' : who, in the *Tatler* satirised Mary
Astell of the 'Serious Call'. *Gulliver's Travels* was still in the future;
Swift's powers, in his short Chelsea period, in revenge for Whig
apathy towards the claims of the Irish church, were being diverted
to masterly political journalism on behalf of the Tory cause. He
went often to London for parleys with Harley and Bolingbroke : and
walked back 'up the Pall Mall, through the Park, out at Buckingham
House, and so to Chelsea a little beyond the church'. It took him
'something less than an hour : it is two good miles, and just five
thousand seven hundred and forty-eight steps'.

'I had no money to lose' : thus he concisely explains the reason
for walking, at any hour, and in spite of the dangers of the road.
One sees the grim figure striding through the Five Fields at one in
the morning counting his paces, careless of highwaymen and foot-
pads, with all the sense of immunity that his cloth, his genius and his
empty purse could give. Once he and his servant Patrick interfered
in a brawl between a drunken parson and a seaman. The seaman
followed them to Chelsea, cursing. 'A pretty scene for one that just
came from sitting with the prime ministers : I had no money in my
pocket and so could not be robbed.' When it rained or was very hot,
he went to London by water (he grumbles because there were no
boats on Sunday) : and in the hot June of 1711, he swam in the
Thames at Chelsea, with all the ceremony of the period, borrowing
a napkin from his landlady for a cap, while Patrick attended holding his nightgown, shirt and slippers. He left Chelsea in the following month, expressing on that account neither satisfaction nor
regret.

The literary annals of Chelsea in the Augustan age of Queen Anne
might be extended to include Thomas Shadwell, playwright and poet

laureate, remembered less for his *Squire of Alsatia* than as the victim
of Dryden's *Mac Flecknoe*:

> The rest to some faint meaning make pretence
> But Shadwell never deviates into sense.

Shadwell died in Chelsea, 1692. His son, Sir John Shadwell, physician to Queen Anne, took a house there from Dr John Arbuthnot,
also a physician but more celebrated for lively satire, like that of
his *History of John Bull* (1712), and in Swift's view 'better at his art
than his trade'. John Gay certainly knew Chelsea and may have lived
there for a while, before 1714—when he fell out of favour with the
Duchess of Monmouth—as her secretary at Monmouth House
(the old Lawrence House). It is in Monmouth House, turned, after the
Duchess's death in 1732, into two dwellings, that we take up a later
thread of literary history. In one of them there settled, in 1753, a
peppery, Scottish ex-naval surgeon, turned writer—Tobias Smollett.

Smollett came to Chelsea, as so many had done 'for the air,'
hoping it would benefit his young and delicate daughter, an only
child. In this, and in most other ways during his ten years' stay, he
was disappointed. His daughter died of tuberculosis at Monmouth
House in 1763, when she was fifteen. Her death caused him to leave
and try to forget his sorrow in those travels through France and
Italy of which he wrote a somewhat peevishly critical account.

In the meantime, his work and fortunes did not prosper. Before
Chelsea he had been unsuccessful as a doctor in London and Bath.
On the other hand he had written two first-rate novels, *Roderick
Random* and *Peregrine Pickle*: but now he committed himself to
a dreary programme of hackwork, his much-criticised *History of
England* being a sad example. An attack in the *Critical Review* on
Admiral Knowles—a commander at Carthagena where Smollett saw
action—earned him a fine of £100 and three months imprisonment
for libel—the period he occupied in writing his worst novel in im-
probable imitation of *Don Quixote, Sir Lancelot Greaves*. Prison varied
a life in Chelsea, spent, he says, 'in the shade of obscurity, neglect-
ing and neglected'. Yet he had kindly memories of the place. 'I cannot help respecting Chelsea as a second native place,' he wrote to a
friend from Boulogne, in August 1763, 'notwithstanding the irrepar-
able misfortunes which happened to me while I resided in it.'

His isolation in Chelsea was from fashionable society ('I have
not spoken to a nobleman for some years'). For this his temper,

8　Holbein's study of Sir Thomas More and his family

9 *Lindsey Jetty, Chelsea. By Walter Greaves*

generous but cantankerous, seems to have been to blame. Distinguished or powerful friends, like Garrick and Wilkes, visited him until he invited enmity by fierce invective against them. He spent his 'vacant hours among a set of honest, phlegmatic Englishmen, whom I cultivate for their integrity of heart and simplicity of manners'. They were, no doubt, his 'brotherhood' of the 'Swan', and frequenters of Don Saltero's, ex-officers, like Captain Robert Mann, 'my neighbour in Chelsea' and 'club companion these seven long years', and the 'unfortunate brothers of the quill' whom he treated on Sundays, to beef, pudding, port, punch and Calvert's entire butt-beer.

Leaving Chelsea, he did not forget it; his last and best novel *Humphry Clinker* refers entertainingly to it, though written after seven years absence, in his final retirement at a cottage near Leghorn. Carlyle in 1834 was near enough to Lawrence Street to 'shoot a gun into Smollett's old house (at this very time getting pulled down)'; added the briskly garbled description 'where he wrote "Count Fathom" and was wont every Saturday to dine a company of hungry authors and set them fighting together'.

At the beginning of the nineteenth century Chelsea found an admirable historian in Thomas Faulkner, bookseller and printer, whose shop was at No 1 Paradise Row, on the site later occupied by the 'Chelsea Pensioner' public-house. Born in 1777, he was a member of that race of antiquarians who were giving a new perspective to English architecture and history. He began writing as a contributor to the *Gentleman's Magazine*, produced his *Short Account of Chelsea Hospital* when he was 28 and the first edition of his *History of Chelsea* five years later, then, at intervals, Histories of Fulham, Hammersmith, Kensington and Brentford, Chiswick and Ealing. He lived to be 78, died in Smith Street in 1855 and was buried in Brompton Cemetery. It is pleasant to think of such an essentially local person, surrounded by dusty folios, looking absent-mindedly up at a customer from some ancient volume, poring with insatiable interest over the lists of Baptisms, Marriages and Burials in the Parish Register, the minutest details of family record. He was capable of prefacing an account of Chelsea Manor with a history of the feudal system, though his leisurely approach has a period charm. He was inaccurate in his copies of epitaphs in the church, yet he did go to original sources. He scrutinised the finances of the parish workhouse with the closeness of an accountant; but if some small particulars bulked too large, many more were of value. After contemplating his modest industry with due respect we come again into the mainstream of literature in considering the Chelsea of Thomas Carlyle.

It was indeed Carlyle's Chelsea, in so masterful a fashion did he survey and appropriate it as his special domain. He came, like so many settlers, in early middle-life, in the year 1834, that is, when he was 39. He was nine years married—to the daughter of a Dumfriesshire doctor, Jane Baillie Welsh, who disappointed in her love for Edward Irving, the friend of Carlyle, had accepted him after considerable doubt and wavering. For six years they had lived on the small estate she inherited at Craigenputtock, not far from Dumfries. There was the silence there, by which he always set so much store, broken only by the bleating of sheep on the lonely grasslands between the house and the Solway Hills: but too much silence, even for him, absorbed in the production of reviews and essays, his history of German literature, the philosophy of *Sartor Resartus*. With a typical relish of the worst side of things, he called it 'the dreariest spot in all the British dominions'. The silence was certainly too much for the sociable Jane Welsh. It was a relief for both of them when, with £200 at his command, he obeyed Jeffrey's injunction to 'bring your blooming Eve out of your blasted Paradise' and in June 1834 they set up house in London at No 5 (now No 24) Cheyne Row.

Quite apart from philosophy, Carlyle had a wonderful gift of observing and recording his observation, and his first impressions, less critical than usual, make one intensely feel what he saw. He gave a picture, that was both like and unlike the old Chelsea, a nineteenth-century view, that is, of the eighteenth-century scene. The social ambience was altered. Cheyne Row was no longer a minor, aristocratic elegance but 'a genteel neighbourhood, two old ladies on one side, unknown character on the other, but with "pianos" '. Modern sympathy with Queen Anne and Georgian architecture is so intimate that examples still seem modern with that modernity of which the eighteenth century so much approved: but this quality is blurred by the focus of Carlyle's vision. His description of Cheyne Row 'flag-pathed, sunk storied [i.e. with basements], iron-railed . . . all old-fashioned and tightly done up' is tinged with the spirit and style of a romantic period. The house was aged, massive and rambling to his eyes: 'antique, wainscoted to the very ceiling', the balustrade 'massive . . . (in the old style)', 'the floors thick as a rock, wood of them, here and there worm-eaten, yet capable of cleanliness . . .' the presses and shelved closets 'queer' and 'old'. He exaggerated the capacity of the 'china-room or pantry, or I know not what ... fit to hold crockery for the whole street', the places 'to hang, say, three dozen hats or cloaks in', the 'many crevices'. On the whole he approved the 'roomy and sufficient' house, and the rent of £35 a year.

As to the surroundings, something, perhaps, of uncongenial formality in the 'tree avenues, once a bishop's pleasure-grounds' beyond the garden, caused him to describe the view as 'unpicturesque but rather cheerful'. On the other hand, 'Our row, which for the last three doors or so is a street, and none of the noblest, runs out upon a "Parade" (perhaps they call it) running along the shore of the river, a broad highway with huge, shady trees, boats lying moored and a smell of shipping and tar.' The verbal Dutch picture merges into an early-Victorian print in words. Its placidity is disturbed by 'white-trowsered, white-shirted Cockneys dashing by like arrows in their long canoes of boats; beyond the green, beautiful knolls of Surrey ... a most artificial green-painted yet lively, fresh, almost operatic-looking business'.

There was no doubt he liked Chelsea from the first. His remark that it was 'a singular heterogeneous kind of spot, very dirty and confused in some places, quite beautiful in others' was without rancour and portended reluctant affection. He remembered in later years the London journey to Cheyne Row, in a hackney coach with his wife and the canary 'Chico' she had brought from Craigenputtock; 'the cheerful gipsy life we had among the litter and the carpenters for three incipient days' : and there was a literary neighbour 'in the next street'—Leigh Hunt.

Leigh Hunt, too, had recently moved, with his wife and seven children, 'from the noise and dust of the New Road', to 'a corner in Chelsea', No 4 (now No 22) Upper Cheyne Row. He was a struggling writer of fifty, whose more exciting personal experiences, his friendship with Shelley and Byron, his residence in Italy with 'my noble friend', were already behind him. He, too, had his description of his new address, though more gently framed than that of Carlyle and more receptive to the spirit of the eighteenth century, from which, in date, he was not so far removed. He used the same adjective as Carlyle 'old-fashioned', but identifying himself with it :

The house was of that old-fashioned sort which I have always loved best, familiar to the eyes of my parents, and associated with childhood. It had seats in the windows, a small third room on the first floor, of which I made a *sanctum* . . . and there were a few lime trees in front, which in their due season diffused a fragrance.

That riverward Chelsea was quiet then, in the eighteen-thirties, no present-day visitor would doubt. It was a quietude beautifully analysed in Hunt's *Autobiography*. 'A little backroom in a street in London is farther removed from the noise than the front-room in a country town.' In Chelsea this sudden remoteness conveyed the delightful feeling of being 'at the end of the world'. 'The air of the neighbouring river was so refreshing and the quiet of the "no-thoroughfare" so full of repose that although our fortunes were at their worst, and my health almost of a piece with them, I felt for some weeks as if I could sit still for ever, embalmed in silence.' Carlyle was to blame the street cries and crowing Chelsea cocks for an infinity of dyspeptic and neurotic torture. More placid in temperament and better in digestion, Leigh Hunt found in these noises the gentlest accompaniment and accentuation of stillness; in the cries of street vendors, a timbre different from that 'in other quarters of the suburbs'—the 'quaintness and melodiousness which procured them the reputation of having been composed by Purcell and others.' There was, he says, 'an old seller of fish, in particular, whose cry of "shrimps as large as prawns", was such a regular, long-drawn, and truly pleasing melody, that in spite of his hoarse and, I am afraid, drunken voice, I used to wish for it of an evening, and hail it when it came.'

In those 'old-fashioned', panelled rooms of Cheyne Row, the two men subjected each other, each to his own variety of searching examination. It is curious that, on the whole, Carlyle should have liked Hunt, curious, that is, because Hunt was so much a being of another world and company, for whose intimates, Shelley and Charles Lamb, Carlyle reserved the fiercest and nastiest of his remarks. 'A good man' is the summing up in Carlyle's *Journal* of 8 September 1834: though this goodness was to be differentiated from a mode of life that was by no means to be admired and the light, polished manner of an earlier age that Carlyle found it hard to understand and could only describe as 'idle' ('free, cheery, *idly* melodious as bird on bough').

Yet the description of Hunt, visiting No 5 Cheyne Row, talking amiably to his Scottish hosts, listening with every sign of pleasure to Jane Welsh's old Scotch tunes on the piano, bending graciously over the frugal morsel of porridge which he found 'endlessly admirable', is Carlyle at his most, and even most comically, effective. How well he calls up the 'fine, clean, elastic figure', leaning on the mantelpiece ' "as if I were a *Lar*", said he once, "or permanent Household God here!" (such his polite *Ariel*-like way)', or taking leave with the words '(voice very fine) as if in sport of parody: While I to sulphurous and penal fire ...' In Upper Cheyne Row, however, the Victorian energy of words seemed intended with more, if unconscious, cruelty to pin the Regency butterfly—if such a term can be applied to as hard-working a person as Leigh Hunt. His house, said Carlyle, 'excels all you have ever read of—a poetical Tinkerdom, without parallel even in literature'—already Carlyle foreshadows the attitude of Dickens to Mr Skimpole in *Bleak House*. 'In his family room where are a sickly large wife and a whole school of well-conditioned wild children, you will find half-a-dozen old rickety chairs gathered from half-a-dozen different hucksters and all seeming engaged, and just pausing, in a violent hornpipe. On these and around them and over the dusty table and ragged carpet lie all kinds of litter—books, papers, egg-shells, scissors and last night when I was there, the torn heart of a quartern loaf.' In these surroundings and sat on a window-sill, in his printed dressing-gown, Hunt would engage on 'the liveliest dialogue on philosophy and the prospects of man (who is to be beyond measure happy yet)'.

To Carlyle the household disclosed 'hugger-mugger, unthrift and sordid collapse'—he says nothing of Hunt's industry, knew nothing of the expense of seven children and was not immune from the fear of contamination by failure. The 'hugger-mugger' had 'to be associated with on cautious terms'. Yet, while he pitied, Carlyle was aware that his neighbour was repelled by what 'he would call "Scotch", "Presbyterian", who knows what', qualities in Carlyle and his wife which he himself preferred to describe as 'something of positive, of practically steadfast'. He may have been mistaken. In Hunt's expressed view, Carlyle was 'one of the kindest and best, as well as most eloquent of men' : but not immune from criticism. 'Mr. Carlyle sees that there is a good deal of rough work in the operations of nature; he seems to think himself bound to consider a good deal of it devilish, after the old Covenanter fashion, in order that he may find something angelical in giving it the proper quantity of vituperation and blows ...' His 'antipathy to "shams" is highly estimable and salutary ... But the danger of the habit of denouncing—of looking at things from the antipathetic instead of the sympathetic side—is that a man gets such a love for the pleasure and exaltation of fault-finding, as tempts him, in spite of himself, to make what he finds . . .' Save for a passing glimpse, the Hunts quickly vanished from the Carlyle's ken. Struggling with his casual journalism, London essays, his anti-war poem *Captain Sword and Captain Pen*, his unsuccessful drama *A Legend of Florence*, Leigh Hunt remained in Chelsea for seven years, though except in his *Autobiography* he has left no account of the district. With his wife and family, he moved in 1840 to Kensington and 'although my health was not bettered, as I hoped it would have been by the change, but on the contrary, was made worse in respect to body than I ever experienced . . . yet I loved Kensington for many reasons'. It was to Kensington, not to Chelsea, that he devoted a memento of his 'suburban' life—in his *The Old Court Suburb* of 1855.

The seven years during which he saw (less and less of) Leigh Hunt were, on the contrary, only the first stage of Carlyle's attachment to Chelsea. With his 'practical steadfastness' he remained there, and in Cheyne Row, for the best part of 47 years. For 32 years he wrote, lectured, preached and stormed at the Victorian age, suffered in his own peculiar, physical and mental fashion. For the same length of time, Jane Welsh Carlyle, suffered and was kindly, unkindly and brilliant in her fashion. For fifteen years after her death (in 1866), looked after by a niece, his work done and his partner gone, he was still in Cheyne Row, 'a gloomily serious, silent and sad old man gazing into the final chasm of things'.

In so long and remarkable a tenancy, it was only natural that the people and the house should grow together: that even in the gradual accumulation of material objects, it should assume something of their personality and tell of their history in a hundred silent ways. Open to everyone, and now under the auspices of the National Trust, it has inevitably acquired the austerity of a museum, of a place 'stripped for action', as it were, the display of 'specimens', yet it is heavy with its Victorian memories. An oil painting by R. Tait makes up for some present deficiency of décor by showing us the ground-floor dining-room in 1857, the table (on which the visitors' book now rests) covered with an ornamented cloth, the floor, with a flowered carpet, the panelling with a patterned wallpaper. And there, resting no doubt from his struggle (just ending) with his 'Minotaur', the *History of Frederick the Great*, is Carlyle himself, in his striped dressing-gown, with the long pipe that, in deference to Jane Welsh, he habitually puffed up the chimney; while

76

she listens, with hand to her lips, in an attitude that may signify attention, reverie—or pain.

Victorianism accumulated everywhere; the mahogany chairs with their horsehair seats, the cane and Venetian blinds, the sofa covered with red chintz, where Jane Welsh lay in the tortures of migraine, the steel Bramah grate in the drawing-room, the leather armchair (presented by John Forster) and swivel writing-desk, the elephant letter-weight ... The engravings, of Goethe and Frederick and Cromwell speak of Carlyle's hero-worship. We seem to see him, on the ground floor, eating his '(*dietetic*, altogether simple) bit of dinner'; or with his wife in the evening taking his spoonful of brandy in the first-floor drawing-room. 'It was she who widened our poor drawing-room (as if by a stroke of genius) and made it (zealously, at the partial expense of three feet from *her own* bedroom) into what it is now, one of the prettiest little drawing-rooms I ever saw.' It was here in the first Chelsea year that he wrote the first volume of the French Revolution; and received with the stoicism that he had long substituted for 'whining sorrow', the news, from the pale and trembling John Stuart Mill, that one of Mill's servants had used the manuscript to light the fire; set to work to rewrite and continue it, with the help of £100 from Mill who added in the fullness of his agonised regret, a set of the *Biographie Universelle*. Here at a later date, famous as reformer— the arch-prophet of many prophets—he entertained his fellow great Victorians, Ruskin, Tennyson, Dickens, Kingsley, Huxley, Owen; his neighbour, the Italian patriot Mazzini, and, on his occasional visits, Ralph Waldo Emerson.

The 'sound-proof' room, a converted attic at the top of the house, flimsy and jerry-built as he accused it of being 'mere work of Belial, father of lies', remains, a reminder pathetic or humorous as one chooses to look at it, of the crescendo of noise, that subjectively assailed him in what, for others, was the calm and quiet of Chelsea in the 1850s during his struggle with the history of the Prussian King. The triumph—'all softer sounds were killed and of sharp sounds scarce the thirtieth part could penetrate'—was quickly modi-fied by the fact, the visitor can readily appreciate, that the place was icy in winter and unbearably hot in summer. It is pleasanter to imagine him writing in the garden against the Queen Anne house background that might have been painted by Vermeer. A feeling of discomfort is given to the sound-proof room by the numerous doors, two of which open into the same cupboard. They recall the occasion when an admirer made his way to the top of the house, only to be ignored by Carlyle who sat at his desk, writing. At length, in confusion, murmuring apologies, the visitor backed to the door, and found himself in a cupboard. He tried another with a similar result, embarrassment grew frantic. After the third attempt the great man pointed, without looking up. 'There, sir, is the door'; and went on with his labours.

The interior intensity of life in Cheyne Row was only one aspect of Carlyle's life in Chelsea. As the 'sage of Chelsea' he dominated the district. The extraordinary position he came to occupy as the mentor of the Victorian age, not solely as historian or man of letters, but as one with some essential secret of wisdom or recipe of improvement, surrounded even the course of his walks by the river with reverence. The beginning of this special reverence may be traced to the works in which he attacked the social and industrial problems of the 'hungry forties'. He was 'the master', whose *Chartism, Past and Present* and *Latter-Day Pamphlets* inspired the *Hard Times* of Dickens, the *Unto this Last* of Ruskin. Yet as the century advanced, and, after the death of his wife in 1866, he relapsed into rarely broken silence, his long life and continued residence in the one place, as well as his printed works, seemed to foster totemic veneration. The images of which the Victorian artists made so many, the medallion by Woolner in the fifties, the portraits by G. F. Watts and Millais, the portrait by Whistler of 1874, were the icons of the Chelsea print shops; added to the number of visitors who came to waylay the original, and catch a glimpse of the grizzled beard, the clear blue eye, the thin cheek brightly tinged with red, the Inverness cape and wide-brimmed hat of which through the years Mr and Mrs Robert Heath made for him so many replicas: which finally seemed inseparable from his main promenade, Cheyne Walk. Not even Sir Thomas More is identified more closely with Chelsea than Carlyle. Woolner's relief on the façade of the present No 24 Cheyne Row, the bronze statue by Sir Edgar Boehm, erected (1882) in the garden on the Embankment, the year after Carlyle's death, are the fitting local tributes of his era.

In contrast, other Victorian writers are the merest transients. It may be noted that Elizabeth Cleghorn Stevenson, better known as Mrs Gaskell, was born (1810) in the terrace known as Lindsey Row at No 93, but has no other connection with Chelsea, her mother dying less than a month afterwards and the child being promptly placed under an aunt's care at Knutsford in Cheshire (the *Cranford* of Mrs Gaskell's most celebrated book). 'George Eliot' at the other extremity of life was there as short a time. George Henry Lewes, the main prop of her existence, was dead two years, she had been married to John Cross for seven months, when early in December 1880, she and her husband came to No 4 Cheyne Walk. The great woman novelist was 61 and in a melancholy and ailing condition. The move produced the hopeful comment usual on such occasions: 'I find myself in a new climate here—the London air and this particular house being so warm compared with Witley.' Yet in less than three weeks (22 December 1880) she died of a chill caught at one of the St James's Hall concerts. The arrangement of her books 'as nearly as possible in the same order as at the Priory'; a few chords on the piano 'played with all her accustomed enjoyment', a reading with Mr Cross of the *Data of Ethics* and the *Study of Sociology* by her old friend Herbert Spencer, a last visit from Spencer himself; such are the slight components of her evanescent association with Chelsea.

At about the same time and for some time after new and exotic currents of thought, opposed to the High Victorian culture, were flowing in the district. They are to be discerned in Tite Street, whence Whistler conducted his campaign against the Victorian artist critic, and public: where in 1884, Oscar Wilde, just married to Miss Constance Lloyd, came to live, with his bride, at No 16. Wilde was in his thirtieth year. His youthful displays of audacity and brilliance had already made him well known as poet, wit and 'professor of aesthetics'. The *Poems* of 1881 had passed through several editions (though each edition, it is true, consisted of only 200 copies). The comic opera *Patience* in the same year, had established the popular conception of Wilde as a 'Bunthorne', a posturing, soulful figure in strange garb. The lecture tours of 1882 and 1883, in America and Britain, had triumphantly preached 'the principles of true artistic decoration', the error of antimacassars and waxed peaches under glass. He now appeared (after a visit to Paris) still brilliant but transformed, correctly and fashionably dressed, prepared to cut a figure in Society, together with his 'grave, slight, violet-eyed Artemis'.

There was more than one reason for settling in Chelsea. His mother, Lady Wilde, the poetess 'Speranza', after the death of Sir William Wilde, in 1876, had transferred her salon from Merrion Square in Dublin to Oakley Street. Her house in Oakley Street, Chelsea had become the meeting-place of Irish nationalists, lovers of poetry and disciples of her son's 'aesthetic' creed. 'All London,' said Speranza, 'comes to me by way of King's Road ... Americans come straight from the Atlantic steamers moored at Chelsea Bridge.' In

Tite Street, moreover, he was not only near the 'salon' of which he was the star, but in the same road as Whistler, from whose conversations on art he had already so much profited. An angry and unfriendly Whistler in these days, bankrupt after the libel action against Ruskin, deprived of the White House which he and E. W. Godwin had designed, but installed since 1881 in another studio at No 13 Tite Street.

The home of the Wildes at No 16, a plain, red-brick, basement house of four floors, with a front bay window passing through three floors, was, as far as the interior was concerned, a challenge to the taste of one which had so much to say about 'The House Beautiful'. Wilde called in Godwin to help him in the scheme of decoration and that curiously interesting architect (whom Sir Max Beerbohm has described as 'the greatest aesthete of them all') added the eclectic flavour characteristic of him and something of the restraint on which Whistler had insisted. There was no trace of William Morris's ideas of furnishing, though Wilde in his lectures had frequently quoted him. The peacock feather motif, so frequent in the late-Victorian aesthetic decor, was banned by his superstition: but chairs copied from Greek vase paintings expressed the classical leanings of both Godwin and Wilde and a general simplicity and freshness of colour may be traced to Whistler's influence. The regularity of the continuous frieze of framed etchings that ran round two walls of the drawing-room (after the fashion of Ruskin's Turner water-colours) would not, perhaps, have been disapproved of by Whistler himself. The walls and woodwork of the study on the top floor were painted white, in the lower rooms the walls were buttercup yellow, the woodwork lacquered a golden red, the interior doors replaced by curtains. The objects of art included some Whistler studies, and in Wilde's own room, a Monticelli, a Japanese print, a drawing of the triumph of Eros by that favourite artist of the Aesthetic Movement, the decadent Pre-Raphaelite, Simeon Solomon; while a cast of the Praxitelean Hermes stood by the writing-table that had once belonged to Carlyle. There were few of those aesthetic 'properties', the fans, the sunflower-patterned screens, with which Du Maurier surrounded his pictorial parody of Wilde, Mr Jellaby Postlethwaite: yet the many, accustomed to mahogany and horsehair, thought, or took it for granted, that the interior was odd and even vulgar; incurring the mild rebuke that 'Vulgarity is the conduct of others'.

For eleven years, until the thread of his career was broken by the trial of 1895, Wilde lived at No 16 Tite Street. The exchange of witticisms and telegrams that followed his criticism of Whistler's 'Ten O'Clock' lecture in 1885, gains in piquancy from their being close neighbours. It is under the heading *Tenderness in Tite Street* that Whistler expresses his sarcastic acknowledgment to Oscar of 'your exquisite article in the *Pall Mall*'. Wit by telegraph ('when you and I are together we never talk about anything except me') goes over the electric wires ('from Whistler Tite Street to Oscar Wilde Chelsea').

There were receptions at Tite Street. During the period when Wilde was editor of the *Woman's World* and, with Godwin, interested himself in dress reform, Constance on occasion received her guests in the 'modified form of Greek dress' advocated by her husband and his architectural friend. Brilliant stories, essays and plays between 1887 and 1893 were written in the top floor sanctum: yet the association of their author with Chelsea grew steadily less. The artists of the region (including Whistler) were not aesthetes. His friendships flourished elsewhere. His plays—and pleasures—took him into the undomestic and centralised area of theatres, restaurants and metropolitan meeting-places; while his wife stayed at home with the two children. The House Beautiful became the colourless background of a life lived elsewhere. It is only for a moment or two that Chelsea is lit by a sinister flash from the bonfire of his career. The Marquis of Queensberry makes his furious appearance at No 16 Tite Street in 1894 and is thrown out. The lurid light briefly illuminates the Cadogan Hotel, Sloane Square, in April 1895, where in the company of Lord Alfred Douglas, the unfortunate man gulps his hock and seltzer, puffs at cigarette after cigarette, idly turns over the pages of the *Yellow Book* or gazes dully at the newspaper reports of the law court proceedings, while he awaits arrest, a scene of tragedy with a pungently period setting that has incited John Betjeman to a poem. In a final sinister gleam, one sees the disruption of the Oakley Street salon (Lady Wilde died while her son was in Reading Gaol) the dispersal of the House Beautiful's contents at a sale that was little better than a pillage.

It is a contrast to turn to the sojourn in Chelsea of Henry James —so different in every way from Wilde (whom he is said to have called a 'fatuous cad', and whose *The Importance of Being Earnest* he is reported, by Hugh Walpole, to have described as 'miserable trash')—tenaciously clinging to respectability and social conformity as almost aesthetic ideals. It was towards the end of Henry James's 40 years' residence in England that he came to Chelsea; in 1911 when he was 68. Since 1896 his headquarters had been the delightful Lamb House at Rye. In 1910 he had made his last visit to America. On his return he felt the need of town. Lamb House had to be abandoned, at least for the winter. He could 'no longer stand the solitude and confinement, the immobilisation of that contracted corner in these shortening and darkening weeks and months'. He took rooms in Cheyne Walk, where he began the fragmentary autobiography contained in *A Small Boy and Others* (1913), *Notes of a Son and Brother* (1914) and *The Middle Years* (1917). 'I apply myself to my effort every morning at a little *repaire* in the depths of Chelsea, a couple of little rooms that I have acquired for quiet and concentration.' Presently, his secretary, Miss Bosanquet, found him permanent quarters at 21 Carlyle Mansions, Cheyne Walk. In this modern block of flats no nostalgia for old cream-panelled rooms. The rooms at Carlyle Mansions, looking over the river were 'admirable and ample . . . so still and yet so animated . . . ideal for work'. He found, like Leigh Hunt, repose in the atmosphere. 'I sit here,' he wrote to his sister-in-law, 'with my big south window open to the River, open wide and a sort of healing balm of sunshine flooding the place.'

Gouty, dyspeptic, shortsighted (though not incapacitated), he enjoyed a bath-chair as a luxury: 'the long, long, smooth and really charming and beguiling Thames-side embankment' offered, he thought, an ideal promenade for meditation, 'in the sense of variety and tranquillity . . . of jostling against nobody and nothing'. His seventieth birthday (15 April 1913) brought many tributes: a 'huge harvest of exquisite, of splendid sheaves of flowers', a 'golden bowl' (materialisation of one of his titles) 'a very brave and artistic exact reproduction of a piece of old Charles II plate' which sat 'with perfect grace and comfort on the middle of my mantelpiece where the rare glass and some other happy accidents of tone most fortunately consort with it'.

Then came the war; destroying his conception of the age he lived in but decisively confirming his affection for Britain. The titles of his two, last, projected novels *The Ivory Tower* and *The Sense of the Past*, seemed dissonant in the changed conditions. He chafed to do more than minister to Belgian refugees in Chelsea. 'My hands, I must wash them,' he said to Logan Pearsall Smith, 'My hands are dripping with blood. All the way from Chelsea to Grosvenor Square I have been bayoneting and hurling bombs.' There was little he could do except to identify himself with Britain. To be naturalised, would, he jokingly remarked, enable him to say 'We' when the Allies advanced. But how did one become naturalised? He asked Ford Madox Hueffer. 'You go to a solicitor' the latter suggested. 'Good, I will, at once,' said James, with fewer words than usual.

It was as a British subject that he died in Chelsea early in 1916 after a stroke. Before the end, Edmund Gosse approached the bed where he lay and whispered 'Henry, they've given you the O.M.' There was no sign from the apparently unconscious writer: but when Gosse had gone, he said cheerfully enough to the nurse: 'Nurse, take away the candle and spare my blushes.'

The memorial tablet in the old church identifies him with Chelsea as with the nation and a memorial service was held in the church, where it had always pleased him to remember Sir Thomas More sang in the choir. With the end of a modern epoch and of a remarkable genius it seems appropriate to conclude a brief account of the Writer's Chelsea. It is tempting to wander on into Carlyle Square and pause there in 1916 where, at the performance of *Façade* and with some adaptation of Futurist ritual, an invisible poet, Dame Edith Sitwell enounced her poems through drawn curtains and an improved megaphone (called the 'Sangerphone'), to the music of William Walton. The influence of Chelsea on the development of Arnold Bennett is an interesting study in itself, yet here it may be enough to remark that Chelsea has not lacked distinguished writers down to the present day.

CHAPTER FIVE

The Artist's Chelsea

Popular usage terms painters 'artists' and though, of course, they are, or should be, so, a somewhat awkward distinction thus tends to be made between them and others who pursue an art, or a craft in which there is a measure of creative and imaginative effort. As far as Chelsea is concerned, painters, numerically, and in their individual importance, are its characteristic artists, but allowance must be made for the others and apology need scarcely be offered for beginning a chapter on 'The Artist's Chelsea' with some reference to its eighteenth-century porcelain.

It is true that our history, at its beginning, couples the great name of Holbein with that of Sir Thomas More: we look with interest at his delineation of the More family at home, not only for the persons assembled, but for what indications it gives of the Tudor Chelsea interior—all too slight as they are. We speculate on the life of the Dutch flower painter Van Huysum during his stay in Sir Robert Walpole's household: and in the course of the eighteenth century the record of painting in Chelsea is not entirely blank. The Venetian Sebastiano Ricci who stayed in London c. 1710–15, painted 'The Resurrection' for the apse of the Royal Hospital's chapel. Giovanni Battista Cipriani, who was born at Florence in 1727, came to London in 1755 and was a founder member of the Royal Academy in 1768; decorator of the State Coach and author of so many designs skilfully engraved by his fellow-countryman Francesco Bartolozzi; had his connection with the district and was buried in the old churchyard at Chelsea, in 1785, his friend Bartolozzi erecting a tomb to his memory. Paradise Row had its sprinkling of minor painters. The German portraitist John Giles Eccardt, assistant of Vanloo and protégé of Walpole, who painted (1747) the portrait of Thomas Gray, now in the National Portrait Gallery, died in Paradise Row in

1799. Samuel Cotes (1734–1818), miniature painter and brother of the better-known Francis Cotes, lived there: so did John Collet (?1725–80), a disciple of Hogarth, and William Hamilton, R.A. (1751–1801), one of Boydell's Shakespeare illustrators (and a native of Chelsea). James Northcote, R.A. (1746–1831), whose altarpiece 'The Descent from the Cross' is in the present St Luke's Church, Sydney Street, was staying in 'Cheyney Walk' in 1781.

Yet in spite of this muster of worthy but minor painters, the eighteenth-century 'artist's quarter', in a more coherent and brilliant sense, was not to be found in Chelsea but in the region of Long Acre, St Martin's Lane and Leicester Fields. If Chelsea then attained European fame as an 'art centre', it was because of its potters rather than its painters. The history of the Chelsea China Factory is not closely documented. Reginald Blunt's exhaustive enquiry into its site led him to conclude, substantially in agreement with Faulkner, that it stood at the upper end of Lawrence Street at the corner of Justice Walk, near 'Mr Tobias Smollett's'. In the cellar of the little 'Prince of Wales' public-house, Blunt himself examined 'some remains of cylindrical, domed-topped brick structures, which can hardly have been anything but kilns'.

It seems to have been established some time before 1745, like the other English factories at Bow and Derby, seeking to rival the products of Meissen ('Dresden') and of the French industry. In its early days it produced much uncoloured porcelain, creamy white with a satin glaze, and some Oriental designs in blue and white. In its most flourishing period, towards 1760 (by which time the French factory at Sèvres and the factory at Tournai, in the then Austrian Netherlands, were in full swing), it became 'rococo', its products notable for moulded ornament, gilding, and a rich claret colour and 'mazarine blue'. Success coincided with the management (1749–65) of the Belgian, Nicholas Sprimont, who came from Liège, and had also worked as a silversmith in Soho. It has been suggested that he, and through him the Chelsea factory, had close connections with the Tournai works founded in 1751; an Anglo-Belgian exhibition (1954), at the Anglo-Belgian Institute in London, illustrated the link. There were artist-craftsmen, Duvivier, Willems, Gauron, who worked for both. Resemblances can be found in colour and gilding between some Tournai porcelain and that of Chelsea's 'gold anchor' period.

Sprimont, who lived at the nearest house to the old church, in Church Row or Prospect Place as it has also been called (No 63 Cheyne Walk, largely demolished by bombing in 1941), remained active until 1764. By 1752 the factory was selling porcelain to the value of £3,500 a year, employed a hundred hands and was training a hundred lads, 'taken from the parishes and charity schools', in designing and painting. At a somewhat later date, Mr Boreman, or Bowman, the chief landscape painter, received 5s. 3d. a day, assistants skilled in painting birds, flowers and insects rather less. The paintings included botanical specimens copied from Miller's *Figures of Plants* and an advertisement of the time refers to 'plates enamelled from Sir Hans Sloan's plants'. The Royal patronage, first of George II, then of George III and Queen Charlotte, contributed to the Factory's celebrity. The story, related by Faulkner, after a Mr A. Stephens, who had it (in 1814) from the foreman of the China Factory (then in the workhouse of St Luke's, Middlesex), that Dr Johnson baked his own compositions in the ovens of Lawrence Street, has been often repeated. It is not impossible; and that Johnson by his own unaided efforts should fail to arrive at the right soft-paste mixture is entirely credible; but the story remains an unverified piece of Johnsoniana; its truth scarcely proved by the fact that a set of Chelsea ware came from the Doctor to Mrs Piozzi.

The first traceable reference to the Johnsonian experiment in Chelsea, appearing in the Monthly Magazine, 1821, under the heading 'Stephensiana', is as follows:

I was told by the foreman of the Chelsea China Manufactory (then in the workhouse of St Luke's, Middlesex) that Dr Johnson had conceived a notion that he was capable of improving on the manufacture of china. He even applied to the directors of the Chelsea China Works, and was allowed to *bake* his compositions in their ovens in —— St, Chelsea. He was accordingly accustomed to go down with his housekeeper, about twice a week, and stayed the whole day, she carrying a basket of provisions along with her. The Doctor, who was not allowed to enter the *mixing* room, had access to every other part of the house, and formed his composition in a particular apartment, without being over-looked by anyone. He had also free access to the oven, and superintended the whole process; but completely failed, both as to composition and baking, for his materials always yielded to the intensity of the heat, while those of the company came out of the furnace perfect and complete. The doctor retired in disgust, but not in despair, for he afterwards gave a dissertation on this very subject in his works; but the overseer, who has read this, assured me in the

10   *Ranelagh: the Rotunda (1754). By Canaletto*

11   *Ranelagh: exterior of the Rotunda*

12 *At the Swan Inn, Chelsea*

13 *The race for Doggett's Coat and Badge finishing at the old Swan Inn, Chelsea. By Thomas Rowlandson*

spring of 1814, that he was still ignorant of the nature of the operation. He seemed to think that the Dr imagined one single substance was sufficient, while he on the other hand asserts that he always used sixteen, and he must have had some practice, as he has nearly lost his eyesight, by firing batches of china, both at Chelsea and Derby, to which the manufacture was afterwards carried.

The life of the factory in Chelsea was not long. Sprimont, who became proprietor on the death (1758) of Sir Everard Fawkener, the original owner, retired in 1769; William Duesbery took over; the remaining stock and moulds were moved to Derby, when the factory was finally closed and the buildings pulled down in 1784. Yet the china itself—the tureens and dishes moulded in the form of rabbits, doves, partridges, melons and cabbage-leaves; the typical figurines, the scent bottles and trinkets—charming rococo trifles; always retained prestige. Of the four periods distinguished by their marks —'Triangle', 'Raised Anchor', 'Red Anchor' and 'Gold Anchor' —the Red Anchor Period—1754 to 1758—is outstanding in its charm.

To painters the attraction of the river grew with the development of the landscape art itself. It is a tribute to Chelsea Reach that Turner, who knew so well the waterways of Britain and Europe; Severn, Humber and Tyne, Rhine and Seine, Tiber and Arno, the Thames in every phase, should, in his old age, choose this particular stretch of river (one imagines him to have chosen the view rather than the house at Cheyne Walk) for daily contemplation. That he liked the view may, of course, be far from the complete explanation of his going to Chelsea (at some unspecified date in his later years). His secretiveness, his natural tendency to lead two lives, both of which had elements of mystery, led him, no doubt, to 'hide' there as an alternative to his main hiding-place in Queen Anne Street. His biographer, Walter Thornbury, makes much of his puzzling absences from his principal address, the perplexity they caused his house-keeper, Hannah Danby, her tracking him to the cottage by the riverside. 'The adjoining cottage they [she took a friend with her] found to be devoted to the sale of light refreshments, one of which was the conventional ginger-beer; and the outlay of twopence enabled them to hold a gossip with the proprietor, in the course of which a little judicious interrogation soon satisfied them that the lady and the old gentleman next door must be the great painter and his landlady. They were grieved, however, to learn that the gentleman had been very unwell and that he had seldom been out for the last two months.' This, it would seem, was in 1851, for Turner is reported to have died soon after. 'On that final day—I believe within an hour of his death—his landlady wheeled his chair to the window, to enable him to look upon the sunshine in which he delighted so much, mantling the river and illuminating the sails of the passing boats.'

He had apparently known his landlady at Margate, but perhaps took her name, 'Booth', to convey that any name would do to preserve his anonymity. Thornbury discounts the tale of his flourishing a roll of banknotes and declaring he could buy the house—a gesture that does not seem in character, but, garrulous and circumstantial as he was in apocryphal matters, silent on many things it would be useful to know, Thornbury gives no coherent account of the Chelsea period, though it must be admitted his subject did much, in advance, to prevent it. Yet even the atmosphere of mystification causes our fitful glimpses of Turner at Cheyne Walk to be curiously clear. It is evident that locally he stood out as a 'character'—the 'Puggy Booth' the urchins jeered at, the retired 'Admiral Booth' the shopkeepers supposed him to be: through their eyes one can see the short, sturdy figure with that seafaring look he had always had, his face, weatherbeaten by a lifetime so largely spent in the open air, typically that of an old salt. He is plainly in view in the little public-house where he repels the friendly greeting of an artist who recognises him. 'I shall often drop in now I've found out where you quarter'—'Will you? I don't think you will,' replies Turner, getting up to go. Or on the early morning steamboat to the City, parrying the curiosity of 'the gentleman who knew him' and was so surprised to see him there.

As a corrective, however, to Thornbury's, and other highly coloured accounts, one may consider the reference to Turner in Chelsea made by Leopold Martin in his reminiscences of his artist father, John Martin. The two Martins paid a visit to Turner at Queen Anne Street, Cavendish Square, at about the end of 1838. At this comparatively early date (Turner was 63 and had thirteen more years of life) it would seem he already had the Cheyne Walk cottage; what is more, did not mind saying so. Martin, it may be added, gives the impression of a clear-headed witness of precise memory.

'Mr Turner intimated that on my father's arrival he was on the point of walking over to his small place at Chelsea. If inclined for a walk, would he accompany him? This my father willingly agreed to. Crossing Hyde Park, Brompton and so on by the footpaths through market gardens to Chelsea, a very pleasant ramble, Mr Turner introduced us to a small six-roomed house, on the bank of the Thames at a squalid place past Lindsey Row, near Cremorne House.' The respectable Leopold was somewhat offended by its meanness: 'the house had but three windows in front' and apart from its magnificent view was 'miserable in every respect', furnished in the poorest fashion. An old woman (Mrs Booth, presumably) brought them porter and bread-and-cheese. 'Mr Turner', however, seemed delighted with it all. He 'pointed out with seeming pride the splendid view from his single window, saying: "Here, you see my study; sky and water. Are they not glorious? Here I have my lesson, night and day!"'' This is an unexpectedly genial Turner, whose words it may well be give the real secret of the supposedly furtive and eccentric episode —simply, indeed, the quiet study of nature. The roof of the house (Nos 118–19 Cheyne Walk) was, as one can still appreciate, a good vantage point, from which (wrapped in his dressing-gown) Turner could watch the sun rise and the changing aspects of the river. He is said to have put up the balustrade on the parapet himself and may have bought it second-hand as it is earlier in style than his day. The engraving, in Thornbury's *Life*, of the little bedroom in which Turner died on 9 December 1851 (top hat and umbrella tell, no doubt, of the departed tenant), is spartan enough to justify Leopold Martin's criticism of the furnishing: but for modern eyes, the house itself, as restored by C. R. Ashbee, retains, or has acquired, considerable charm.

Some ten years after the walk from Cavendish Square, John Martin, who as the painter of prodigious, romantic effects was at that time freely compared with Turner, settled with his family in Cheyne Walk at Lindsey House. The year was 1848. Turner was still there, in what Ruskin described, in awful capitals, as the House of a Stranger; but Martin, aged 60, famous for *The Fall of Nineveh* and other stupendous works, probably came to Chelsea because it was cheaper, and considered healthier, than Marylebone where he had previously lived.

The beautiful old mansion was then known as Lindsey Row (Nos 1–7). Martin occupied the central part (No 4): which he preferred to call 'Lindsey House'. It had had distinguished tenants since the days of Count Zinzendorf and the Moravian brotherhood: Joseph Bramah, inventor of the Bramah lock and the modern water-closet;

the brilliant engineers, the Brunels, Sir Marc Isambard Brunel, creator of the Thames Tunnel, and his son, Isambard Kingdom Brunel, engineer to the Great Western Railway and designer of the marine colossus, the *Great Eastern*. Martin was the second of several artists to live at No 4 Lindsey Row, following the Pre-Raphaelite precursor, William Dyce, R.A., who was there 1846–7.

The Victorian arrangement of the house (afterwards No 98 Cheyne Walk) is carefully detailed by Martin's biographer, Thomas Balston. The hall had its plaster busts of Queen Victoria, King Leopold and the painter himself. The front drawing-room on the first floor overlooking the picturesque foreshore, the back drawing-room on the garden, were rich with rosewood furniture. A smaller back-room was Martin's studio. The second floor consisted of bedrooms— a mahogany four-poster in the chief bedroom. Servants slept in the two attic bedrooms above. Martin's libary included such appropriate works of reference as Whiston's *Josephus*, Bonomi's *Nineveh and its Palaces* and Abington's *Chaos and Creation*. An impressive piece of furniture was the great carved cabinet of black wood, with its shelves of the medals and jewels he received from European sovereigns, its drawers containing his plans for scientific improvements that recall the inventiveness of the Brunels. It was at Lindsey House that Martin embarked on his last huge set of apocalyptic pictures, the 'Judgment' series. The Rev. A. Cleveland Coxe, Rector of Grace Church, Baltimore records a visit there in *Impressions of England*, *1851*. 'We called on Martin. He was engaged on a picture of the Judgment. Full of his mannerisms and sadly blemished by offences against doctrinal truth but not devoid of merit or interest.'

Like Turner, he studied effects of sky, from the balconies on the first and second floors of Lindsey House. He pressed into service the Chelsea boat builder, Charles Greaves, who rowed Turner about the river and whose sheds, rowboats and barges contributed to the picturesqueness of the foreshore. The Greaves family lived near-by at Belle Vue Cottage (No 91 Cheyne Walk). Charles Greaves' son, the remarkable painter, Walter Greaves, was a child then but lived until 1930, and was able to recall for Sir John Rothenstein (*The Artists of the Nineties*, 1928) how 'whenever there was a storm and my father had to stay up all night to look after the boats, Martin used to say to him, 'If there are good clouds and a good moon ring my bell!' When the bell rang, Martin would appear on the balcony to make his sketches—it is, perhaps, in origin a Chelsea sky that looks on the sensational incidents of *The Great Day of His Wrath* (1853).

The Martins left Lindsey House and the contents were sold after the death of the painter in 1854 (when on a visit to the Isle of Man). The next artist to arrive was Daniel Maclise, who occupied the house from about 1861 to his death in 1870 (he was then 73). His supreme effort on the wall-paintings for the Houses of Parliament, his disappointment at their cold reception (they are still disregarded) are said to have affected the health and spirits of this previously popular and sociable Victorian. He became a recluse, keeping indoors, sitting with his sketchbook at one of the windows looking on the river. He was given, like Carlyle, to complaints about noise, yet his annoyance produced a lively account of the old 'free wharf' where, said Maclise, in a letter to *The Times*,

for ever come sailing and oaring in, even in the dead of night, with peculiar cries, as they hoist or lower their masts . . . certain barges called Billy-boys, laden with every kind of material from a brick to a balk of pine 40 feet long. Masses of granite arrive here . . . Three, four or five horses are necessary to pull these importations up an inclined plane from the river and the horses are immersed before my eyes, above their hocks on the coldest of winter days . . . and daily maimed in their goaded endeavours to bring up their load . . .

Meanwhile, the artists' Chelsea, after its earlier nineteenth-century romantic phase (Turner and Martin), had passed into what may be called its Pre-Raphaelite phase with the arrival (severally) of Dante Gabriel Rossetti; William Holman Hunt, William Bell Scott and William De Morgan. The house, No 16 Cheyne Walk, to which Rossetti came in 1862 (aged 34), can be considered, apart from his striking and eventful tenure, as a distinguished building in its own right. It belongs to a period for which Pre-Raphaelites, in theory, had no love, having been built, three years after the death of Queen Anne, in 1717, though subsequently it had been much altered. The added bay window to the first and second floors, incongruous though it appears, does not entirely spoil the simplicity of the façade with its tall well-proportioned windows. Interior alterations had somewhat disturbed the original simplicity of plan and done away with the main staircase leading to the upper rooms, but though they produced a small labyrinth of corridors, the rooms were still spacious and ample. As well as the large room at the back used by Rossetti as a studio, a drawing-room, 40 feet long, runs across the front of the house, and gave him a delightful pre-embankment view of the jetties and beached sailing boats on the shore. The house remains especially distinguished in the beautiful ironwork of railings and gateway. The old description, 'Tudor House', was clearly a misnomer; so too, it has been shown, was the later description, 'Queen's House'. The initials, R.C., on the gate having no reference to 'Catherina Regina' (Catherine of Braganza) but to Richard Chapman 'of St Clement Danes, appothecary', for whom the house was built by an unknown but very capable architect in the reign of the first George.

The lover of the Middle Ages in this classic setting might seem out of place, yet the personality of Rossetti took command as decisively as that of Carlyle at Cheyne Row. There was in 1865 that wonderfully Pre-Raphaelite evening party at Cheyne Walk, assembling Edward and Georgiana Burne-Jones, William and Jane Morris, the Ford Madox Browns, Arthur Hughes, William Bell Scott . . . yet many links were snapped or straining. There were later acquaintances present, Swinburne, Whistler and that fascinating 'villain of the piece', Charles Augustus Howell. Rossetti's wife was dead and he tried to forget the past in new friends, new diversions and new work. The sitting- and bed-rooms capable of housing three guests, accommodated, off and on, Swinburne, William Michael Rossetti, and Theodore Watts-Dunton—though not, as originally planned, George Meredith, who speedily decided the ménage was not for him. It was a period when Rossetti began to paint with a professional ease in marked contrast with his earlier efforts; and found a ready market, employing assistants who lived on the premises, W. J. Knewstub from 1863 to 1867, later H. Treffry Dunn. The house by degrees took on the casual, extravagant personality of its tenant.

The garden, then an acre in extent, with an avenue of limes giving on the lawn, witnessed alike his fondness for animals—and mysterious phenomena. A varied procession of birds and quadrupeds, for some of which wire cages were provided, formed the celebrated menagerie : the owls—'Jessie' and 'Bobby', rabbits, dormice, hedgehogs, wombats, a woodchuck, a marmot, kangaroos and wallabies, armadillos, a deer, an Irish deerhound, a raccoon, squirrels, peacocks, a jackdaw, a raven, parakeets, chameleons, lizards, salamanders— as well as the zebu (whose eyes, Rossetti said, reminded him of Jane Morris) which cost £20 and proved unmanageable. The shrill cries of the peacocks gave rise to so many complaints that Lord Cadogan thereafter inserted a paragraph in his leases that peacocks were not to be kept.

It was in the garden, too, that the mesmerist Bergheim performed, throwing women assistants into a trance, during which one of them picked up a heavy man with no difficulty at all: while in the house, Rossetti and his friends, encouraged by Howell, conducted the spiritualistic séances, at one of which, he tried to call up the spirit of his dead wife.

The spacious and rational conceptions of the early Georgian architect were gradually overlaid by the mystic profusion of objects and ideas. Pre-Raphaelite green crept over the cream-coloured panels, Rossetti's passion for collecting, stimulated both by Howell and Whistler, filled the rooms with a diversity of things. The antique four-poster in his bedroom overlooking the garden was hung with curtains of seventeenth-century crewel work: this and other rooms were littered with brass repoussé bowls, old musical instruments, antique chests filled with jewels, crystals and historic costumes, Japanese screens and fans and specimens of the 'Blue and White' Chinese porcelain to which Whistler was especially addicted.

Theodore Watts-Dunton was a constant visitor in the early 1870s. He would put in a morning's work for the *Athenaeum*, sitting at the bay window overlooking the new embankment, before Rossetti came down for his midday breakfast of poached eggs (grumbling at the 'baneful and unpoetic habit of early rising'). And Watts-Dunton's bedroom was so sombre in furnishing and crowded with 'old carved heads and grinning gargoyles, and Burmese and Chinese Buddhas in soapstone of every degree of placid ugliness' that it acquired the reputation of being haunted. A pencilled note on the fly-leaf of the present writer's copy of *The Life and Letters of Theodore Watts-Dunton* by Hake and Compton-Rickett reads as follows:

Mrs Daniel writes: 'No wonder this room of Mr T. W.'s had the reputation of being haunted for every bit of furniture was black, upholstered with very dark green velvet curtains, the only bit of colour being the famous blue china which was kept in this room.' Mrs Daniel added 'West Cliff Bungalow was a bright cheerful place after 16 Cheyne Walk. I often went to Mr John Marshall, D. G. R.'s doctor with notes and messages before taking the journey. Mr H. C. looked after everything. Miss Lilly H. C. was a very cheerful companion.'

It seems quite possible that these pencillings were the work of someone directly interested in the compilation of the *Life* (perhaps of Clara Watts-Dunton who added her personal reminiscences) and that the Mrs Daniel whose words are recorded was the attendant who accompanied Rossetti to Birchington-on-Sea in 1882 shortly before his death, together with Hall Caine (no doubt the 'Mr H. C.' of the notes). Hall Caine's sister, presumably, being the 'very cheerful companion'. Here, in that case, is a fresh fragmentary side-light on the growing sombreness of No 16 Cheyne Walk in Rossetti's later days.

It is in the early days of his twenty-years' tenancy—when Swinburne was composing *Atalanta in Calydon* in the drawing-room overlooking the river, when he, Howell and Rossetti sallied forth in the evening to taste the pleasures of the town, that we find apparent gaiety: in the 1860s, that we visualise the little poet, the bearded painter and their swarthy familiar sampling the *Hermit's Cave*, the *Fairy's Bower* and other raffish attractions of Cremorne.

Then the singular psychological drama that followed the exhumation of Rossetti's poems from his wife's grave, their publication, and the savage attack on the 'Fleshly School of Poetry', in the *Contemporary Review*, in 1871, introduces us to a period of trial—and another Chelsea house, then belonging to Rossetti's friend, William Bell Scott.

This was Belle Vue House (No 92 Cheyne Walk) described by Bell Scott as 'a lovely old house close to the Chelsea end of the picturesque old wooden bridge to Battersea, a house built by the Adamses [*sic*], with a garden buttressed up from the river, and a studio behind to be easily made out of a music-room in which its first owner indulged himself and in which Handel's organ had stood in these former years'. Dating back to 1771, with a doorway, masterly in its spacious effect, it may have been the work of Robert Adam, though there appears to be no verification of this. A retired art master, Scott went to live there in 1870 (and remained until the beginning of his last illness—he died in 1890). He tells of the excited appearance of Rossetti at Belle Vue House, wildly shouting 'Buchanan', after the appearance of the dreadful article by Robert Buchanan; and of the day in 1872 when William Michael Rossetti (who also lived near by) summoned him to No 16 Cheyne Walk where 'we found our friend [Dante Gabriel] in a condition painful to witness'.

Rossetti's various changes of scene in the following period of disorder and malady are no direct concern of this narrative; but we have to take our final (nineteenth-century) look at the house—later renovated by Sir Edwin Lutyens, and today freshly revived in aspect—with Hall Caine in 1880. The façade was smothered in ivy, weeds pushed through the flags of the courtyard; there was worn coconut matting on the marble floor in the hall: the cry of the peacock was no longer heard in the silent and neglected garden: the 'Blue and White' had vanished from the shuttered rooms: the tenant was a despairing recluse, in two years to end his days at Birchington.

It was Pre-Raphaelitism in more hopeful guise that came to Chelsea in 1872 with William Frend De Morgan, a man then in his thirties, a disciple of William Morris in craftsmanship, friend of Morris and Burne-Jones, determined to revive the craft (and art) of the potter, 'within a stone's throw of the old Chelsea China Works'. He lived at No 30 Cheyne Row and rented No 36, known as Orange House (later replaced by the Roman Catholic Church of the Holy Redeemer) as show-room and workshop, an old coach-house alongside, sheltering a large kiln. With idealism, boyish enthusiasm and the impetuosity of the amateur he there began these efforts that so often (though not always) resulted in delightful tiles. Impatience to complete an order for a thousand tiles 'of a fan-shaped flower pattern' caused him to overheat and blow the top off the new kiln. 'Many a time', says Miss May Morris, 'when our Hammersmith quartette paid a visit to the Chelsea trio, we would go round to Orange House after tea and spend part of the long summer evening wandering through the house and garden eager over the latest experiment'. 'Experiment' rather than commercial certainty was the word. 'There were times when a kiln spoilt cast a slight cloud on the gathering.' On the other hand sometimes, from expected ruin would come 'a triumph of shining colour': and there were ' "spoilt pieces" that one could not help loving for some special quality in them'. Yet if a vase, that might to others, appear satisfactory did not satisfy De Morgan himself he would hurl it to the floor where it smashed in a thousand fragments.

The good work went on in Chelsea until 1882 when De Morgan joined William Morris at Merton Abbey. He conducted his pottery there until in 1887 he married Evelyn Pickering (a Pre-Raphaelite painter in the Burne-Jones manner) and they settled at No 1 The Vale: a little cul-de-sac, along the King's Road, nearly opposite Paulton's Square and rural in atmosphere. A. M. W. Stirling speaks of the house as a 'quaint, rambling dwelling, shrouded in creepers with a veranda back and front ... on one side stretched the former deer-park and opposite to it was the lovely spot where Whistler grew his larkspurs and Alfred Austin was inspired to pen "Farewell summers from a garden that I love" '. Inside it was 'full of unexpected nooks and irregularities, spruce with Morris papers and decorated with De Morgan pots and rich-hued paintings'.

The association of the De Morgans with the Vale was a long one, though until 1905 he had his pottery at Sands End, Fulham, before beginning the last remarkable experiment of his old age—the celebrated novels. They were at the Vale in 1909 when the demolition and rebuilding (described in *The Old Man's Youth*) threatened it. The 'house-cooling' party, as he termed it with defiant humour, held in that year, recalls the earlier fêtes of Chelsea:

> The guests wandered into an unexpected Fairyland. Old Chelsea Pensioners in their scarlet coats guarded the lane, which was festooned with glowing lanterns. The three houses [those of De Morgan, Professor Oliver and Stirling Lee, the sculptor] and their respective gardens were open to the guests of all . . . in one, a band played softly while nymphs drifted over the turf in picturesque dances . . . in the De Morgans' garden choral singing was interspersed by the song of a living dryad among the bushes, hard by where the head of Pan looked out wickedly from a grove of grass-green lamps . . . in the flower-scented dimness. . . . Then, by-and-by, there was supper and song in the old deer-park beneath the doomed trees wreathed with fairy lamps . . .

It was, said De Morgan himself, 'like Cremorne'.

Two houses converted into one at No 12 Church Street were the alternative to the Vale and there De Morgan died in 1917. The tablet to his memory in the old church, designed by Halsey Ricardo, Past Master of the Art Workers' Guild, with wording by Reginald Blunt, was unveiled in the following year.

It was Holman Hunt who unveiled the Rossetti monument in the Embankment Garden (fountain by J. P. Seddon, bust in relief modelled by Madox Brown) in 1887: though long before Rossetti's death their Pre-Raphaelite ways had considerably diverged. Perhaps that occasion recalled to Hunt the youthful period when they had thought of taking the 'Queen's House' together: but Rossetti in 1850 had gone to Newman Street: and Hunt to one of the houses, east of Chelsea Church, No 5 'Prospect Place' (destroyed later to make way for the Children's Hospital). The front room 'facing the mid-day sun, was essential for my "Druid" subject' (*Christians escaping from Persecuting Druids*). On moonlight nights at Chelsea he painted the tendrils of ivy (brought from Surrey) that appear on the door in the *Light of the World* (working from about 9 p.m. to 4 a.m.); attaining a moonlight effect that Carlyle approved when he was induced to pay a visit (doubtful as Carlyle was of 'papistical fantasy' in the whole). Between 1850 and 1854 Hunt produced some of his best works at the Chelsea studio, notably *The Hireling Shepherd*. Many years later, in 1879, at another Chelsea studio, this time in Manresa Road, he toiled on the last stages of his *Triumph of the Innocents* and, as he thought, triumphed over the Devil. The Devil it seemed, announced defeat by an explosion that shook the building at the precise moment when Hunt realised he had solved the difficulties of his theme. The diabolic presence (which has less than the usual Pre-Raphaelite definition of outline) may have been the product of the artist's overwrought imagination. Where exactly the studio was in Manresa Road, history does not specify.

The Chelsea of Whistler is less intense and takes on a more realistic air than the various aspects of Pre-Raphaelitism have given it. In spite of his friendly relation with Rossetti at Cheyne Walk, Pre-Raphaelitism was outside his radius : one recalls his sardonic remark on the idealistic craftsmanship of William De Morgan : 'Can one forgive a plate for a peculiar shine?' How far it was 'Whistler's Chelsea' may, in part, be shown by the fact that between 1863 and 1903, the date of his death, he had some eight different Chelsea addresses.

His first introduction to the district was via the unhistoric region of Victorian expansion, Sloane Street. A young painter, straight from his student experiences in Paris, Whistler stayed in the late 'fifties with his sister and her husband, the surgeon and amateur artist, Francis Seymour Haden, who lived at No 62 Sloane Street at the corner of Hans Place. Though they shared an interest in the graphic process of etching and at this time made some sketching expeditions together, these were outside Chelsea itself. For preference Haden went westwards along the river, in search of the rural distances he drew exquisitely. Whistler on the other hand was attracted to Limehouse and Wapping, producing those superb Thames etchings which remain classics of the copperplate. More relevant to Chelsea are the interiors, which admit us into the placid comfort of an upper middle-class home in Victorian Sloane Street; the etching *Reading by Lamplight* and the painting of the music-room, with Mrs Haden playing the piano while her daughter, Annie, listens, *Au Piano*, exhibited at the Royal Academy in 1860.

It was natural enough that after a while the young Whistler should wish to live independently; a variety of circumstances took him deeper into Chelsea. He fell out with his respectable brother-in-law, who was offended not only by the Bohemian friends Whistler freely invited over from Paris, but by his association with the *belle Irlandaise* (so much admired by Courbet), the model Joanna Heffernan. He came under the spell of Dante Gabriel Rossetti, and this had its influence probably in bringing him to No 101 Cheyne Walk in 1863. He stayed there for three years and then in 1866 moved to Lindsey Row (No 96 Cheyne Walk) with 'Jo', and remained there until 1878.

For the best part of ten years, he and his neighbour Rossetti were on most intimate terms. The magnetic personality of the latter exerted its usual effect, No 16 Cheyne Walk provided a Bohemian circle, a combination of strange characters that Whistler could enjoy, the adventurer Howell with his fantastic stories, Swinburne intoxicated by poetry and life : as well as those beautiful women who came to the house, as models, including the Spartali sisters, Christine and Marie (Marie was to appear in Rossetti's last big picture *Dante's Dream*, Christine was Whistler's *La Princesse du Pays de la Porcelaine*).

There is a point at which Whistler and Rossetti are close as painters and collectors. The handsome, contemplative, self-absorbed feminine type, with traits taken from a whole succession of 'stunners', was during this period, the theme of both. It was Whistler who incited the collecting of Japanese prints and 'Blue', though both in different ways became enthusiasts. With Whistler, the enthusiasm was creative in result : it led to that Oriental care for placing and subtle colour harmony that makes his paintings of the river at Chelsea at once so independent of time and place and yet essentially of the district.

The Whistler of the Chelsea 'nocturnes' dates from 1866, and after his curious and not entirely explained visit to Valparaiso at the age of 32. The river grew on him in the late 'sixties and early 'seventies. Its subtle evening air was like the blue compounded by Japanese artists for printing their wood-blocks. The old wooden Battersea Bridge was like one of those bridges in which Hiroshige found such decorative possibilities. One imagines the small dandified figure walking in the dusk by the shore, reciting aloud, so as to memorise, a list of the tones, shapes and lights the river presented to his eyes. Sometimes he had himself rowed along the stream by the sons of the boat builder Greaves, Walter and Henry. His relation with what he called 'the boat-people, a sort of Peggotty family' is another fascinating aspect of the continuance of Chelsea tradition.

The Greaveses knew the ways of painters, of old—Turner and Martin among them. Walter and Henry, captivated by Whistler, themselves turned painters—or were encouraged by him to pursue a natural bent. As boys they had painted heraldic devices on the boats. Walter, who was to become famous, born in Chelsea in 1846, was drawing the river spectacle at the age of fourteen. His famous *Boat Race from Hammersmith Bridge* (Tate Gallery) appears to have been painted about 1862 when he was sixteen. Something more than a masterpiece of 'child-art'—a kind of superb 'primitive'—it clearly owed nothing to Whistler, though later, both in pictures and in personal appearance, Walter Greaves, who remained Whistler's devoted slave until 1887, did his best to ape 'the Master'. At the time when the latter broke off relations, Walter was still only 35 though he continued to dress like Whistler and imitate, as far as possible, his mannerisms. The time was to come when certain critics hailed him as greater than Whistler (while being his victim), though as Walter Sickert remarked apropos the sensational Greaves exhibition at the Goupil Gallery in 1911: 'To be dragged out of your orbit round the town like a tin-kettle at the tail of a dog, by a stronger personality may appear to the unphilosophical an experience merely painful. The truly philosophical kettle returns, dented it is true but enriched by, and grateful for, ecstatic experience ... Any nagging about mutual indebtedness is sordid and trivial in such a case. It is as if two lovers should quibble under the bough of a lime tree about which made the other happy.' Greaves did not flourish in later years, was eventually admitted as a Poor Brother to the Charterhouse (where he continued to paint Chelsea from memory) and died there in November 1930: but, though overshadowed by Whistler, he made a great personal contribution to Chelsea's pictorial record.

Yet in the 'seventies Whistler stood alone. Chelsea's 'Japanese artist' brought it triumphantly under the control of his unusual vision—which subordinated even the 'Sage of Chelsea' himself to its aesthetic demand. To Carlyle, Whistler was 'the creature', incomprehensible (as all painters were); to Whistler, Carlyle was an old man, simply, divested of the Victorian aura, in the famous portrait art proclaimed its triumph over nature. Achievement and comparative success caused Whistler to desire a house of his own. It was at

the age of 44 (and in the year of his libel action against Ruskin—
1878) that he moved into the White House in Tite Street, built for
him by the architect Edward William Godwin.

They planned the 'ideal house' together, a studio, school for pupils
and residence in one; a large studio at the top, (47 feet by 30 feet),
a studio drawing-room (30 feet by 20 feet), five bedrooms, dining-
room and kitchen; very simple (Godwin proposed a limited application of Greek motives to the mouldings); windows and doors where
they were wanted ('and not in Baker Street regularity'); something,
indeed (for the time), of an architectural revolution. A light yellow
was dominant in the scheme of interior decoration. 'To be in
Whistler's house,' remarked Charles Augustus Howell, 'was like
standing inside an egg.'

His occupancy was a matter of months. He moved in, in October
1878. The trial, with its unfortunate financial result, followed. The
bailiffs knocked at the grey-blue door of the new house. Whistler
was declared bankrupt in May 1879. The last reception was the
scene of Whistler's climbing a ladder to write his witticism over the
door. 'Except the Lord build the house, they labour in vain that build
it. E. W. Godwin, F.S.A. built this one.' It was sold, during Whistler's
absence in Venice for £2,700 to Harry Quilter, the art critic, whom
Whistler never forgave either for his art criticism or for buying and
altering the building. The alterations made by Quilter provoked
Whistler's protest in the *World*—'history is wiped from the face of
Chelsea. Where is Ruskin? And what do Morris and Sir William
Drake?'

It was in the 'seventies that Whistler had his closest and most
affectionate relations with Chelsea as a subject for paintings and
drawings, at the Grosvenor Gallery in 1877 that he exhibited the
famous nocturnes the *Blue and Gold—Old Battersea Bridge*, the
Black and Gold—The Falling Rocket, that so greatly aroused the ire
of Ruskin. The latter picture was the original cause of contention
and at the court (where this nocturne was brought in upside down)
it was argued whether it could really be said to be anywhere.
Whistler, of course, disclaimed topography. It was not, queried the
Attorney-General cunningly, a view of Cremorne? to which the
artist made his reply that 'If it were called a view of Cremorne, it
would certainly bring about disappointment on the part of the be-
holders.' It was 'an artistic arrangement'.

Nevertheless, in spite of his disclaimer, he caught the very atmosphere of the river. In a sense he may be said to have created an

aspect of Chelsea—which, the eye having once been directed to it, now seems essentially a part of the scene.

A more precise delineation is to be found in the etchings of this decade. Perhaps from one of the Greaves' boats he made his delicate distant view of 'Lindsey Row' in 1878: and in 1879 of the old 'Adam and Eve' inn. This building (demolished in 1889 in the clean sweep that got rid of a whole row including the tobacco-shop patronised by Carlyle) with its rambling balconies over the water, called forth that feeling for the linear picturesque which Whistler had shown 20 years before in his etchings down-river. The etching of Old Battersea Bridge, also of 1879, is decidedly more descriptive than the painted Nocturne.

In words, Whistler was almost as good about Chelsea as in pictures. The celebrated passage from the *Ten O'Clock* lecture, unwontedly tender, has the mystery and softness of his tone and colour and, unspecific as it is, would merit its place in any Chelsea anthology: 'And when the evening mist clothes the riverside with poetry as with a veil, and the poor buildings lose themselves in the dim sky, and the tall chimneys become campanili and the warehouses are palaces in the night and the whole city hangs in the heavens before us—then ... Nature, who, for once has sung in tune, sings her exquisite song to the artist. ...'

Chelsea, however, was the headquarters from which, in less tender mood Whistler conducted his fiercely witty campaign against the 'priests of the Philistine', the dilettante, the aesthete, and the 'intoxicated mob of mediocrity'. The development of Whistler's wit would be an interesting study. A certain pointed gaiety was always typical of him. A natural raciness of expression was refined and sharpened by his stay in Paris, his acquaintance with a man of such formidable intelligence as Degas. *L'esprit moqueur* of the Parisian was combined with an American drollery: but the razor's edge was undoubtedly added by Ruskin's attack, the failure of fellow artists to support his case, and the unsatisfactory outcome of his lawsuit. Dispossessed of the White House, he had an understandable bitterness, fomented by the fact that at No 13 Tite Street, to which he moved in 1881, he was constantly reminded of his loss; and by the delinquency of the White House's new owner, Harry Quilter (the 'Arry of *The Gentle Art of Making Enemies*); as well as the aesthetic pretensions of his neighbour, Wilde, at No 16.

Whistler, as depicted by 'Spy' (Leslie Ward—another Chelsea artist who lived in Cheyne Row at Leigh Hunt's old house) in the

1878 *Vanity Fair* cartoon, is a sardonically awesome figure: and this effect was heightened during the 'eighties by his assumption of a quite personal dandyism that was intended to complement and, as it were, illustrate, the wicked polish of his remarks. The monocle screwed in his eye glittered with disdain. A black frock coat was not, in itself, unusual, but Whistler's was longer than fashion decreed, his tall silk hat, taller and distinct in its flatness of brim. His cane was the elegant staff of an eighteenth-century grandee. His white duck trousers, together with the black coat, were deliberately conceived, according to his friend, Mortimer Mempes, as the 'harmony in black-and-white which he loved': a calculated relief of colour being provided by the coloured bows in his patent leather shoes: or the salmon pink of a prominently displayed silk handkerchief.

In this attire he was as remarkable a Chelsea figure as Carlyle— or Wilde. There is some comedy in the rival dandyisms of Tite Street. Both Wilde and Whistler, in their respective exaggerations of fashion, considered themselves the apex of the *beau monde* and were critical of exaggerations not their own. Thus Wilde's green, frogged overcoat seemed fantastic to Whistler in the flashy reticence of black-and-white, and to require the alliterative rebuke: 'restore those things to Nathan's and never again let me find you masquerading in the streets of my Chelsea in the combined costumes of Kossuth and Mr. Mantalini'.

The wordy warfare with Wilde reached its height in the exchanges that followed Whistler's exposition of 'Art for Art's Sake' in the *Ten O'Clock* lecture delivered at the Prince's Hall (February 1885); though Whistler's bolts were now hurled from a new address. He rented a studio, No 454 Fulham Road, in 1885, in the following year was installed at No 2 The Vale, with Maud Franklin who had replaced the red-haired beauty, Joanna Heffernan, as 'Mrs Whistler'. It was, like the house of William De Morgan opposite, a comfortable, verandaed early nineteenth-century piece of domestic architecture, semi-detached but with a large garden. Straitened circumstances or good taste, or the two combined, gave the interior, with its sparse furniture, yellow-washed walls and matting on the floor, an almost Japanese simplicity. Here, if the words of William De Morgan's biographer are to be taken literally, Whistler 'cultivated his larkspurs' (an unexpected condescension to nature). It was in this house, at a later date, that Charles Ricketts and Charles Shannon, established the Vale Press, which has its place in the history of fine book production

14 *Cremorne Gardens, Chelsea, in 1858*

15 *Cheyne Walk photographed before the Embankment was built*

16 *Cheyne Walk from the Old Church*

and has helped to preserve the memory of the now demolished little rural cluster of four houses.

Oscar Wilde, a great friend of Ricketts and Shannon, took William Rothenstein with him to see them at the Vale in the 'nineties. The place was still simple and fresh in colour, with its primrose walls and apple-green shelves, though the pictures on the wall (besides Shannon's lithographs)—a fan-shaped water-colour by Whistler, a drawing by Hokusai—already hinted at the treasures these fastidious collectors would later amass. As Rothenstein describes them they seem a strangely Pre-Raphaelite couple (they were, indeed, in that tradition), bent over their blocks for wood-cutting 'like figures from a missal'. Oscar Wilde, a regular visitor, compared the pale, ascetic Ricketts with his red-gold beard to an orchid, Shannon, fair and fresh-complexioned, to a marigold; while their taste, conversation and the idealism of their own work, attracted a circle in which the craftsman, like Sturge-Moore and the connoisseur, like the young Roger Fry, both joined.

Whistler, to go back a little, remained at No 4 The Vale for four years. While he was there he married the widow of his architect friend, E. W. Godwin (who died in 1886). In 1890 they moved to No 21 Cheyne Walk. Two years after, Whistler's exhibition at the Goupil Gallery proved a great success, the tide of opinion had turned in his favour, as a painter of European fame, he decided to leave London for Paris.

In theory, at least, Whistler attached little importance to a place (or a country) of residence. The artist in his sublime independence could live anywhere. If he chose Paris to live in, it was for the understanding company of confrères, a climate of opinion more congenial than he had found in London. In anticipation of the respect he would enjoy as a Master, he was able to uproot himself without pain from the Chelsea to which he had given the personal and possessive adjective 'my'.

Yet Chelsea was his one refuge in emergency, his point of rest. In the rue du Bac in Paris he kept open house and revived those hospitable breakfasts that had been an institution of the Tite Street days; but painting in Paris was moving into a new phase, unsympathetic to his delicate art. The writers—Mallarmé and Huysmans among them—paid him tribute, but the younger painters showed no wish to sit at the feet of 'the Master'.

He returned to England when his wife fell ill; her death in London, in 1896 made him homeless indeed. In the last seven years of his life, he stayed, fitfully, in several places but returned at last to Chelsea. It was at No 74 Cheyne Walk, in a house built by C. R. Ashbee on the site of a fishmonger's shop (of which Whistler had made a lithograph), that he died in July 1903 at the age of 69. Once again the memorial service of an illustrious man was held in the old church, attended by a few artists and people who had known him (among them Joanna Heffernan, the *White Girl*, now an old woman): though the grave of Whistler, with that of his wife, is at Chiswick. The two contemporaries in Britain whom Whistler most admired were Albert Moore and Charles Keene. Topographically, Moore belongs to Kensington—a fact which recalls how far the classic (and academic) school of the late Victorian age was centred in the Royal Borough, Chelsea never possessed so imposing a constellation of studios as that of Melbury Road and Holland Park Road, where the representatives of what Ruskin termed a 'senatorial and authoritative art' reigned in grandeur. This may be fortuitous. It would be stretching generalisation too much to say that Kensington was 'classic' while Chelsea was 'realist' or 'impressionist'. The gentle and unsenatorial Moore might as well have lived in the King's Road as in Holland Lane—though it is less easy to imagine Lord Leighton than Whistler in Chelsea haunts. It excites no surprise, however, that Keene should have lived in Chelsea. He moved in 1873 (while Whistler was at No 96 Cheyne Walk) from rooms over Elliott and Fry's in Baker Street to 'Paradise Row' (No 11 Queen's Road West). He rented rooms there from F. Wilfrid Lawson, one of two painter brothers, the other, Cecil Gordon Lawson (*d.* 1882), who painted several pictures of Cheyne Walk and neighbourhood, being considered, in his own time, of unusual promise.

Here the bachelor Keene, aged 50 at the time of the move and famous as *Punch* artist, made his beautiful drawings amid a jumble of illustrator's 'properties'—old swords, iron gauntlets, the torso of a wooden horse with saddle, old female costumes, rustic smocks and waistcoats, musical instruments, bagpipes and folios of prints collected through many years. In the small kitchen, if not dining out, he would concoct his own evening meal, a stew of beefsteak, potatoes and onions, left to simmer on a gas jet, and this he would eat at five o'clock, reading a book the while and invariably concluding the meal with bread and jam. This mildly Bohemian routine continued at No 239 King's Road, to which Keene moved in 1879— the apparatus by which he cooked his meals here appears to have comprised a jam pot and the spring from a 'gibus' hat over a gas burner brought by a long tube to a stool in the middle of the room. He smoked the hideously pungent mixture provided by the caked dottles of many past pipes and lamented that in these respectable quarters, where there were other tenants, he was not permitted to make that melancholy drone on the bagpipes which was his favourite recreation.

A tall man, with straggling pointed beard, habitually dressed in loosely cut tweeds and wearing a 'billycock' hat, he added to Chelsea's curious medley of fashion in the 'eighties, though in appearance he was, more than others, the 'typical artist' as the layman has come to imagine him. His life in the King's Road (where he stayed until 1839, three years before his death) seems very self-contained, though he had his acquaintances in the district as well as his quietly satisfactory friendships elsewhere. We should not expect to see him at breakfast with Whistler and his disciples in Tite Street —though it is pleasant to remember that they knew and respected each other's art with equal admiration. On the other hand, while a *Punch* draughtsman had little in common with what Keene called 'the Pre-Raphaelite set', he was friendly with Bell Scott, whose collection of first editions he admired at Belle Vue House where he astonished Bell Scott by revealing an unexpected intimacy with 'Fitzgerald, the old scholar at Woodbridge, Suffolk.'

A letter in which Keene records this Chelsea conversation is interesting not only in its attempt to imitate, or caricature, the 'Pre-Raphaelite' manner of speech but also in its awareness of the gifts of the 'old scholar at Woodbridge'. It is not likely that the translator, or creator, of Omar Khayyam, saw a great artist in Keene; it is certain the latter could not believe Fitzgerald capable of a poetic masterpiece; but on Keene's casual mention of their acquaintance (1881) Bell Scott 'jumped off his chair! "Do you know him? Why Ram Jam" (some wonderful Persian name he gave it) "is the most quite too exquisite work of the age and Rossetti considers the translations from Calderon the finest thing ..." etc. etc. So [continues Keene] I shall tell the old man. I don't know whether he'll be pleased.'

It is a commentary on the overlap of artist generations that Keene, who was a star of *Punch* in 1860 should have known Walter Sickert (who lived until 1942), put him up for the Arts Club and at the time of his last illness gave Sickert a choice of what drawings of his he liked to have. Keene, indeed, seems nearer to the 'Impressionism' of the end of the century than Whistler himself. When he died, Chelsea was already in a post-Whistlerian phase, with the 'impressionists' of the New English Art Club, who included Sickert; although, in more general terms, the combined magnetisms of its great men had really, at last, constituted it an 'artist's quarter', irrespective of any particular faction. Even so cosmopolitan an artist as Charles Conder settled there at last, living at Belle Vue Lodge from 1901 to his death in 1909. When the young William Rothenstein arrived in London from studentship in Paris, Whistler observed, 'Of course you will settle in Chelsea,' as if an artist could settle nowhere else.

That Sickert 'settled' there, would be too much to say, in view of his lifelong restlessness and also of that love for the shabbier districts of London that associates him with Camden Town and Kentish Town, Clerkenwell and Islington. It is not easy to follow his movements with precision from the 'eighties when he gave up acting and became a 'Follower', helping Whistler prepare his etching plates in Tite Street. He went to France, met Degas, lived at Dieppe, married and took a house in Hampstead, painted the music-halls of North London; all before he paused in the Vale in 1893, and for a time, rented No 1 from the De Morgans and received pupils in a 'school', as the prospectus asserted, 'under the patronage of Whistler'; the pupils at evening classes including William Rothenstein, Roger Fry and that historian of the New English Art Club, Alfred Thornton. Sickert, according to Thornton 'loved the red-faced sporting men with big-buttoned, box-cloth coats, who thronged the King's Road, and the racy retorts of the dingy little London *gamine* as she strolled the streets of Chelsea'. According to Rothenstein, he had a place of work, other than Mrs De Morgan's studio 'a small room at the end —the shabby end—of the Chelsea Embankment, west of Beaufort Street. Needless to say, this room was in one of the few ugly houses to be found along Cheyne Walk.' Sickert's interest in plebeian life and décor was a puzzle to his contemporaries. He is said, when passing a rag and bone shop with Steer, to have remarked, 'That's how I should like my pictures to look.' Steer, a man of few words which sometimes achieved the effect of wit by accident, said, 'They do.'

Otherwise, he appears simply as a visiting confrère among those who assembled socially round Philip Wilson Steer, the leading light of the New English Art Club and most firmly and indisputably settled in Chelsea from 1898, when, at the age of 38, he took No 109 Cheyne Walk—where he remained for 44 years. It was one of the late-eighteenth-century houses, given, externally, a Victorian appearance by altered windows. Steer had a studio built at the top but did not use it for long. The spacious first floor with its three tall windows overlooking the river provided both a sitting- and painting-room. Here, in placid bachelor state, he entertained his friends, would doze in peace while George Moore talked endlessly of Manet, or Henry Tonks, the martinet of the Slade School and D. S. MacColl, critic, watercolourist and 'the Ruskin of the Impressionists', argued about regrettable modern tendencies in painting.

There had always been collectors in Chelsea, and in this respect Steer followed in the steps of a More, a Sloane or a Rossetti. By degrees he filled the house with the finds of the sale-room and the little antique and lumber shops of the King's Road: Chelsea china, coins and medals, Oriental screens, paintings and bronzes. Sickert's portrait of Steer as a young man, a nocturne by Walter Greaves, water-colours by Sargent, Tonks and other friends hung on the walls. The cosiness of the interior is reflected in one of Henry Tonks's humorous conversation pieces, where the light gleams on the Chelsea figures behind the scrupulously polished glass of the cabinet and Steer, a bulky foreground presence, pours out tea for his old nurse and housekeeper, Mrs Raynes, and a party of her friends. Mrs Raynes, whose portrait by Steer hangs in the Tate Gallery and who lived to be 90 (she died in 1925), must be numbered among Chelsea characters, if only for her excellent remark, when complimented on a pudding—'There's art in everythink, even in painting pictures.' Steer was greatly attached to her and hardly less to his tabby cat, 'Mr Thomas', who lived to the ripe feline age of 18.

The years passed quietly. Every winter, Steer laid his plans and took infinite precautions against the enemy that annually invaded the snug house on Cheyne Walk—the common cold. Regularly as clockwork, he packed up in the summer and went off for his sketching outing, often accompanied by his close friend, Ronald Gray (a painter, Chelsea born, whose father had an engineering business in Danvers Street). Steer loved shopping and, with his string bag and his dog 'Peter', was a familiar figure at the fruit and vegetable stores of World's End.

Few events rippled the gentle surface of Chelsea existence. 'Flo', a girl from Fulham, took Mrs Raynes's place as housekeeper and served 'Father', as she called Steer, until the end. The great 'Mr Thomas', the cat, died of influenza in 1924 and was replaced by a 'powerful striped tabby', who stalked seagulls on the mud banks of the shore. The Thames flood of 1928 that swept into Chelsea and

Millbank (destroying many works in the basement of the Tate Gallery) invaded the basement of No 109 Cheyne Walk, the dog being rescued from water six feet deep. Steer was still living in Chelsea when war began in 1939 and stayed there until the year of his death, 1942. The fabled labyrinth of underground Chelsea provided an air-raid shelter, the main wall of the basement being discovered, as Steer's niece, Miss Hamilton, has recorded, 'to be of great strength and age, being part of one that had run down to the River since Tudor times'. Old and nearly blind, he endured patiently the discomforts of the period. His back windows were blown in, and the roof of the house damaged by bombs, though a greater source of grief towards the end was the destruction of the old church. Steer's house was again damaged by rockets after its owner's death.

So long a life is both near to and far from our own day. More distant in every way is John Singer Sargent, yet for many years he and Steer were Chelsea neighbours and great friends. Sargent, the young cosmopolite, an American born in Florence, arrived in London from Paris in 1885, taking a studio at No 13 Tite Street in succession to Whistler and, in the following year, joining in the 'Impressionist' venture of the New English Art Club, with Steer, Charles Furse and lively spirits of the time. He took a 21-years' lease of these premises in 1900, though he also had a large studio, Nos 12–14 The Avenue, Fulham Road, where he worked on his decorations for the Boston Library and Museum (it was here that he painted the generals of the 1914 war and the war picture *Gassed*).

It was during the 'nineties that he began to paint the portraits which made him so much sought after. Sir Max Beerbohm has depicted the fashionable queue outside No 31 Tite Street, the burly painter peering from the window at the row of distinguished would-be sitters, including Lady Faudel Phillips and the Duchess of Sutherland, a number of messenger-boys keeping the place of others. The Hon. Evan Charteris has related in his Life of Sargent that on one occasion a 'famous personage' asked to bring some of her friends to a sitting. He having doubtfully agreed, a crowd of 'curiously dressed representatives of the aesthetic movement' arrived, the pressure of arrivals forced the painter into a corner, and the sitting had to be abandoned.

His real home in Chelsea was the flat of his sister, Emily, in Carlyle Mansions, where he dined with her, another sister, Mrs Ormond, and their mother in a room hung with red damask overlooking the Thames, or they jointly entertained friends, Steer, Tonks,

Henry James and some of the American painters who in the early years of the century had not yet abandoned London for Paris. On these occasions, Sargent, who was tongue-tied on public occasions, would talk freely, expressing definite views on art, in which he was curiously bigoted (seeing that his appreciation of music and literature was quite wide). In some ways, and certainly in antipathy to public speaking, he and Steer were alike. They differed, obviously, on the score of travel.

Unlike the stay-at-home Englishman, Sargent found Chelsea, and the English climate, possible for only four months of the year. Within this period, his current portrait commissions had to be completed: the months remaining were spent in Venice, Rome or elsewhere in Europe. His bags were always packed ready for instant departure, his transatlantic crossings were a record in number: and to this extent Chelsea was less a part of his being than it was of Steer's. It was in Chelsea, however, though on the eve of a visit to the United States, that he died in 1925. He had gone home after a farewell dinner at No 10 Carlyle Mansions (Steer and Tonks, as so often, among the guests), the next morning the maid at Tite Street found him dead—an open volume of Voltaire's *Dictionnaire Philosophique* by his side.

His Chelsea studios were full of paintings, studies and the water-colour landscapes which were his recreation. Steer, who helped to arrange a public sale was astonished when the first day brought £146,000.

In outward appearance, and as a whole, Tite Street (named after the architect Sir William Tite) is far from being one of the most attractive thoroughfares of Chelsea. It does, however, represent interestingly that late-nineteenth-century phenomenon, the studio-house. There can have been few, if any, specially designed, top-lit studios in London before the 'sixties: though the unmoneyed painter would find an incidental advantage in the skylight of his attic. Others painted happily, as the old masters did, in the spacious rooms of old houses, not being over-particular as to the direction in which the tall side-windows faced. This was the practice of Wilson Steer at No 109 Cheyne Walk. He did not care to use the studio he added and was not averse from the entry of the sun into his painting-cum-drawing-room.

Yet, the professional studio, properly so-called, with a large top, or top-and-side north light, was considered desirable on various counts. It reflected, from the 'seventies to the early years of this century, a growing opulence and the uniqueness of the artist's professionalism. It reflected an attitude that set importance on the faithful reproduction of a given object under a steady and unchanging (north) light. For both reasons it had its value for a portrait painter like Sargent. He received his sitters in appropriately magnificent surroundings, and was able to study them without the distraction of shifting shadows and fugitive gleams. These considerations applied generally; but the studios of Tite Street also reflect the tendency of Chelsea to become a community of painters and sculptors: and something of a community feeling caused the same architect to be employed on the design of their homes and workshops—E. W. Godwin.

The White House designed for, and in conjunction with, Whistler, by Godwin, encouraged others to commission him. The young Archibald Stuart-Wortley, who bought three plots of ground adjoining the White House, required a larger house to be built on this site. George Francis (Frank) Miles, a devotee of Japanese art and portraitist in pencil, was another client, for whom Godwin devised a house of nine rooms with a studio at the top, 40 feet long. It was not an easy specialisation. 'The artist,' said Godwin, 'is the most extraordinary client that you can deal with—every individual painter has his individual idea as to what a studio should be. One tells me that he wants the light to come straight down from the roof. Another says he must only have a window light. While Pellegrini ['Ape' of *Vanity Fair*] declares he will have nothing but light—walls and roofs, all must give light. One would be driven mad if he had many artists as clients.' On the other hand, difficult too was the Board of Works, where the plan submitted for Miles's house was considered 'worse than Whistler's', and would only pass with the addition of what Godwin described as 'a number of reminiscences of a visit to Holland'.

In all, Godwin was responsible for No. 35, the White House of 1879, demolished in 1964, No 33 (The Studios), No 29, and opposite, No 44 and the neighbouring Tower House. No 31, where Sargent died, was the work of another architect, R. W. Edis. In view of this and the varying requirements of client and authority, it is hardly surprising if the group is not altogether coherent as an architectural composition, though that it is a group is apparent enough.

Tite Street and Cheyne Walk were not by any means the whole of the artist's Chelsea in the late nineteenth century. The penurious painter or sculptor could get a workshop converted or easily convertible into a studio, at a very small rent. Thus, the Avenue Studios in the Fulham Road, where Boehm, Alfred Gilbert and Poynter worked were previously the workshops used when the Onslow Gardens estate was built. In Manresa Road, the site of the Public Library and L.C.C. Technical School was occupied by a row of ramshackle buildings used as studios, facing the Trafalgar and Wentworth Studios on the other side of the road (where Wilson Steer, Sir Frank Brangwyn and Sir Frank Short among others worked in their early days). The specially built studios in Glebe Place, completed about 1890, were, the late Ronald Gray records (in some interesting unpublished notes on the origin of the Chelsea Arts Club), considered 'very smart'. Gray then had 'one of the glass shacks in Glebe Place opposite Bramerton Street'.

That famous institution the Chelsea Arts Club came into being very naturally and spontaneously in this studio world. As Chelsea was still somewhat cut off from the metropolis, the local deficiency in congenial places of resort and refreshment was all the more obvious. Two small Italian café-restaurants served the growing artist population, one, Manzoni's, almost opposite Carlyle Square, the other, the Monaco in the King's Road, which later became the 'King's Head'. Some would go for food and drink to the 'William IV' in the Fulham Road, or to the 'Six Bells' which was then pretty much like a country inn: but socially there was still something lacking. Artists began to meet as a group, for beer, bread-and-cheese and talk, in the studio of one or other. It was a logical step as well as a greater convenience to form a club; in 1891 the Chelsea Arts Club was launched at No 181 King's Road, in premises belonging to a Scottish painter, James Christie.

Whistler was one of 90 artists who expressed their willingness to join. The story is told of a foreign painter with a pronounced accent, who proposed that meetings should be held at the Pier Hotel. 'Oh, no! not a *beer* hotel,' said Whistler, affecting to misunderstand the pronunciation of the labial. There was some fear that Whistler's fame would require his election as president of the club. The memory of his stormy presidency of the Royal Society of British Artists, when, as he said, 'the artists went out and the British remained', was still fresh. It seemed a happy solution to have no such permanent office. A sculptor, Thomas Stirling Lee, acted as the first chairman. He is described in A. S. Hartrick's reminiscences as 'the most innocent and inoffensive of men' who became notorious because of a nude in a panel for St George's Hall, Liverpool, which aroused an acute fit of morality. With Lee as chairman and Whistler safely relegated to a committee of rules, the Chelsea Arts Club started off smoothly and quickly acquired the distinct and genial individuality it was to retain.

This distinct character was due in part to the fact that only practitioners in some branch of visual art were eligible as members —a rule in which it is unique among London clubs: to the fact also that it was purely social and not concerned with exhibiting works of art. An early proposal for annual exhibitions was quickly shelved: nor did it propagate any particular theory, though Whistler's brilliant exposition of 'Art for Art's Sake', the *Ten O'Clock* lecture, was re-read at the club on a memorable evening in 1891.

In 1902 the club moved to the premises it still occupies at No 143 Old Church Street, a pleasant building with its low, asymmetrical façade, its informal and varied garden front; the garden itself, with its trees and flowers and cupid fountain, by Henry Poole, R.A., as delightful as any of those for which Chelsea is famous.

The history of such an institution is better conveyed by personalities than dates. Retrospectively one sees Whistler arriving in his hansom to deliver some carefully prepared *bon mot*; or at the dinner given in his honour when he spoke of being misunderstood, likening himself to the Traveller in the old tale who drew his cloak more closely about him when the stormy winds blew, to cast it open when the sun shone again—the sun being the genial atmosphere of the Chelsea artists in their club. Or Sargent in the agonies of after-dinner speaking, scoring the table with deep scratches from a fork clutched in nervous hand; or his equally inarticulate friend, Wilson Steer, bent over the chessboard. . . .

With its resources of talent and gaiety, the Club inspired that long popular event, the Chelsea Arts Ball. Its origin has been traced to the fancy-dress dances and Mardi Gras parties organised by the members, among whom the sculptor Stirling Lee was particularly active in the attempt to create a Parisian verve. The parties became progressively more ambitious: and according to the reminiscences of Ronald Gray, one of them, held at the Chelsea Town Hall, was the direct precursor of the Chelsea Arts Ball, which except for the war years was held annually from 1908 to the 1950s. With the Albert Hall interior as background the effect was that of a tumultuous Ranelagh in a still larger Rotunda. The decors designed by members of the Chelsea Arts Club formed an interesting episode in British theatrical design.

CHAPTER SIX

Images of Chelsea

Having surveyed the history of painters and other artists in Chelsea one asks what record of it they have left; and even whom one might elect as best conveying the spirit and character of the region. The obvious answer to the latter question is Whistler. Has he not given us that dimly exquisite and poetical Battersea Bridge? distilled the subtle magic of riverside atmosphere and echoed distant festival in the slow golden descent of the rockets of Cremorne? All this is true, yet of course we should not call Whistler a topographer, nor say that his images are, on the whole, local. There is the same atmospheric poetry in his picture of Valparaiso Bay. In his cultivation of art for its own sake, for the sake, that is, of some beauty of form or colour, he escapes from particular association. His Battersea Bridge of the nocturne is an element in a generalised design (though he painted a more detailed view). Similarly, his Thomas Carlyle is scarcely to be studied as a character portrait of the Sage of Chelsea, the 'man in his time'; it has more to tell us of Whistler's flawless sense of arrangement.

Topography, in which there is fact and description is more pedestrian though, in the present context, that is, to tell us what Chelsea has looked like, it has a more definite use. Kip's famous view of Beaufort House, 1699, admirable specimen of the engraver's craft and not without its aesthetic attraction of design, is primarily of value for the information it gives. The 'arrangement' here is not that of the artist's invention but objectively of Chelsea at the end of the seventeenth century. In the right foreground we see 'Duke Street' and the beginning of Lombard Street, and the ferry boat starting on its way across. Behind Duke Street is the trimly laid out orchard and the terrace of Beaufort House, the quay of which appears to the

left. The eye travels from the landing-stage, along the Front Court of
Beaufort House, past the lodges with their pointed roofs, to the
Inner Green Court and so to the great house itself, the formal gardens
behind it and, in the distance, the King's Private Road. In the left
foreground is Lindsey House, behind it Gorges House and garden,
and then the stables of Beaufort House. To the right of the engraving
is the garden (with circular lay-out) of Danvers House, behind it,
Dovecote Close, the kitchen-garden of Beaufort House. As a document, this engraving is indispensable for the historical study of
Chelsea.

That topography and the representation of architecture and art
of a high order are not incompatible, there is Canaletto to remind us.
His painting of the interior of the Ranelagh Rotunda (National Gallery), executed, as the inscription in his own handwriting on the
back of the canvas records, in London, 1754, is both delightful to
look at and of value in the confidence it gives us that we have now
seen exactly what Ranelagh was like. It was towards the end of
Canaletto's several years stay in England, when a certain mechanical
dexterity was becoming noticeable in his style; yet the groups of
figures here are natural-looking, and the Venetian master's skill deals
superbly with the chandeliers, the ornament and intricate perspective imparting an Italian stateliness to the setting which is lacking in the popular prints of Ranelagh by Bowles of about the same
time.

The early English water-colourists were to some extent in the
Canaletto tradition (did not Girtin learn much from the Canaletto
drawings in Dr Monro's collection?) and their own combination of
architecture, social life and landscape has included views of Chelsea
that interest us from each of these points of view. The obscure James
Miller, who exhibited views of London and its environs at the Royal
Academy and the Incorporated Society of Artists from 1773 to 1791
made a charming picture of Cheyne Walk in 1776, a little west of
the end of Oakley Street, showing the sign of the old Magpye Inn
hanging on a beam over the road, and the inn's convivial box built
over the shore, one of several in the days before the Embankment.
It is delightfully intimate and the play of shadow from the tree on
the brickwork (which is, convincingly, Cheyne Walk brick) is a
typical effect still to be appreciated in photographs of modern
Chelsea. There is a sensation of cheerful noise (such, however, as
would have maddened Carlyle) of gossip along the fenced walk, the
clack of hooves, the shout of a carter or riverside character who

somewhat dwarfs his surroundings by his over-heroic proportions, the rumbling of barrels, trundled along a gangway to a barge. In the distance appears the White Windmill of Battersea.

A later water-colour of Cheyne Walk (1811) shows that unequal and prolific painter John Varley at his best. The church, which still has the original cupola that was removed four years after the date of Varley's water-colour, is tenderly silhouetted, the piers of Battersea Bridge make an enticing and delicate pattern in the intervals between the dark foreground trees, composed with all Varley's art-master science, but less than usually conventional. The wooden awning of the shop on the right survived into Victorian times.

The spirit is the same, though bonnet, shawl and crinoline tell of the new age in the lithograph (c. 1850), looking along Cheyne Walk, by Church Row, or Prospect Place, from the old church (with Sir Hans Sloane's tomb on our right). The trees and wooden rail along the river were as before, but since Varley's time the houses had evidently been somewhat remodelled, early-Victorian balconies add their gaiety; the first house visible behind the church is No 63 Cheyne Walk (shattered in the twentieth century by bombs) and taking the numbers consecutively one can just see at the corner No 59 and the window of the first floor in which, at the time of this lithograph, Holman Hunt was painting, or at all events was very soon to paint, *The Light of the World*. The conspicuously new item in the scene is the portentous gateway (suspension bridge in embryo) of the Cadogan Pier. Its air of modern improvement, not unpleasantly combined with quasi-rustic leisure, is seen to closer advantage in the minor Victorian painter Brownlow's open-air genre-piece, where the eye strays from the goat-carriage in the foreground to the admirably realised group shirt-sleeved lounger, apple-woman, plodding Chelsea pensioner, and brisk top-hatted man of business making no doubt for the steamboat to the city.

To revert to our water-colours, art and fact mingle in Thomas Rowlandson's drawing of the finish of the race for Doggett's Coat and Badge at the Old Swan Inn, though Rowlandson, always interested in any sporting event, concentrates attention on the action of the watermen and the cheering crowd, on the shore and in the line of barges drawn up for the finish and treats a little summarily, although with spirited 'calligraphy', the 'Swan' itself, while church and farther distance seem hazily remembered. It is, however, a triumph of graphic vigour. Girtin's *White House* must be numbered among the masterpieces that Chelsea has inspired, though, like Whistler's nocturnes, of which it may be considered an anticipation, it transcends topography.

It is sad that no masterpiece by Turner has come down to us depicting the Chelsea he studied so attentively—perhaps surprising also. It would seem that in those later days, the sky and river he saw from his Cheyne Walk eyrie became an inner or imaginative vision, that the sun was converted into the sun of Venice, that he looked beyond the Thames to stranger and wilder waters. While it is certain he found Chelsea inspiring it is equally certain he did not make it his theme.

For our early nineteenth-century picture of Chelsea in water-colour, apart from such rare examples by practised hands as Varley's Cheyne Walk and Bonington's view from the Red House, Battersea, we descend to the worthy though amateur level of the Gulston Collection in the Chelsea Public Library which provides fifty views of buildings, unique in many cases as record but marked by a primitive simplicity of execution. They were painted by, or for, Miss Eliza Gulston, Faulkner's assistant in the preparation of his History of Chelsea. 'From local sources we learn,' says Reginald Blunt, in his introduction to the catalogue of *Chelsea a Hundred Years Ago*—an exhibition held at the Town Hall in 1929, 'that Miss Eliza Gulston lived at Ashburnham Cottage, which stood near the river just west of Ashburnham House, at the western end of Chelsea. . . . The water-colour drawings in this collection may have been her work, but it seems more probable that they were done for her by either Mrs Jane or Mrs Honour Rush, the mother, or the wife, of the first assistant minister of the Old Church.'

With the help of Miss Gulston or Mrs Rush we can form some idea of a number of houses that otherwise would be mere names. 'Church Place' for instance, otherwise known as 'Essex House', the 'Palace' and 'Queen Anne's Laundry', which stood at the corner of Paulton's Street and Church Street, opposite the Rectory, and is described in Henry Kingsley's *The Hillyars and the Burtons*. The Burton family lived in this 'very large house called by us indifferently Church Place or Queen Elizabeth's Palace. It had been in reality the palace of the young Earl of Essex' [Parliamentary General and son of Elizabeth's favourite]. One can, moreover, peep into Lady Walpole's grotto and greenhouse, into the World's End tea gardens (at the corner of King's Road and World's End passage), see the last of Shrewsbury House (which the artist mistook for Sir Thomas More's) or be transported to the rural Chelsea of Blackland's Farm, the more rural for the naïvety of the artist's brush, which quaintly details latticed windows and thatched barn, hens and pigs, the thresher with his flail and the farm-hand in rustic smock, milkman's yoke on his shoulders. Blacklands Farm stood on the site of the Duke's of York Headquarters, its cows pastured in the early nineteenth century on what remained of Chelsea Common. 'The Family of King George III', the title of the drawing informs us, 'stop most mornings here to take milk.'

The Gulston picture of another old farmhouse, Hutchins's Farm, which stood on the north side of the King's Road between Arthur Street and Carlyle Square, on the site afterwards called King's Parade, shows the scene of a murder and robbery in 1771, of which Faulkner gives a circumstantial account, quite in the vein of the Newgate Calendar. A desperate gang arrived one night, tied up the maids, robbed and ill-treated Mrs Hutchins, 'One of them struck her so forcibly on the mouth as to loosen a tooth, on which, in the dread of still further violence, she went upstairs with them and gave them sixty-four guineas'. They shot one of the menservants, who after they had gone approached Mrs Hutchins, and saying 'How are you, madam, for I am dead,' dropped on the floor. Seven men came up for trial; four of them were hanged at Newgate; and as they were Jews, for some time afterwards 'a Jew could scarcely pass the streets but he was upbraided with the words "Hutchins" and "Chelsea", a wanton unfairness which Faulkner very properly condemns'. The farm was also the final setting of the famous stag-hunt that Faulkner witnessed in 1796 when 'the animal swam across the river, from Battersea, and made for Lord Cremorne's grounds; and upon being driven from thence, ran along the waterside as far as the Church and turning up Church Lane at last took refuge in Mrs Hutchins's barn where he was taken alive'. It would be ungrateful to wish these water-colours were more accomplished in execution for they illustrate so much of Chelsea's past, and apart from associations they suggest something of the mellow warmth of brick of vanished mansions, of Dutch-seeming neatness and orderliness, of placid and happy bowers.

The combination of fact and aesthetic feeling is well represented in the nineteenth century by Walter Greaves, who if we leave Whistler out of account, is to be considered as the artist of Chelsea *par excellence*. Greaves (1846–1930) had two objects of adoration : one was Whistler; the other was the Chelsea in which he was born and bred, which he knew the more intimately and from every aspect as a boat-builder's son and habitual waterman.

He spent the whole of his life painting and drawing Chelsea, sometimes after the manner of Whistler, sometimes with that precise and primitive vision so remarkably evidenced in his *Boat Race from Hammersmith Bridge*. The result is a very large number of splendid works, including Whistlerian nocturnes like *The Balcony* (painted from 'the Master's' window in Lindsey Row) which Walter Sickert described in 1911 (the year of Greaves's sensational first one-man show at the Goupil Gallery) as 'an august nocturne with a quality of intricate and monumental design that Whistler never reached'. It is the 'primitive' or *douanier Rousseau* Greaves on the other hand that we see in the early picture of Lombard Street, looking east (1862) where the absolute distinctness of buildings, lamp-posts and a Carlylean figure looking towards Danvers Street attains a certain magic. The same quality appears in his view of the foreshore and houses on the south side of Lombard Street (like the picture previously mentioned now on permanent loan from the Chelsea Society to Crosby Hall). Affection is implicit in the care he has lavished on every brick gable, the tower of the old church, the picturesquely stepped galleries of the 'Adam and Eve'; on every crack and stain in the river wall; while boats and barges are rendered with the mastery of their structure we should expect. These, like many later works, are signed 'H. & W. Greaves', but though Henry, the brother, did paint, he is as shadowy a figure in the combination as Hubert, the brother of Jan van Eyck, and Walter, there is no doubt, was the genius of the two. Lindsey Wharf and the family landing-stage are subjects of some of his best paintings. Of Battersea Bridge, he painted several versions—an especially beautiful version with foreground figures was exhibited in London at the Roland, Browse Galleries in 1947. The great frost of 1891 inspired another remarkable series depicting the Frozen Thames and Chelsea in snow. Greaves's *Cremorne Gardens in the Evening* showing the entrance to the theatre, the Stooping Venus fountain, and groups of visitors is fascinating in its union of tawdriness and mystery.

In 1890 'H. & W. Greaves' executed a series of wall-paintings in what was then the Wandsworth Town Hall, reputedly of Chelsea subjects, reported after the Second World War to be in a state of bad repair. Curious to see them I discovered that the Wandsworth Town Hall had become a warehouse and through the courtesy of the Streatham Engineering Company was able to look at them in the

17   Holland House in 1800

18   Old Campden House, Kensington. From a drawing by Hollar (1647)

19 Gore House, Kensington. From a watercolour by T. H. Shepherd

20 The Grill Room at the South Kensington Museum

firm's premises, the former 'mayor's parlour'. It was both mournful and exciting to have a last view of these works which were already on the verge of dissolution. Painted actually on the wall (frames are also painted round the pictures) they were pitted with numerous holes and gashes in the plaster. They were of the Thames rather than Chelsea in particular; the Pool; Mortlake with a lively crowd watching an American crew rowing on the Boat Race course; the old riverside inn at Battersea, the Red House; but they included a view of the faintly oriental 'Dancing Platform' at Cremorne with a number of the artist's typical black-coated figures standing round: and if rather cruder in style than his canvases, it conveyed, as a music-hall backcloth might—though on a smaller scale—a sort of shabby glamour.

If we turn to human iconography Chelsea is also well served. Sir Thomas More and his family circle come to life in the famous conversation piece which has also its interesting suggestion of the Tudor interior, the clock, the sideboard with linenfold panelling, the pewter plate and jug by the leaded casement, the books scattered round, the footstool on the rush-covered floor. The image of Sir Thomas himself, as first conceived by Holbein and copied by other hands, has thus been made almost as generally familiar as that of Henry VIII. The National Portrait Gallery half-length is one version that brings the Chancellor intimately before us, the keen reflective gaze, the philosophically clasped hands, the mouth at once earnest, determined and with the capacity of humour.

The National Portrait Gallery, indeed is full of Chelsea notables. Here is Sir Theodore Turquet de Mayerne, physician and chemist, a native of Geneva, knighted by James I and celebrated as the medical adviser of four kings, Henry IV and Louis XIII of France, James I and Charles I of England. He appears, old, courtly, plump and bearded in the portrait painted by some assistant of Rubens in 1652. Mayerne was then 79 and living at Lindsey House, the old farmhouse belonging to Beaufort House, rebuilt some years after his death in 1655. Sir Theodore must have been interested in art for his friend Edward Norgate, the Herald, refers to his desire 'to know the names, nature and property of the several colleurs, of Limning commonly used by those excellent artists of our Nation (which infinitely transcend those of his)'. He left to 'the poore of Chelsea where I now dwell, the sum of £50'. One of his daughters, Elizabeth, wife of Peter de Caumont, Marquis de Cugnac, died during his lifetime, in 1653, and a monument to her memory was put up on the south wall of the chancel in the old church. The Chelsea parish register records that another daughter, Adriana, was married there in 1659 to 'Armand de Coumond, Lord Marquest of Monpolion'.

A portrait painted on copper by an unknown artist suggests the opulent charm and striking appearance of the Duchess of Mazarin (who died in 1699 at the age of 53); while J. Parmentier represents the aged and quizzical features of her friend, St Evremond, in 1701, at which time he was well over 80. Sir Godfrey Kneller (1711) does justice to the florid countenance of Richard Steele (in his Chelsea period) in one of the Kit-Cat Club portraits acquired by the National Portrait Gallery in 1945. In the painting of Smollett, in the year before his death and during his exile at Leghorn, an unknown Italian artist (1770) seems to have caught a look of pain and trouble that clouds and embitters what would otherwise have been a genial face. Among eighteenth-century notables there is the celebrated physician and collector, Dr Richard Mead (who had a house in Paradise Row), in a portrait coming from the studio of Allan Ramsay (1740); a group of Count Zinzendorf and his Moravians of about the same date: Sir Hans Sloane, tranquil and learned, in S. Slaughter's half-length of 1736. If one wishes to see what Leigh Hunt looked like at the time of his residence at Upper Cheyne Row, there is the sensitive portrait by S. Lawrence (1837) which so well bears out the description given by Carlyle.

The unfortunate Dominiceti does not appear in the National Hall of Fame. One would like to have seen the picture which hung in No 6 Cheyne Walk where 'a human subject is extended on a table in a lecture room, the Doctor looks on with a scalpel in his hand; around him stand the allegorical forms of Europe, Asia, Africa and America in postures of veneration and homage; while the Doctor, the chief personage in this awful scene, tramples upon the utensils and nostrums of the Galenical art'. This portrait was sold to the son of the Doctor's assistant at an auction 'for the relief of his numerous and most clamorous creditors', but its whereabouts, if it still exists, is not known.

The iconography of Thomas Carlyle is a subject in itself. In view of his contempt for art and artists, the number of sittings he accorded must remain a matter of surprise. They were a mysterious rite to be patiently endured, though portraits of him and Tennyson were icons in world-wide demand—as Thomas Woolner discovered when he quitted the Pre-Raphaelite Brotherhood for his brief adventure in Australia. Woolner's sculptured medallion of Carlyle (1855) was one of the principal bases of his fame and fortune in later Victorian days. Each time he sat, the Sage of Chelsea had some crusty remark to make. He expressed surprise at the magnificence of Millais's house ('Has paint done all this, Mr Millais?'); he denounced the Greek gods to G. F. Watts as characterless beings; to 'the creature', Whistler, he gave the order 'Fire away'—'When you are fighting a battle or painting a picture, the only thing is to fire away.' Yet the artists were not to be deterred, and though the nineteenth-century painter R. Tait is not a Holbein, his picture of Mr and Mrs Carlyle in the ground-floor front at Cheyne Row adds to the portraits of Woolner, Millais, Watts and Whistler, a conversation piece which in interest can be compared with Holbein's More Family. How frequently also the Carlyles endured the ordeal of photography! and the photographs are perhaps the most interesting of all the Victorian likenesses, both psychologically and in the period character which even the camera subtly appropriates. The character of Carlyle seems grandly and gloomily etched into the photographic plate of 1880: in the thin worn features of Jane Welsh Carlyle the camera sums up for us the long affectionate martyrdom of Cheyne Row. It is an impressive experience to look into the haunting and haunted eyes of Dante Gabriel Rossetti, so instinct with life and personality in one of the several photographs taken by Charles Lutwidge Dodgson ('Lewis Carroll') at No 16 Cheyne Walk.

In a category apart from the photographic or painted portrait, something more than caricature, though it contains the elements of caricature and humour, a kind of graphic historical narrative, is the series of twenty-three water-colours (now in the Tate Gallery) of the Pre-Raphaelite Brotherhood by Sir Max Beerbohm, in which Rossetti's Chelsea household with its garden, zoo, stunner and pervading eccentricity is one of the most entertaining pictorial chapters. Sir Max has taken certain, though pardonable, liberties with history and chronology in the gathering. John Ruskin, who appears on the right in a scandalised attitude, had ceased to be an intimate of Rossetti by the time the latter settled at Cheyne Walk and did not visit him there. Burne-Jones (extending a flower to a wallaby) and William Morris, declaiming a poem, had also by that time ceased to be intimates in a household by no means in harmony with their tastes. George Meredith, who is seen leaning dreamily on the garden wall was never so much at home and more than one account of his projected stay indicates a brief and uncongenial contact. An account, approved by the novelist, is as follows. Mr Meredith had, rather irresponsibly, agreed to occupy a couple of rooms in Queen's House. One morning therefore, shortly after Rossetti moved in, Mr Meredith who was living in Mayfair drove over to Chelsea to inspect his new apartments. 'It was,' says the unhappy co-tenant, 'past noon, Rossetti had not yet risen, though it was an exquisite day. On the breakfast table, on a huge dish, rested five thick slabs of bacon upon which five rigid eggs had slowly bled to death! Presently Rossetti appeared in his dressing-gown with slippers down at heel and devoured the dainty repast like an ogre.' This decided Mr Meredith. He did not even trouble to look at his rooms, but sent in a quarter's rent that afternoon and remained in Mayfair. One has alternatively Rossetti's version, which was that, taking exception to something Meredith said, he threatened to throw a cup of tea in his face. Meredith repeated his remark; Rossetti threw the tea and Meredith left at once: the outcome however is the same. This nevertheless is a minor matter. Swinburne (pulling Whistler's white lock of hair while Watts-Dunton reproves him) is certainly in place, and the model is no doubt intended to represent the redoubtable Fanny Cornforth who was for so long the virtual mistress of Cheyne Walk; though she had her own place of residence in Chelsea, No 36 Royal Avenue. It was to that address, during the time of his illness that he wrote letters to his 'dear Elephant', as he described the amply proportioned Fanny, chiding her, among other matters, for the disappearance of a cherished pot from No 16 Cheyne Walk. In a light-hearted vein also, we have of Whistler as Chelsea knew him, the brilliant sketch by Phil May; and on the walls of the Chelsea Arts Club one may find a whole series of caricatures of more recent Chelsea notables in art, including the magnificent presence of Augustus John.

Old photographs of Chelsea, as well as of its notabilities, are strangely impregnated with the spirit of their period. The late-Victorian Chelsea stands still for us in the photograph of the corner of Lawrence Street and Cheyne Walk, with the Thames Coffee House (uproarious with music-hall advertisements); while village characters in fur caps and velveteens stand with sturdy passivity save where an incautious movement has resolved one into ectoplasm. The trees and railings lean at the historic angles to which the early water-colours have accustomed us in the pre-Embankment photograph of Cheyne Walk. The Chelsea Public Library has others of much interest including a fine panorama of roofs and chimneys with the old Battersea Bridge behind still gallantly spanning the stream. Even modern photographs have their tale to tell of vanished charm, like that of

Lombard Terrace, with the café-restaurant that essayed continental atmosphere. 'The Good Intent' here finds approving mention in the Survey of London. 'If it had remained it might have inherited some of the fame of the eighteenth-century coffee-house of "Don Saltero" which was started close by in Lombard Street. Like its prototype, it had its show of antiquities (if not of curiosities), it provided good fare, and attracted to its benches the celebrities of the neighbourhood.' Yet this, the continuous ironwork balcony of intricate cobweb-design, the curved early-nineteenth-century shopfront so typical of its period, in beautiful condition as they appear in the photographic print, vanished a quarter of a century ago.

CHAPTER SEVEN

Chelsea Characters

The unusual people we call 'characters' form a category that does not exclude the writer and painter. Turner, Rossetti, Carlyle, Whistler, these indeed were 'characters', apart from their gifts, with all that the word conveys of the peculiar, idiosyncratic and amusing (consciously or otherwise) in person and behaviour. Yet there are in addition many not possessing such creative ability who deserve the title even better because they did not write a book or paint a picture and they too have their place in Chelsea history.

An example is Dr Messenger Monsey, Physician to the Royal Hospital, noted in the eighteenth century, for his wit and learning, rhymes and rudeness. The son of a clergyman in Norfolk, he spent some years at Oxford, studied medicine at Norwich and set up as a country practitioner at Bury St Edmunds. He seems to have successfully treated Lord Godolphin when the latter was suddenly taken ill on the way to his country estate, and through him was appointed to the Royal Hospital. 'He will,' says Faulkner, 'be remembered for the vivid powers of his mind and the marked peculiarity of his manners,' the peculiarity consisting in a license of speech which Dr Johnson condemned. 'He was vehement,' we find in Boswell, 'against old Dr Monsey, of Chelsea College, "as a fellow who swore and talked bawdy".' Yet both Godolphin and Sir Robert Walpole found this no obstacle to liking the 'Norfolk Doctor'. Walpole wondered why 'nobody will beat me at billiards or contradict me but Dr Monsey?' 'They get places,' said the Doctor, 'and I get a dinner.' He lived to be 94, complaining on the morning of his death that he would 'lose the game . . . the game of *a hundred* which I have played for very earnestly many years'. The length of time he held his office, burying, he remarked, five wishful successors, is perhaps more striking than his wit, but the impression remains (to which a grotesque engraving in Faulkner's History adds) of an eccentric such as one might find in a Fielding novel.

Another eighteenth-century 'character' was Michael Arne, son of the composer Dr Arne, and a belated alchemist, who built a laboratory at Chelsea in 1767 with a view to discovering the Philosopher's Stone. Having failed and lost his money in this enterprise, he became until his death in 1786 a Bohemian type of musician, composing some music while in prison for debt. He has a certain distinction also for having conducted at Hamburg in 1772 the first performance of Handel's Messiah to be given in Germany.

Among women 'characters' of the eighteenth century must be included two of those 'British Amazons' who contrived to serve in the army. One of them was Christiana Davies (1667–1739), an Irishwoman otherwise known as Mother Ross. She enlisted as a dragoon in the Enniskillens under the name of Christopher Welsh without its being discovered (until she was wounded in the body at the battle of Ramillies) that she was not a man. She subsequently acted as a vivandière in Flanders and in 1712 received, for her gallantry, an allowance of a shilling a day from Chelsea Hospital. This warrior had three husbands, all soldiers, the third being a Chelsea Pensioner. She died in Chelsea in 1739 and her grave, over which three volleys were fired at her request, is in the Hospital Burial Ground, though no monument to her has been found.

The similar, chap-book adventures of Hannah Snell are likewise those of a heroine that Defoe might have imagined. Born in Worcester in 1723, she went, we are told, to live in Wapping and when she was 17 married a Dutch sailor who ill-treated her and left her destitute. In a borrowed suit of man's clothes, she enlisted in an infantry regiment from which she deserted to join the Marines; served in the East Indies in a ship of Admiral Boscawen's fleet and later was wounded at Pondicherry. She received a pension from the Duke of Cumberland and also became a pensioner of the Hospital. She appeared for some time on the stage, singing and going through military exercises, but finally went mad and died in Bedlam in 1792. She too is buried in the Hospital Burial Ground, though, like Mrs Davies, lacking a monument.

Henry Constantine Jennings, also known as 'Dog' Jennings, from his being supposed to possess a sculpture of Alcibiades' dog, was one of Chelsea's numerous collectors and connoisseurs who is described as 'an extremely quaint character, short, thin, much bent and singularly dressed'; though at the beginning of his career he had a commission in the guards and long continued daily exercise with a heavy broadsword. He travelled in Italy, developed a taste for collecting, and then for horse-racing in which he lost his fortune. Somehow or other he made a second fortune, lost that also and was for a time imprisoned in Chelmsford Gaol. He was over 60 when he settled at Lindsey Row in 1792, continuing to spend money on his collection until a third and final debacle consigned him to the King's Bench Prison where he died in 1819 at the age of 88.

'He came,' says Faulkner, 'into the world at a time when *virtu* was held in high estimation'—not to speak of betting and the turf: and the 'Museum' he accumulated (and lost, like his money, rapidly and completely) was at least as varied as that of Sir Hans Sloane. It included a great many shells, minerals, gems, crystals, cameos, intaglios; stuffed birds and animals; souvenirs of his Italian travels, prints, after Raphael and examples of ancient sculpture; some paintings, including a miniature of the Princess Elizabeth said to be by Holbein; and a library of first editions, described by Faulkner as 'both classical, and of the entertaining kind'.

The passion for objects of art and curiosity appears, indeed, with persistence throughout the story of Chelsea. Distinguished in other respects, Sir Thomas More, Sir Hans Sloane and Dante Gabriel Rossetti may be studied as collectors: and the 'characters' of the district, a Jennings, a Don Saltero, repeat the pattern, occasionally with an element of unconscious parody. Though a collector is not necessarily a 'character', the length of the list may be noted in passing. It would include Dr Mead, whose books, pictures, coins and medals and antiquities were sold at his death for some £16,000; the chemist, Charles Hatchett (1765–1847) who lived at Belle Vue House and wrote a treatise on *The Spikenard of the Ancients*, and had paintings by Salvator Rosa, Gainsborough, Bellini?, George Barrett, R.A., manuscripts and rare printed music (Palestrina, Purcell, Handel, Mozart) and 'Mongol Idols' brought by his friend, Professor Pallas, from Tibet. George Aufrere, who took the lease of Walpole House, there displayed the splendid collection of old masters he acquired in France and Italy, which passed to his son-in-law, Lord Yarborough. And then, at Stanley House in the early nineteenth century, there was William Richard Hamilton, the great virtuoso and watch-dog of antiquities who, as Lord Elgin's secretary during the Napoleonic Wars, was able to prevent France from carrying off the Rosetta stone; and shares with Elgin the credit for transporting the Parthenon sculptures to England. It was Hamilton who built the large hall on the east side of Stanley House, and by inserting in it casts from the Parthenon frieze set an example much copied later—for instance in the studio of Lord Leighton. Mme. D'Arblay records (1821):

> Luckily the house rented by Mrs Gregor from William Hamilton, Esq. (who accompanied Lord Elgin into Greece) abounds with interesting specimens in almost every branch of the fine arts. Here are statues, casts from the frieze of the Parthenon, pictures, prints, books and minerals, four pianofortes of different sizes and a excellent harp. All this to study Desdemona (that's me) seriously inclines and the more I study, the more I want to know and see. In short, I am crazy to travel in Greece.

To call this distinguished, efficient, diplomat and scholar a 'character' would scarcely be appropriate but an account of collecting in Chelsea brings us finally to a character of characters, Charles Augustus Howell, the 'wonderful man' of Whistler's description, to Ford Madox Brown the 'Baron Münchausen of the Pre-Raphaelite Movement'. As far as residence is concerned, he did not, in a strict sense belong to Chelsea. He lived at North End, Fulham and in Putney for a considerable time and alternatively at Selsey Bill. On the other hand he was so constantly in Chelsea, and in and out of Whistler's studio and Rossetti's house at No 16 Cheyne Walk, so closely linked with them in selling their pictures, and furnishing them with amusement and specimens of the 'Blue and White' they both delighted in; that he is inseparable from the story of the district and its great personalities. Howell was a collector in the most comprehensive sense of the term. With an immense plausibility and an imagination prolific of fantastic fictions, he was capable of turning any given object into whatever he wished. Whistler one day made a slight sketch of Brompton Oratory to illustrate some point in conversation. That the piece of paper was passed to Howell and not returned was a small matter, disregarded; but the sequel demonstrates his gift of invention. A short while after Whistler was staggered to find the drawing in a Chelsea shop window with an attached label: 'Michelangelo's original design for St Peter's, Rome'.

He was tireless in collecting Oriental porcelain for his artist friends and others whom they infected with their enthusiasm. One of Rossetti's assistants who lived in the house, Treffry Dunn, tells how Rossetti and Howell tried to outdo each other. Rossetti made off with a rare piece of 'Blue' that Howell had discovered and bought, and hid it at Cheyne Walk, intending to produce it later to Howell's confusion: but the latter was not to be tricked, guessed what had happened, found the piece at Cheyne Walk and substituted for it a worthless piece of cracked Delft. Rossetti, taken aback, when he unwrapped the boasted treasure, said, 'Confound it! see what the spirits have done'.

Indeed, the way in which an object of art would detach itself from its owner and come into Howell's possession by so mysterious and complicated processes that even the original owner eventually doubted whether it had really been his, is the subject of countless anecdotes. There was that beautiful drawing by Rossetti which he and Dunn came on in a sketch-book at Cheyne Walk. 'Howell, with an adroitness which was remarkable, shifted it from the book into his own pocket and neither I nor Rossetti ever saw it again.' There was the pile of eleven etchings by Whistler, of which, next day, there were only five. 'We must have a search,' said Howell, 'no one could have taken them but me and that of course is impossible.'

A comic legend grew round Howell's legerdemain: and one of the best stories about him, posthumous in every sense, was told by Oscar Wilde. The ghost of Howell, related Wilde, appeared one night to Ellen Terry, and after it had vanished she found that a diamond necklace had gone too.

Chelsea was reputedly the scene of the last sensational episode in the 'wonderful man's' career. He was, so it has been generally understood, found in the gutter, one night in 1890, outside a public-house in the district, with his throat badly cut and a ten-shilling piece clenched between his teeth; and died a few days later at the Home Hospital in Fitzroy Square. The present writer, having first accepted this account, which (at once circumstantial and mysterious) seemed too strange to be anything but true, later made some tentative but fruitless enquiries. The records of the Home Hospital did not go so far back: nor had any such event come to the attention of Scotland Yard. Perhaps it had all been somehow hushed up: though it still seemed strange that Whistler or Ellen Terry or Graham Robertson should not have anything to say about it. Ellen Terry, it is true, wrote to Graham Robertson, 'Howell is *really* dead *this* time —do go to Christie's and see what turns up.' (He had previously shammed being dead and arranged his own sale of his effects): but she makes no remark on the cut throat or ten-shilling piece. Graham Robertson gave a list of items to Whistler who identified many of them. 'That was Rossetti's, that's mine, that's Swinburne's ... You couldn't keep anything from him and you did exactly as he told you. He was really wonderful.' But Whistler does not refer to the sinister end. It may be as Mrs Helen Rossetti Angeli holds, in her *Life of Howell* (*Pre-Raphaelite Twilight*, 1945) that the first written version of Howell's death was that of T. J. Wise in preface to the Swinburne papers. The question arises whether Wise invented it. That eminent bibliophile, was not, as we now know, immune from the temptations of literary invention. He might have thought it poetic justice that a man who told so many tall stories about others should have a final tall story told about him. One would, in that case, be inclined to probe further into Wise's intention. Why the ten-shilling piece? Some kind of symbolism? or was it a picturesque touch at random? The vision of that lean frock-coated figure sprawling under the gas lamps on the King's Road, the sallow visage blood-smeared, the lantern jaws shut on the little coin of gold remains vivid but without sure foundation.

Another fabulous nineteenth-century character connected with Chelsea was the 'last of the dandies', Alfred Guillaume Gabriel, Count d'Orsay, who had a house in Manor Street (rebuilt in 1888), the then 'Gothic House', No 10: the perfect Disraelian nobleman, tall, handsome, well-bred, full of charm, talented as painter, sculptor and writer, and suitably romantic in his attachment to the brilliant Lady Blessington. One might have anticipated, in his encounter with the Carlyles, the clash of opposites, yet it was precisely this contrast, of which he was quite conscious, that delighted and even flattered Carlyle himself, and elicited the memorable description of the Count's arrival in Cheyne Row:

Chelsea, April 16, 1839. I must tell you of the strangest compliment of all which occurred since I last wrote—the advent of Count d'Orsay. About a fortnight ago, this Phoebus Apollo of dandyism, escorted by poor little Chorley came whirling hither in a chariot that struck all Chelsea into mute amazement with splendour. Chorley's jaw went like the hopper or under-riddle of a pair of fanners, such was his terror on bringing such a splendour into actual contact with such grimness. Nevertheless, we did amazingly well, the Count and I. He is a tall fellow of 6 feet 3, built like a tower, with floods of dark, auburn hair, with adornment unsurpassable on this planet, withal a rather substantial fellow at bottom, by no means without insight without fun and a sort of rough sarcasm rather striking out of such a porcelain figure. He admired the fine epic etc., hoped I would call soon and see Lady Blessington withal.

Finally he went his way, and Chorley with reassumed jaw. Jane laughed for two days at the contrast of my plaid dressing-gown, bilious, iron countenance and this Paphian apparition.

Hardly less effective, though tinged with more visual colour, is Jane Welsh Carlyle's account of the incredible visitor: '... the sound of a whirlwind rushed thro' the street, and there stopt with a prancing of steeds and footman thunder at this door, an equipage all resplendent with skye-blue and silver ... like a piece of the Coronation Procession, from whence emanated Count D'Orsay!' She agreed with her husband that 'in the face of all probability he is a devilish clever fellow'; while the servant Helen was reported to have exclaimed, 'such a *most* beautiful man and most beautiful carriage'.

It was in the sombre 'forties that Count d'Orsay made his second call at Cheyne Row: and with a nice sense of what was due to the period into which he had unaccountably strayed, the 'Prince of Dandies' had shed much of his former resplendence: 'all in black and brown ... that man understood his trade', approved Mrs Carlyle, 'he had the fine sense to perceive how much better his dress of today sets off his slightly enlarged figure and slightly worn complexion than the humming-bird colours of five years back would have done'. Lord Jeffrey was present on this occasion and she noted 'How *washed out* the beautiful dandiacal face looked beside that little clever old man's.' It was the last intimate glimpse of him though they met again at a dinner party, in 1848, the year of revolutions, that was to give D'Orsay's friend, Louis Napoleon, his opportunity. That D'Orsay should go bankrupt was in the dandiacal tradition; that he should not have lived to take up the post of Director of Fine Arts in Paris which the newly-instated Prince-President offered him in 1852 was an unkindness of fate. In his career of empty and fruitless magnificence he pauses for a moment in Chelsea for our close inspection, a bright butterfly seen through the Venetian blinds of Cheyne Row.

Perhaps the supreme Chelsea 'character' is Jane Welsh Carlyle, though her fine, sometimes mockingly concealed intelligence, and the lively expression of her letters make it a question whether she should not be included among the writers. If we speak of her here as a personality it is certainly without disrespect to her pen. With a sudden crackle and thunder of description, Carlyle himself creates their visitors for us, throws his swift flash of light on the townscape, but in the constant domestic awareness of day-to-day events, experienced acutely with a nervous tension that communicates itself, it is she who informs us about the house and its relations with the outside world, and composes the drama which is so perpetually at the moment of climax—even if it is only poor Mrs Leigh Hunt's request for a spoonful of tea.

Mrs Hunt I shall soon be quite terminated with I foresee. She torments my life out with borrowing. She actually borrowed one of the brass fenders the other day and I had difficulty in getting it out of her hands—irons, glasses, tea-cups, silver spoons are in constant requisition—and when one sends for them the whole number can never be found. Is it not a shame to manage so with *eight guineas* a week to keep house on!

A Scottish Mme Récamier on a horse-hair sofa, she had her salon, took pleasure in the presence of young, interesting and romantic men, like John Sterling or the romantic European exiles, the scarred soldier of fortune, Garnier, or the Italian Count de Pepoli 'one of the first poets of Italy, the handsomest and best-mannered of men', commanding them all with witty small-talk as her husband did with genius. She liked to think that Sterling 'would go through fire and water for me; and if there were a third worse element would go through that also'. She called him the 'Stimabile'—a result of the Italian lessons received from the Count and Countess Pepoli: while with that leader in the fight for Italian freedom, Giuseppe Mazzini, she skirted flirtation.

Servant trouble was a steady source of interest and crisis. The crash of plates dropped by a Chelsea native, Sarah Heather (Sereetha the Peesweep as Jane nicknamed her), sent Carlyle bounding off in fury to Annandale to fetch a Scotch cook, returning with one 'full of wild Annandale savagery, which causes the Cockney mind here to pause astonished. Broader Scotch was never spoken or thought by any mortal in this metropolitan city.' Raked by the combined powers of observation of master and mistress the position of servant at Cheyne Row cannot have been altogether easy. In spite of her accent, Anne Cook was quickly replaced by a girl from Fife—Helen Mitchell ('Kirkcaldy Helen') who made them laugh and was travelled enough to compare Cheyne Row with the Boompjes in Rotterdam, but unfortunately got 'more and more into the habit of tippling' thus inciting a high-light of description when Jane found her in the kitchen 'dead-drunk—spread out like the three legs of Man ... in the midst of a perfect chaos of dirty dishes and fragments of broken crockery'.

She was, she liked to think (for she was not, as Charles Darwin observed, a natural or unselfconscious woman) 'demure and devilish', and in her account of those strange ructions that went on at Cheyne Row, she is sarcastically if affectionately aware of the irrationality of her husband's behaviour. Thus she writes to the good friend of both, the second Lady Ashburton. 'You have heard, I think, of our troubles in long past years from neighbouring *Cocks*! How I had to rush about to one and another Householder, going down on my knees and tearing my hair (figurately speaking), to obtain the silence of these feathered Demons that broke Mr C's Sleep with their least croupy crow; when you might have fired a *pistol* at his ear without waking him! Thro' efforts that I still shudder at the recollection of, the neighbouring gardens were quite cleared of Cocks; and Mr C. forgetting all the woe *they* had wrought him has been free latterly to devote his exclusive attention to—*Railway Whistles!!*' She proceeds to describe her horror on hearing loud crowing, the arrival of a fresh Cock just under their bedroom windows. But this time, 'Thanks to the prepossession of *Railway Whistles*, Mr C. never heard the *crowing* under his nose.' Her ill-health which matched his—the pains, the sick-headaches, the insomnia—were induced in part by her nervous apprehension of his nervousness of, at night, that moment when thumping and tapping would announce that some irritation of his senses had banished sleep. Yet it was encouraged also by her own in-turned character which subjected her symptoms to a similar exaggeration; and at times, her letters, even when they gossip lightly and discuss trivialities, seem like a prolonged scream.

The evident strain often gives the impression of having some other than its ostensible cause and has led to some theorisation on the sex life of the Carlyles, the matter being considered in the proper, impartial light in an appendix to the Life of Jane Welsh Carlyle by Laurence and Elizabeth Hanson. Controversy has gone on between those who maintain that Carlyle was impotent, and others who claim that this was not so but that his wife's ill-health prevented normal relations. One piece of evidence put forward by the biographers mentioned above is contained in letters to Sir James Crichton-Browne from Charles G. Fall of Boston, U.S.A., from which it would appear that Mr Thos Appleton, Longfellow's brother-in-law, was told by Sir Lyon Playfair that he had been consulted at one time by Mrs Carlyle for her nerves and had found her a virgin. This it is true is far from direct evidence and roundabout enough to be called hearsay. It may be enough to conclude that they were not sexually well-matched and not unreasonable to suppose that this was in part the cause of the evident neurosis of the household.

This tense psychological drama, that has its moments of laughter and is also sad, has produced, since Froude controversially presented it, in the 1880s a whole succession of books, one effect of which has been to make the Carlyle's Chelsea home one of the most famous houses in the world, and to invest it for ever with the character of its so closely bound and yet disparate inhabitants.

CHAPTER EIGHT

Growth and Change

The Embankment made in 1871 was one of the major alterations of Chelsea's aspect and those who love the district, still are apt to feel a pang as if at some quite contemporary inroad of modernity. Any embankment has the drawback of interposing a barrier between town and river, of disturbing the organic relation that one feels should exist between them. The river becomes a spectacle, that, leaning over a wall, one contemplates with an absence of any feeling of participation that amounts to a sense of unreality.

It was not so in the old days when the river bank was a picturesque path under stately trees that seemed like the edge of a Dutch canal and had, as late as the nineteenth century, an atmosphere of the time of William and Mary: when the balconies and steps of the old 'Adam and Eve' and the 'Swan' had an intimacy with the river that is now only fragmentarily to be found at Wapping or Greenwich: when the gates and landing-stages of private houses emphasised the fact that the water was another main road for the use of Chelsea tenants, and as crowded with rowboats and private barges as the streets of London with omnibuses and carriages.

The connection and continuity of life on land and water is pleasantly illustrated in the old prints, for example, in Bowles' view (1792) of Chelsea Hospital and Ranelagh Rotunda from the Thames. The gateway is open, invitingly whether viewed from one side or the other, skiffs are tethered by the stairs; some wealthy person's barge, with covered deck cabin and six oarsmen paddles downstream, smaller boats dodge about among the sailing barges. The architecture gains in effect from this foreground bustle, the dignified plan of the Hospital becomes lucidly apparent. The Physic Garden had its barge-house; its relation to the river is interestingly

21 *Kensington Gardens: the Fountains*

22 *The Albert Memorial (1863–72): designed by Sir George Gilbert Scott (overleaf)*

shown in the engraved plan of the architect. Edward Oakley (1732), and with decorative elegance in the plan by John Haynes (1751); the picturesqueness of its watergate with a background of the famous cedars is conveyed in a lithograph from a water-colour by the nineteenth-century artist James Fuge (who lived for some time at No 1 Upper Cheyne Row).

There must have been a special pleasure in surveying the water traffic from the pavilions and garden houses, like those of Walpole House as shown in the water-colour drawing in the Guildhall copy of Lyson's *Environs* (reproduced in the Survey of London, *Chelsea* (Part 1); or of Gough House (1720) as visualised in a lithographed illustration to Faulkner's *Chelsea*.

Yet improvement was not to be withstood. The proposal to embank the Thames, made as early as 1839 by Her Majesty's Commissioners of Woods and Forests, offered the advantages of a new main road and of a certain amount of reclaimed land. The work hung fire for many years. The plan approved by Parliament in 1846, which allowed for the construction of an embankment and roadway between Vauxhall and Battersea bridges and of a suspension bridge at Chelsea was halted for lack of funds, road and embankment getting only as far as the western end of Chelsea Hospital gardens. The need for an extra sewer from Cremorne eastwards, and also of a thoroughfare along which to construct it, revived the scheme. The Government, however, refused to disgorge the unexpended balance of something over £38,000 from the amount originally raised. Sir William Tite urged that the Metropolitan Board of Works take over (it was allowed to do so in 1868), the whole undertaking being complete by 1874.

The design of an embankment, a road and a sewer, is not one of the more spectacular opportunities of the town planner and the engineer responsible, Sir James Bazalgette, is not perhaps to be criticised for several aesthetic shortcomings. The stretch of hammer-dressed granite wall is undeniably stern and monotonous and one imagines the old brick-built water-front to have been more cheerful, human and entertaining. The Hospital and Physic Garden have become somewhat remote from the river, which was once an integral part of their effect as a composition. Without consciously thinking of town-planning, one may be vaguely aware of an unresolved problem in the double roadways of Cheyne Walk, where the old trees that once marked the river's edge are set somewhat confusedly behind the newer planting of the embankment itself. Many changes were inevitable, among them the disappearance of the ancient Lombard Street and the Arch House which spanned the entrance to it. This building, the history of which goes back to Elizabethan times, formed a curved archway and is thus represented in the water-colour by Thomas Malton in the Chelsea Public Library, though at some time during the Victorian period the arch was converted into the bluntly rectangular opening which appears in photographs taken, prior to demolition, in 1871.

Carlyle was one of those who warmly approved the Embankment as a notable sign of Progress. Faulkner, at an earlier date when the scheme was in the discussion stage, had looked forward to a 'handsome terrace' providing a '*coup d'œil* that would not then be surpassed in any city of Europe, not even by the celebrated terrace at Cologne'. One may nowadays withhold superlatives, but regard it, not without fondness, as an accomplished fact.

The bridges of Chelsea are another aspect of its growth : and the old Battersea Bridge—for a long period, *the* bridge—is, like the unembanked shore, a vivid memory and the cause of lament for a lost and unique landmark. It superseded, in the eighteenth century, the ancient horse-ferry (which figures in the song of Dibdin's waterman) and had been in use since Elizabethan times. 'Chelcheyhith' ferry, granted in 1618 by James I to his 'dear relations, Thomas, Earl of Lincoln and John Eldred and Thomas Henley, Esquires', changed ownership several times, being promptly sold by James's 'dear relations' to William Blake (then owner of Chelsea Park) becoming, Faulkner tells us, the property of Bartholomew Nutt in 1695 (and rated some years later at £8 per annum); later belonging to Sir Walter St John and passing with the Bolingbroke estate to Earl Spencer who in 1766 obtained leave by Act of Parliament, to build a bridge, at, or near, the ferry, at his own expense.

The Earl having formed a company to finance it, the bridge was begun and completed in 1771, costing between £15,000 and £20,000, though its wooden structure was an economy as compared with stone. The result was, as paintings, drawings and photographs inform us, remarkably picturesque, in the variety and pleasant irregularities of form which came from the material employed. It was 726 feet in length and 24 feet wide, the spans varying from 15 feet 6 inches to 32 feet. At first the toll of a half-penny for footpassengers and fourpence for a one-horse cart brought no profit, but the increase of population on both sides of the river during the nineteenth-century eventually made it a financial success. Lit by oil-lamps in 1799, by gas lamps from 1824 onwards, it must have been poetically impressive by night. Improvements were made from time to time. Iron railings were introduced at the same time as the gas lamps. A carriage road was made with a raised footpath on each side and a series of bays where the stroller could stop to admire the view. Faulkner records the interesting fact that in his time each of the fifteen shares which controlled the property entitled each proprietor to vote for the counties of Middlesex and Surrey.

That the bridge was a delight to painters is well known and easy to appreciate; it retains its hold on the affections by Whistler's superb nocturne alone. It gained even a kind of superstitious respect, for the legend grew up (it finds mention in the Life of William De Morgan) that the particular confluence of airs, to be met with halfway across, possessed some strange curative and healthful magic nowhere else existing. On the other hand, Beaver remarks that 'the old bridge was utterly detested by "practical" people, being to them nothing but an eyesore and an encumbrance'. Bargees and tug captains would evidently find it difficult to negotiate; while, for its purpose, and in spite of the massiveness of its beams and ties, it was fragile. Severe weather put it out of action for some time as early as 1795. While it aged beautifully it also grew unsteady. The Albert Bridge Company, which bought it in 1873, strengthened the foundations with concrete and threw two spans into one for the convenience of river traffic: but by 1883 it was too unsafe for wheeled traffic and in 1885 was pulled down and replaced by a temporary foot bridge until the new iron bridge was completed in 1887.

There was nothing especially characteristic of the eighteenth century in its appearance. It had the natural and primitive functionalism that might belong to any age; and, for a decade, presented an odd contrast with its Victorian neighbour, the Albert Suspension Bridge of 1873, between Beaufort Street and Battersea's Albert Bridge Road, essentially of its period in style and the decorative importance that ironwork then assumed. The third of Chelsea's Bridges, Chelsea Bridge, linking the eastern side of the borough with Victoria Road and the eastern side of Battersea Park, is a suspension bridge of 1934. 'An instructive comparison can be made,' says Dr Pevsner, 'between the prolixity of the Victorian construction and the conciseness of the 1934 work of G. T. Topham Forrest and E. P. Wheeler.'

If one considers the history of Chelsea in terms of invasion, it is clear that the main attack on its rural detachment began, as one would expect, in the nineteenth century when the population of

London as a whole was increasing so vastly. The population of Chelsea itself is given as 12,000 in 1801, 40,000 in 1841, 88,000 in 1881, and (peak figure) 95,000 in 1901. Why, between 1901 and 1931, it should have decreased again, losing some 36,000 inhabitants, is not at once obvious, though the outward extension of suburbs and the intermediate position of Chelsea between suburb and metropolis may go some way to explain it.

The earlier stages of the development are effectively recorded in surveys and maps. Thus in the 'Map of Chelsea', surveyed in the year 1664 by James Hamilton and continued to 1717, 'Church Lane' is virtually Chelsea's only street; and apart from the 'palaces', riverward, only one or two widely separated houses break the vista of park, common and arable land. In Richardson's Survey of Chelsea, 1769, Little Chelsea appears on the Fulham Road, Cheyne Walk and Paradise Row are populous, and a series of new buildings begins to define the King's Road, though this was still a private and privileged way. In M. Thompson's Map of Chelsea, 1836, the area on both sides of King's Road, a public thoroughfare since 1830, is seen to be rapidly filling in. The old garden tradition persisted in the form of numerous nurseries: the less pleasant tradition of footpad and highwayman, grimly indicated in Thompson's Map by the 'Great Bloody Field' adjoining the King's Road, was eradicated by force of bricks and mortar.

To give a connected and coherent view of King's Road, Chelsea and its neighbourhood is impossible, for no coherence exists. It is random in its architecture, genially and cheerfully nondescript, and an account of it is entitled to be random. Try to visualise its early twentieth-century aspect and as likely as not you will have a picturesque mental montage in which colourful fruit and flower stalls, antique shops and would-be Parisian restaurants are confused with a few exquisite old houses and the florid front of the Town Hall. At a more recent date the picturesque confusion is the more confounded by boutiques, discotheques and the modern parade of anti-fashion in all its curiosities of attire.

Yet the old houses, No 211 (Argyll House) and Nos 213, 215 and 217 are indeed beautiful examples of early eighteenth-century architecture; Nos 213 and 215 built as a pair in 1720, Argyll House in 1723, and No 217, at the corner of Glebe Place, about 1750, when Glebe Place was a passage across glebe land (originally to the back of Shrewsbury House). No 215's survival to the present day is the more welcome because of its celebrated tenants: as the home, for one, of the composer, who according to Wagner expressed the whole of the English character in eight notes (the opening strains of *Rule Britannia*), Dr Thomas Augustine Arne. Arne (1710–78), apart from this classic contribution to the masque *Alfred* and patriotic music, composed music for the performances at Ranelagh and is further linked with Chelsea as the tutor of Dr Burney, the Royal Hospital organist. In comparatively recent times No 215 was the London house of Ellen Terry, who was living there in the 1920s while still indomitably playing old women's parts at the end of her long and illustrious stage career. Mr James Whitall, who in his book *English Years* has transatlantically idealised the cream panelling, the elegant staircases and fireplaces of the Chelsea house at its best and most typically historic, and sought also for a surviving elegance of life in that setting; was for a time Ellen Terry's neighbour, and describes her, first as a distant distinguished figure, with white face and a mouth of vivid red, surrounded usually by a crowd of female relatives or satellites, later as a charming friend with a fund of Chelsea memories, among them the recollection of Carlyle mounting the stairs at No 211.

The four old houses are a single small oasis of the past or, at least, of the eighteenth century in the King's Road. The Pheasantry, No 152, was an architectural surprise, with its archway adorned by caryatids and quadriga, suddenly intruding the nostalgia of the Greek Revival. The Duke of York's Headquarters, formerly the Duke of York's School for the children of regular soldiers, designed by John Sanders (1801) adds its military plainness to the King's Road approach from the east. Whiteland's House, next to it, a girl's school in 1772 when the Rev. John Jenkins, M.A. lectured on the subject (or presumably related subjects) of 'Female Education and Christian Fortitude under Affliction' was rebuilt in 1890. Architecturally, it preserved the link-extinguishers and wrought-iron gate of the original: sentimentally is to be noted for John Ruskin's interest in it when it became a training college for schoolmistresses, and his institution of a May Day festival, when the gold-hawthorn cross designed by Arthur Severn was presented to the chosen Queen—and, to other girls, many and many a copy of *Sesame and Lilies*.

About 1900 several places of ancient interest disappeared. They included the seventeenth-century farmhouse (Nos 148 and 150), Box Farm, and the artists' hostelry, the 'Six Bells', less famous of old for its architecture than for its garden with its arbours and rockery, its vine-clad walls and mulberry tree, its bowling-green. The medley of nineteenth-century building is completed by the 'Italian' style of J. M. Brydon's Town Hall which constitutes, with the same architect's Public Library and Polytechnic in Manresa Road, as much of a point of focus as the length of the King's Road offers: and, at its western end, by the buildings of St Mark's College, added to Stanley Grove when William Hamilton sold the house to the National Society for the Education of the Poor in 1840, and designed by the revivalist, Blore, 'in the Byzantine style'.

It is to be remarked, however, that the Georgian idea, if not in all points the style of execution, lingered in the orderly plan of the neighbouring extensions, Chelsea Square, Carlyle Square (so renamed in honour of the great man) and Paultons Square, roughly speaking between 1830 and 1850. The plutocratic era of the 1870s and 1880s found its distinctive expression along those channels which linked Chelsea with Belgravia; in the 'Hans Town' region, including Sloane Street, Cadogan Place, Cadogan Square, Hans Place and the neighbouring streets where there is little to remind one of an earlier age, except for some Georgian houses in Hans Place, and otherwise Victorianism is undiluted. The tall red-brick mansions built by and under the inspiration of Norman Shaw were at all times formidable in their suggestion of wealth and exclusiveness and for a considerable period induced in the critical observers of architecture and social life a feeling of discomfort amounting to aversion, though eventually a 'sense of period' came to the rescue and the curious modern mingling of irreverence and respect was nicely summed up in Osbert Lancaster's pictorial appraisal and his description 'Pont Street Dutch'.

The flamboyant gifts of Norman Shaw can be studied in various parts of London, Hampstead and Kensington as well as Chelsea, yet in Chelsea they were exerted to especially brilliant and dominating effect, and Swan House, 1875, though a victim of bombing in the Second World War, was in its way a masterpiece; its projecting first and second floors, its oriels and tall Queen Anne windows giving a new flavour to old architectural motifs.

Part of the terrace on either side of the Physic Garden built along the new Embankment in the 1870s, a modern variation on the theme of Cheyne Walk, Swan House occupied the place where a Swan tavern had carried on the memory of an earlier building 'Old Chelsea residents', said Alfred Beaver in his *Memorials* (1892), could remember its floating pier for steamboat passengers, its arbours and gardens sloping to the river. The new Swan House and its neighbours, though compelled to renounce these amenities, made an impressive addition to this corner of Chelsea. The terrace is substantially Shaw's, including also by him Cheyne House, the Clock House and Nos 9–11 Chelsea Embankment, though other architects contributed, Godwin providing Nos 4–6 and G. F. Bodley the River House (No 3). Altogether Chelsea adds entertainingly to the revivals of the late nineteenth century and the aspirations of the 'art nouveau'. The architect and designer C. R. Ashbee (1846–1942) who has had a growing number of admirers in recent times was responsible for three distinguished houses on Cheyne Walk (Nos 37, 38, 39), the Magpye and Stump (1894) retaining the name of the ancient tavern destroyed by fire in 1886: while the new-art, hand-wrought ironwork of the group has its charm for those who can savour the 'period' character of even a recent age. Viewed in this spirit No 35 Glebe Place becomes of special interest as the design of William Morris's architect associate, Philip Webb (1831–1915) and No 48 Glebe Place as the dwelling (to which he made characteristic improvements) of Charles Rennie Mackintosh (1868–1928), the chief exponent of 'art nouveau'.

In a similar spirit, one nowadays views the later churches which it was once the custom to dismiss as 'imitation Gothic'. Even the destruction of the Markham Square Congregational Church (1860), designed 'in the Gothic style' by John Tarring of Bucklersbury, is lamented by the Chelsea Society (Annual Report, 1953) as that of 'a landmark which has worked its way into the affections of the community'.

An affection of this kind, not proceeding entirely from an aesthetic respect, and at the same time not merely antiquarian, but tender in its regard for a good intention carried out with timid persistence, may be given to the new St Luke's (1820–4), designed by James Savage in the Perpendicular style. This early product of the 'revival of Christian Architecture', neat rather than impressive in its proportions, has a certain cold delicacy not without its appeal. Its principal monument, that of Colonel Henry Cadogan, by Chantrey, has also an agreeable period flavour, with its soldiers of the Peninsular War who grieve over a flag-draped portrait medallion—Colonel Cadogan, son of the Earl, distinguished himself at Talavera and Fuentes d'Onoro, was killed, as the inscription on the sculptured coffin conveys, at the battle of Vittoria, 1813. Among the memorials in the burial ground is that of 'William Jones, Esq., aged 83', one of those otherwise unknown persons whom the industry of Faulkner has so entertainingly re-created for us. Mr Jones, who lived in retirement at No 10 Manor Street after making a fortune as a wine-merchant, was 'eminently skilled in the Hebrew and Greek languages and possessed a happy talent of poetical composition' : in addition 'painted from nature about fifteen hundred species of butterflies in the most masterly and elegant manner' the paintings being 'much admired by the celebrated Fabricius'.

A later and more impressive product of nineteenth-century church architectural ideas, especially as far as the interior is concerned, is Holy Trinity in Sloane Street (1888–90), designed by John Dando Sedding (1838–91). The stiff restraint of earlier revival is now en-riched and coloured by the influence of Ruskin, whose ardent disciple Sedding became, and the Pre-Raphaelites. It is full of those variegated stones and marbles that Ruskin valued so highly—green marble, red porphyry, onyx and alabaster; rich in sculptured angels, gilt and bronze; while William Morris's company made the glass for the east window, with 48 panels showing saints, apostles and archangels, designed by Burne-Jones. Rich also is the metalwork, for example the altar rails by Henry Wilson (1864–1934), Sedding's assistant who succeeded to his practice after 1891 and continued work on the church's unfinished detail. In Holy Trinity, Chelsea possesses a re-markable repository of late-Victorian design, which plans for rede-velopment have menaced but hesitated to attack.

Not a revival but an actual transplantation of past architecture is the Crosby Hall of the international hostel of the British Federation of University Women on Cheyne Walk, brought to Chelsea from Bishopsgate in 1910. It was originally part of the house built about 1470 by Sir John Crosby, M.P., alderman, warden of the Grocer's Company and prosperous wool-stapler, and shows in what magnifi-cent state the merchant prince of the fifteenth century lived. It had famous associations also. After the death of Sir John in 1475, his widow parted with it to Richard, Duke of Gloucester. 'There,' says Sir Thomas More in his *History of Richard III*, 'he lodged himself and little by little all folks drew unto him, so that the Protector's court was crowded and King Henry's left desolate.' Shakespeare in *Richard III* mentions Crosby House (and, alternatively, Crosby Place) several times.

Some 30 years after Richard left it and under a new dynasty More himself owned, and lived in, the house, though he sold it to his friend, the Italian merchant Antonio Bonvici, at the time when he had decided to settle permanently in Chelsea. Until the Civil War, the hall was the scene of many occasions of splendour under a succession of wealthy Londoners: there followed then the period of its decline. During the war, it was a prison for 'malignants'. In 1672 it was turned into a Presbyterian chapel. It survived, two years later, the fire which destroyed the rest of the premises, and remained a chapel until 1769. The contempt for 'Gothick' then prevailing reduced it to a warehouse, though it was rescued from neglect and decay in the romantic 1830s, its restoration being marked in 1836 by a banquet in the Old English style, presided over by the Lord Mayor. Between 1842 and 1860 it was occupied by a scientific and literary institute. After that, it was turned into a restaurant.

The removal from one place to another of an historic building is not usually regarded with favour: but in this case it cannot be looked on as an act of sentimental vandalism. The Gothic hall was hardly suited to form part of the offices of the Bank of India, which bought the site in 1908 in order to build new premises. The Bank of India deserves credit for the compromise preservation; being at much pains and expense to take down, carefully number and store every component of the fabric, these being handed over to the London County Council. And as, in the circumstances, it had to be moved somewhere, congratulations are to be divided between the L.C.C. and the University and City Association of London for the agreement which caused the Hall to be re-erected in Chelsea, and thus to be linked once again with the memory of Sir Thomas More.

The re-erection was carried out in a precise and discriminating fashion: as may be gathered from the detailed account in the Survey of London *Chelsea* (Part II). The original stone windows, doors, fireplace and corbels for roof were set in their proper positions. The fine oriel window and the stone vault with its central boss bearing the helm and crest of Sir John Crosby (a ram trippant, argent, armed and hoofed, or) were put together. The superb fifteenth-century oak roof, stripped of many coats of paint, was refitted. Internally the hall is as More knew it, save that an oak floor replaces the original vanished flooring of Purbeck stone.

It was designed to stand in the same relation to the quadrangle of the University Hostel (the building of which began in 1926) as in Bishopsgate to the rest of the original premises. Strange to think that as recent an addition to Chelsea as Crosby Hall is also the oldest building in it. For the visitor, there is not, perhaps, the same breathtaking fascination that attends the discovery of venerable architecture on its original site. The sense of age has been impalpably disturbed. Materially, however, the building is as dignified and beautiful as ever and could not be more appropriately placed than where Sir Thomas More's own garden was. Appropriately, too, it contains a replica of Holbein's painting of Sir Thomas and his family, presented by the Chelsea Society in 1950.

II KENSINGTON

CHAPTER NINE

A General View

The borough of Kensington—royal borough since 1901—was in the main a Victorian creation, although it had three individual points of interest—royal palace, great house and famous square—of earlier date. These are fascinating survivals, not only as architecture, but in the tale they have to tell of distinguished men and women associated with them. Their history constitutes the whole of the early history of Kensington, and has continued until the present day to be of importance, though a separate and remarkable story is that of the monuments which represent Victorian planning and idealism and of the great surge of domestic buildings that housed the nineteenth-century middle-class.

Kensington, by and large, is, perhaps, the most typical of all Victorian creations. That vision of a magnificent centre, of education, culture, art, ever present in the mind of the Prince Consort, materialises in the 'Cité Universitaire' of South Kensington. The search for an architectural style conveying the aspirations of an age produced results as impressive as the Royal Albert Hall, the Albert Memorial, the Natural History Museum. The pomp of Victorian wealth lingers about the serried porches of streets, squares and 'gardens'. The artists' studio mansions remain, to speak of a picture-loving age when painters made fortunes and lived in state. The simpler houses, rows of cottages, the surrounding 'stable land' remind us of the humbler social strata and the army of coachmen, grooms and others who served the rich: though the mews and the by-ways in which the lower orders lived have acquired in the twentieth century a new or revived charm and desirability.

An earlier Kensington than this is, in effect, Holland House, Kensington Palace and Kensington Square. Before the seventeenth century there is nothing except the far-off source of names and boundaries—and the vague conjecture that once gave a romantic delight to the local antiquarian. Rough Saxons no doubt lived in this wooded, undulating country outside London : but it would be useless to dilate on the Kensingas or Cynesiges, whose 'tun' or communal settlement we must suppose to have been here. A tribesman called Cnotta may have been the Saxon Napoleon of Notting Hill, giving his name to that region: as an Oswulf may have done to the 'Ossulston' Hundred of Middlesex which contained the manor of Kensington : but both may just as well be creatures of myth. The Domesday Survey of 1086 first gives some certainty of facts and figures: the entry establishes that the 'manor' or estate of Cheneslton had a village or township, a number of smallholders and serfs, a priest and therefore perhaps a church. A tendril of history reaches towards the present day in the mention of some three acres of vineyard, for the grape-bearing vine is still to be found in the borough. Mediaeval records are of service in explaining some main points of nomenclature. The Saxon thane, Edwin, who had held the manor, was dispossessed or disappeared with the Norman Conquest. 'Albericus de Ver' (Aubrey de Vere), from Ver near Coutances in Normandy, was granted tenure by the Conqueror's adviser, Geoffrey, Bishop of Coutances. After the Bishop's death in 1093, the manor became the de Veres' property, though part of it was ceded to Abingdon Abbey. This was at the dying request of Alberic's son, Geoffrey, who thus, no doubt, sought insurance, in the fashion of the time, for the welfare of his soul. The division provides the mediaeval flavour of title. The church and some 270 acres that went with it, the gift to Abingdon, became known as Abbot's Kensington and the church itself as St Mary Abbot's.

For a material vestige of the de Vere family one must visit the remarkably well-preserved keep of their castle, Hedingham in Essex : but the progress of the family added another title to Kensington. In the reign of Stephen, the third Aubrey de Vere ('The Grim'), Count of Guisnes by virtue of his marriage to Beatrix, Countess of Guisnes, was made (1155) Earl of Oxford, and the part of the manor remaining to him was styled Earl's Kensington. The echo of chivalry (like that of faith in 'St Mary Abbot's') resounds still in Earls Court Road and Earls Court Gardens, likewise in De Vere Gardens; though the connection with earldom and abbey was severed in the sixteenth century. With the dissolution of the monasteries, Abbot's Kensington went to the Crown, and in 1526 the rest of the manor passed from the de Veres with the succession of the married sisters of John, the fourteenth earl.

Apart from names, the shape of the manor, as indicated by the borough's former boundaries, takes us back to the Middle Ages. There is no other reason for its straggling and anomalous character; it is rather like a miniature map of Italy unintelligibly imposed on the map of London. It has its ancient relation to the other Domesday manors of Harlesden on the north and Chelsea on the south. It reaches northward to the Harrow Road and through part of the Kensal Green cemetery. Kensal, it has been conjectured, was anciently the woodland of the Kensingas—Kensing Holt, the three syllables of which have been smoothed by time into two. The further suggestion has been made that heath or broom land on the borough's south-eastern confines gave rise to the name 'Brompton' and that a broad geography of Kensington is implicit in the contrast which names suggest between rising and wooded areas and heathy flat. Southward the boundary ran along one side of the Fulham Road, taking in the region that used to be known as 'Little Chelsea' and extending to the corner of Sloane Street. The West London railway, following the course of an ancient creek (turned into the Kensington Canal early in the nineteenth century and later filled in), brings its definition to the Hammersmith and Fulham side. West Kensington, however, is, confusingly, not in Kensington but in Hammersmith : and the impingement on the east of lands that anciently belonged to Westminster Abbey adds further confusion. An adjustment of boundaries in the thirteenth century ordains that a north-western segment of Kensington Gardens should be regarded as being technically in Paddington. The very heart of Kensington, by insistence on boundaries, was plucked from it and given to Westminster. Strictly speaking, Kensington Gardens, the Albert Memorial, Kensington Gore, the Albert Hall, part of Queen's Gate and the old Imperial Institute were not within the boundary, though it would be absurd to exclude them from any account of Kensington as they so organically belong to it.

A comparison with Kensington's neighbour and now partner, Chelsea, provides a striking contrast in local history. There is no remnant or even memory of Tudor Kensington, though Tudor Chelsea is still vividly projected by the personality of Sir Thomas More and the record of his life there, as well as by the re-erection of the house, Crosby Hall, in which he lived. The old church of Chelsea, badly damaged as it was in the Second World War, survives and still preserves features of historical value : the More Chapel remains, with the monuments that speak eloquently of Chelsea's ancient families. Kensington's parish church, however, dates only from 1869 : the Victorian Gothic of Sir Gilbert Scott interposes itself between us and the more distant past. Chelsea had its village nucleus which gained a secluded permanence by its position on the riverside; but no such seclusion has been granted to Kensington. Its High Street was a high road, Knightsbridge and Kensington being two of the points at which, until 1860, tolls were levied at turnpike gates. It was one of two originally Roman roads between eastern England and the south-west, the other being represented by the Bayswater Road. One would look in vain for the picturesque houses that so often line the old high street round which a city has grown. No original village is traceable; the early story of the Kensington highways is simply of traffic to and from London.

In the seventeenth century, however, in the midst of pleasant country, there came into being those separate architectural growths of which there is yet some trace. Of these the country seat of the lord of the manor, Holland House, needs to be considered first.

77 *Pelham Crescent (1831–70): designed by George Basevi*

24, 25 No. 9 Melbury Road,
Kensington: the exterior
and the library mantel-
piece (1875–81)

26 *Kensington Gardens: Wren's Alcove*
27 *Kensington Palace: Wren's Orangery (1704)*

28 G. F. Watts in his garden at Little Holland House

CHAPTER TEN

The Great House

It is an extraordinary thing that a country mansion, surrounded by its gardens and park, should survive into the twentieth century in a populous district of London, and from this point of view Holland House has been unique. The past tense is necessary because of war-time destruction and subsequent change. First an incendiary bomb and later a flying bomb reduced it during the Second World War to a shell, impressive still but beyond complete restoration. It has been possible to retain some part of its seventeenth-century aspect but the purchase of the house and grounds from the Earl of Ilchester by the London County Council in 1951 necessarily entailed great alterations.

The main part of the house was Jacobean, built by Sir Walter Cope between 1605 and 1607. Cope, a favourite of James I, who held various official and lucrative posts, Chamberlain of the Exchequer, Master of the Court of Wards and Liveries, Keeper of Hyde Park (1612), aimed at creating an estate of suitable dignity and to this end set himself to reassemble the various parts of the Kensington manor which by the reign of James I had split into four. This involved the purchase of the northern area known as Notting or Knotting Barns; West Town, a small estate on the ground now occupied by Addison Road and its environs; as well as Earl's and Abbot's Kensington. The house was built on the slopes of the hill which came to him with Abbot's Kensington and was originally known as Cope Castle.

Whether or no the architect was John Thorpe, active in the late sixteenth century and the early years of the seventeenth, the designer of Longford Castle and Audley End, seems to be a matter of some doubt or at least the extent to which he had a hand in the work seems debatable. The ground plan in the Soane Museum, which

he certainly drew, shows the central part of the building in black ink
and the wings in brown, while a note in brown ink indicates that
Thorpe 'perfected' it. This could imply that he was responsible for
the wings, though it would not preclude the possibility that he was
also responsible for the centre and earlier block, as Horace Walpole
stated in his *Anecdotes of Painting*. Satisfactory conclusions can
scarcely be drawn from a design which differs in several respects
from the actual building but Thorpe may well be assumed to have
had a hand in the work. It is safe to say also that Walpole was in
error in assuming that Inigo Jones and Nicholas Stone had a part in
its completion. He was perhaps misled, as the Earl of Ilchester suggests in *The Home of the Hollands*, by the fact that Nicholas Stone
(possibly from Inigo Jones's design) provided in 1629 the gate piers
surmounted by heraldic beasts which originally flanked the southern
approach and in the nineteenth century were relegated to the north-
east corner of the building. Certainly the house had none of the
classic or Palladian element which Jones would have introduced.
It was typically Jacobean in its combination of plain red brick with
quaint and cumbrous ornamentation. The shaped gables, the mullioned bay windows, the polygonal porch with its rusticated pilasters
and cupola, the arched loggias with balustrading in the shape of
fleurs-de-lis (chief emblem in the arms of the Copes) made the south
front very impressive and to the modern eye curiously ornate. This
effect was increased by the brick towers with their turrets on either
side. The east front had its three tiers of stone pilasters representing
the three orders of achitecture decorated in a style which shows
some Dutch influence.

Ornateness was repeated in the interior. The original entrance hall,
later converted into a breakfast room (41 feet by 18 feet), with its
ceiling enriched with scrolls in relief, its profusion of strapwork
and its doorways with elaborately carved wooden screens set the
key of decoration. The 'Gilt' Room above the hall on the first floor
was lined with panelling with fluted Ionic pilasters set at intervals.
The Long Gallery, converted into a library, ran impressively the
length of the west wing (100 feet by 17 feet) and contained elaborate
fireplaces. The first floor comprised the principal rooms, Dining-
room and large (the Crimson) Drawing-room being on the north side
and a smaller (the Yellow) Drawing-room intervening between library
and the main rooms of ceremony and entertainment.

Sir Walter Cope died in 1614, leaving the property to his wife,
from whom on her second marriage it passed to her daughter Isabel.

With her marriage to Sir Henry Rich, son of the Earl of Warwick, the name of Holland makes its appearance. Rich, who helped to negotiate the marriage between Charles I and Henrietta Maria, was made Baron Kensington (1623) and in the following year first Earl of Holland. The ceiling of the Breakfast-room has been accredited to his and his wife's taste, while the Gilt Room is supposed to have been decorated for a ball in honour of the royal marriage. The reign of Charles and the Civil War period following brought their calamities. Lord Holland hesitated between the royal and parliamentary parties, to the satisfaction of neither, and finally taking up arms for Charles was captured by the Parliamentarians in 1648 and beheaded. For a time Holland House, as it may now be called, was a Cromwellian headquarters. Tradition leads us to picture Cromwell and Ireton discussing their plans in the seclusion of the grounds, where, if Cromwell's voice was raised to a roar because of Ireton's deafness, it might be supposed that no malignant would hear. The Countess, however, was presently allowed to return and lived there until her death in 1655. Stage plays were surreptitiously performed in the house while the Puritan ban on play-houses and play-acting was in force, and established something of a tradition, for amateur theatricals long continued to be a feature of the Hollands' entertainment.

In 1673 Isabel's son, Robert, the second earl, succeeded also to the title of Earl of Warwick. His son Edward, sixth Earl of Warwick and third Earl of Holland, married (1696) Charlotte, daughter of Sir Thomas Middleton of Chirk Castle, who long outlived him (he died in 1701) and gave to Holland House one of its most interesting associations by her marriage, after 15 years of widowhood, to Joseph Addison. Legends in plenty have grown round this match between the great writer and the dowager Countess of Warwick. He has been pictured as the impecunious tutor of the Countess's son, the fourth Earl of Holland, walking from his country house at Sandy End on the Chelsea–Fulham borders to give him instruction: though, in fact, in 1716, Addison was a man of fame and substance, who had come into money and stood high in political importance among the Whigs, gaining the office of Secretary of State. The marriage has been supposed unhappy, though on this it is now impossible to comment: it may or may not have led to his frequent withdrawal to the White Horse Inn at the end of Holland Lane (rebuilt in 1866 and renamed the Holland Arms). A famous story represents Addison as pacing from one end of the Long Gallery to the other and refreshing himself from a bottle of wine placed at either end, though the degree of intemperance this implies depends on the fancy of the narrator. It is of more value to recall the charming letters he wrote to the young earl, quoted in Faulkner's *History of Kensington*, which evoke the rural surroundings of Holland House; his discovery of the nest 'that has abundance of little eggs streaked with red and blue veins' which he surmised, by 'their turn and colour', to be full of tom-tits. Even better is the Augustan elegance of the 'concert of music' he heard in a neighbouring wood. 'It begins precisely at six in the evening and consists of a blackbird, a thrush, a robin red-breast and a bullfinch. There is a lark that by way of overture sings and mounts until she is almost out of hearing ... the whole is con-cluded by a nightingale that has a much better voice than Mrs Tofts and something of Italian manners in her divisions.' The nightingale long after Addison's time continued to be heard in Holland Park, on Campden Hill and in Kensington Gardens, and its song always re-mained one of the principal delights of the inhabitants of Holland House.

It was at Holland House that Addison was visited by Milton's daughter. He had asked for some proof of her identity but on seeing her exclaimed, 'Madam, your face is sufficient testimonial of whose daughter you are.' It was in the house that he died, uttering those famous last words, 'See in what peace a Christian may die.' The writing-desk of which at least the upper part would seem to have been his, which passed from his daughter (only child of the marriage) to Sir Thomas Lawrence, then to Samuel Rogers and was bought by Lord Holland in 1856, was burnt in the Library in 1940. The portrait which appears in C. R. Leslie's picture of the Library (engraved in mezzotint by Samuel Reynolds) may not have been of Addison but of his friend Sir Andrew Fountaine. Yet apart from material relics the association with Addison is inseparable from the lustre of the house which grew so bright in the eighteenth and nineteenth cen-turies.

It was not, however, until the latter part of the eighteenth cen-tury that Holland House became the brilliant centre of what may be called 'Whig culture'. The property passed in 1721 to William Edwardes, son of Elizabeth Rich, the daughter of the second Earl of Holland, who married Francis Edwardes of Haverfordwest. Edwardes Square perpetuates the family name. It had various tenants and for a while stood empty. There was even some talk of pulling it down, for the author of a *Tour through England* in 1748, quoted by Faulkner in his *History of Kensington*, referred to the 'prodigious

improvements' that might be made by a rebuilding and town planning scheme. By that time, however, it had already been leased to
Henry Fox, who later bought it outright, and the change of ownership brought with it fresh celebrity.

Of the remarkable Fox family with which henceforward Holland
House was to be always associated, it was said that each generation
improved upon the one before it, though some of its vigorous traits
may well be traced back to the father of Henry, Sir Stephen Fox, a
political figure of Charles II's time, to be remembered as one of the
founders of Chelsea Hospital. His vigour and zest for life are effectively shown by the fact that he married a second time at the age of
77 and had by this marriage four children of whom Henry was one.
He had also the flair for place and wealth which was to show itself
again. As Paymaster of the Forces and Commissioner of the Treasury,
he accumulated a large fortune and in the benign era of Sir Robert
Walpole and Whig supremacy, his sons profited by his example.
Stephen, the elder son, born in 1704, found favour with Walpole's
government and in 1741 was made Lord Ilchester. Henry, born in
1705, after gambling away large sums in his youth (a trait which
reappeared in his own offspring) also aspired to political advance-
ment and held government office, though, overshadowed by Pitt (his
contemporary at Eton), he contented himself in the Seven Years' War
period with the post of Paymaster-General and like his father made
a large fortune during the eight years he held this office from 1757
to 1765. He became first Baron Holland in 1763.

It would seem that Lady Holland (Lady Caroline Lennox, the
daughter of the Duke and Duchess of Richmond, with whom Fox
made a sensational runaway match) was fonder of the house than
he was. He grumbled over the purchase price and perhaps preferred
the house he built for himself at Kingsgate in the Isle of Thanet.
Nevertheless, Kensington was the scene of a number of gay and
splendid occasions. In 1753 sixty-two people sat down to supper after
an evening of dancing and card playing. Horace Walpole and George
Selwyn were among the guests, looking on at the games of whist and
cribbage, and making their comments on the dancers in the Gilt
Room. Amateur theatricals began again. Horace Walpole in 1761 was
'excessively amused' by a play at Holland House, acted by children
—*Jane Shore*. 'No Magdalen by Correggio was half so lovely or
expressive' as Lady Sarah Lennox, the grown-up young woman who
took the main role. Sir Joshua Reynolds painted one of these theatrical occasions, at a corner of the house with a view of the grounds, his

group including Lady Sarah, Lady Susan Fox-Strangways and the young Charles James Fox. It was an untoward result of these performances that Lady Sarah fell in love with a professional actor whose services were called on, William O'Brien, whom she married, in spite of family opposition, at St Paul's, Covent Garden. An actor could not be accepted into the aristocratic circle and land was bought for the couple at the safe distance of still colonial America. The later days of Henry Fox were clouded in various ways: by ill health, political disappointment and unpopularity, and by the reckless behaviour of his sons Stephen Fox and Charles James Fox. A witticism was forced from him towards the end by the unpleasant interest George Selwyn took in the state of his health: 'If I am alive, I shall be delighted to see George; and I know that if I am dead he will be delighted to see me.' Disagreeable questions of money were a burden. His vague and lavish handling of large sums as Paymaster made necessary a huge refund to the Government. £116,000, we are told, was still owing in 1783, nine years after his death, and the debt was not cleared until 1805. Both Stephen and Charles James Fox gambled away fortunes, the former owing £100,000 in 1773. Their father died in 1774, their mother a few days after him. Stephen Fox became the second Lord Holland though he, too, died soon after (aged 29), Stephen's son Henry Richard becoming the third Lord Holland when he was only a year old.

It was Henry Richard Vassall Fox (1773–1840) who first took a great and affectionate interest in Holland House, regarding it as both his town and country residence, and who, together with his wife, made it a headquarters of cultivated liberalism. It might well have decayed and been sold if Stephen had lived and a sale of furniture and books in 1775 is an indication of the difficulties already created by his extravagance. The new Lord Holland, however, was able in due course to improve the situation and to give the family a new prestige. In accordance with its tradition he went to Eton, then to Christ Church, travelled about Europe and settled at Holland House in 1797. It was in the same year that he married Elizabeth, the divorced wife of Sir Godfrey Webster, that lady of great ambition and personality who was to become the mansion's famous hostess.

They began to entertain and these occasions not only brought together a circle of intimates but a stream of foreign visitors to Holland House. Among the intimates were Sydney Smith, whom they first knew as a young curate, whose wit sparkled at the dinner-parties; Samuel Rogers, the sharp-tongued banker-poet, whose 'seat' was to become a feature of the gardens; the translator of Aristophanes, Hookham Frere, who scratched on a window-pane in 1811 the lines :

> May neither fire destroy nor waste impair
> Nor time consume thee till the twentieth heir,
> May taste respect thee and may fashion spare.

Lord Holland had literary tastes, occupied himself with translations from Spanish and Italian works, wrote *Memoirs of the Whig Party* (published after his death) and delighted to entertain literary celebrities. Many writers visited Holland House, Sir Walter Scott, Wordsworth, Thomas Campbell, Thomas Moore; from America Washington Irving and—lion for a season—James Fenimore Cooper; from France Mme de Staël. Among artists were C. R. Leslie, Wilkie and Antonio Canova on his visit to England. Lord Holland's liberal sympathy with the exiled caused him to defend Napoleon, for whom indeed he had retained the Whig respect, and several members of the Bonaparte family were his guests. The exiled Italian patriot and writer Ugo Foscolo found refuge at Holland House. Talleyrand as French ambassador to England enlivened its table with his brilliance and his illegitimate son, the Comte de Flahaut, appears frequently in the family chronicles as an intimate of the house. The recorded witticisms of the Holland House circle have often lost some of the savour they no doubt possessed at the moment of utterance but Talleyrand was neatly and maliciously amusing when he scandalised his hostess, by replying, to a lady with a squint who asked him how political affairs stood, 'Comme vous voyez, madame.' Guizot and Thiers were later visitors. Yet perhaps the most vivid association of all is that with Macaulay who looked with favour on the house as a stronghold of the liberal principles he shared and described it with his incomparable vigour. Lady Holland, as he first saw her, was 'a bold-looking woman with the remains of a fine person and the air of Queen Elizabeth'.

She was gracious to Macaulay, though he did not fail to remark the haughty and imperious manner in which she ruled and ordered about her guests. He surveyed the Jacobean interior with a typically Victorian eye, noting 'the very large and very comfortable rooms, rich in antique carving and gilding, but carpeted and furnished with all the skill of the best modern upholsterers'. He was soon an intimate at the breakfast—as well as the dinner—table: and among those oratorical pieces of prose in which he excelled, the passage in which he wrote of Holland House in 1841 stands out: 'The wonderful city, which ancient and gigantic as it is still continues to grow as fast as a young town of logwood by a water-privilege in Michigan, may soon displace those turrets and gardens which are associated with so much that is interesting and noble, with the courtly magnificence of Rich, with the loves of Ormond, with the counsels of Cromwell, with the death of Addison. The time is coming when perhaps a few old men, the last survivors of our generation, will in vain seek amidst new streets and squares and railway stations for the site of that dwelling which was in their youth the favourite resort of wits and beauties, of painters and poets, of scholars, philosophers and statesmen.' The prophecy was only in part to be fulfilled. Macaulay would have wondered to see the public of the twentieth century strolling in the well-kept gardens, the new building of the Youth Hostels Association attaching itself to the east wing, and, at least, some fragmentary part of the old mansion respectfully preserved.

That critical observer, Charles Cavendish Greville, has left in his *Journal* an estimate of both the host and hostess of Holland House, Lord Holland gaining his unreserved praise, for 'his marvellous social qualities, imperturbable temper, unflagging vivacity and spirit, his inexhaustible fund of anecdote, extensive information, sprightly wit with universal toleration and urbanity, inspired all who approached him with the keenest taste for his company, and those who lived with him in intimacy with the warmest regard for his person'. He maintained this cheerful spirit in spite of ill health, gout and the arthritis which led him to nickname himself 'Lord Chalkstone'. Lady Holland was less easy for Greville to describe. 'She was often capricious, tyrannical and troublesome, liking to provoke and disappoint and thwart her acquaintances, and she was often obliging, good-natured and considerate to the same people. To those whom she could show any personal kindness and attention, among her intimate friends, she never failed to do so. She was always intensely selfish, dreading solitude above everything and eternally working to enlarge the circle of her society. She could not live alone a single minute. Her love and habit of domination were both unbounded. No one ever lived who assumed such privileges as Lady Holland and the docility with which the world submitted to her vagaries was wonderful.' Sydney Smith who 'reigned' at Holland House as elsewhere 'without a rival in wit and humour' was able in his inimitable way to cope with the peculiarities of the household and to combine the merriment it inspired with affection. Thus he writes to Lady Holland from Jermyn Street in 1811: 'How very odd, dear Lady Holland, to ask me to dine with you on Sunday the 9th, when I am coming to stay with you from the 5th to the 12th. It is like giving a gentleman an assignation for Wednesday when you are going to marry him on the preceding Saturday—an attempt to combine the stimulus of gallantry with the security of connubial relations.' How wittily he declines an invitation:

> My dear Lady Holland,
> I have not the heart when an amiable lady says 'Come to "Semiramis" in my box' to decline; but I get bolder at a distance. 'Semiramis' would be to me pure misery. I love music very little—and I hate acting. I have the worst opinion of Semiramis herself and the whole thing (I cannot help it) seems so childish and foolish I cannot abide it. Moreover it would be rather out of etiquette for a Canon of St Paul's to go to an opera: and where etiquette prevents me from doing things disagreeable to myself I am a perfect martinet. All these things considered, I am sure you will not be a Semiramis to me but let me off.

That he loved dining at Holland House there is no doubt, though here again he cannot resist a quip: 'I know nothing more agreeable than a dinner at Holland House: but it must not begin at ten in the morning and last till six. I should be incapable for the last four hours of laughing at Lord Holland's jokes, eating Raffaelle's cakes or repelling Mr Allen's attacks on the Church.'

The Mr Allen referred to was the Scottish doctor and political writer John Allen, M.D., a permanency at Holland House as librarian, a sort of major domo and patient slave of Lady Holland. He combined his slavery oddly enough with the post of Master of Dulwich College, which the imperious lady permitted him to visit at intervals —the only occasions when he was allowed to leave Kensington. He appears in Leslie's group in the Holland House Library, though neither in this nor in Sir Edwin Landseer's portrait in the National Portrait Gallery is it possible to observe that stoutness of limb which led Sydney Smith to remark, 'He has the creed of a philosopher and the legs of a clergyman; I never saw such legs—at least belonging to a layman.'

At the Holland House dinner table Macaulay did not immediately make an impression on guests who did not know him. Greville at all events saw him first as 'a common-looking man in black ... I settled that he was some obscure man of letters or of medicine, perhaps a cholera doctor'. When this stranger stood up, 'I was aware of all the vulgarity and ungainliness of his appearance; not a ray of intellect beams from his countenance; a lump of more ordinary clay never enclosed a more powerful mind and lively imagination.' Greville was taken aback indeed when Lord Auckland addressed this commonplace person, 'Mr Macaulay, will you drink a glass of wine?' This then was the famous man, but in the conversation that followed, 'whatever subject was touched upon he evinced the utmost familiarity; quotation, illustration, anecdote seemed ready in his hands for every topic', and Talleyrand who came in after dinner on this occasion paid his own homage to Macaulay as one of the great orators.

The dinners at Holland House had the value of bequeathing us many such interesting observations of the great at close quarters. Macaulay's own description of Talleyrand (1832) among them: 'He is certainly the greatest curiosity I ever fell in with. His head is sunk down between two high shoulders. One of his feet is hideously distorted. His face is as pale as that of a corpse and wrinkled to a frightful degree. His eyes have an odd glassy stare, quite peculiar to them. His hair, thickly powdered and pomatumed, hangs down on each side as straight as a pound of tallow candles. His conversation, however, soon makes you forget his ugliness and infirmities. . . .'

The death of Lord Holland in 1840 marked the end of a brilliant phase. Lady Holland had not the heart to keep up the salon, nor indeed did 'poverty on £5,000 a year' allow of lavish entertainment on the old scale. She stayed sometimes with her sister-in-law, Caroline Fox, at the old farmhouse, Little Holland House, which Stephen Fox had added to the property, but the 'stillness that strikes to the heart' drove her away from the mansion itself. For a time it remained empty and shuttered. Charles Greville in his *Journal* wrote a postscript to Macaulay's prophecy, when Lady Holland died in 1843, on 'the final extinction of the flickering remnant of a social light which illuminated and adorned England and even Europe for half a century. The world never has seen and never will see again anything like Holland House.' A period of revival was again to follow, however, and some restoration of the fabric of the house was carried out by the third Lord Holland's successor.

A curious thing that strikes one about the building, as it can be seen in photographs, is the Victorian look which in some subtle fashion had communicated itself to the Jacobean façade. Like those illustrations of the interior which Joseph Nash (1809–78) made for his *Mansions* (or those of C. J. Richardson), it seemed to belong rather to some slightly fabulous 'olden tyme' than to a specific period. This in part was due to the lavish but not always easy finance which had not permitted any wholesale reconstruction or redesign even if this had been wished for. When repairs were necessary the original materials were used and patched, with, however, some incidental changes of aspect, which were made more obvious by the renovations of 1848. These were undertaken by Henry Edward Fox, the fourth Baron Holland (1802–59), and his wife Mary Augusta. To this time belong the Conservatory near the old stables, the still-existing 'Garden Ball Room' with its ornamental tower that appears more Victorian than Jacobean and yet probably consists of decorative material dating back to the seventeenth century: the arcade and terrace connecting it with the south-west corner of the house, and the terracotta screen flanking Nicholas Stone's gates.

Though the fourth Lord Holland and his wife spent a good deal of time in travel there was some revival of the Kensington Salon in the ensuing decade and until Holland's death in 1859. Macaulay living at Holly Lodge not far away was still a frequent visitor. The foreign visitors included Louis-Philippe, in his exile, and Alexandre Dumas, who washed his breakfast down with a bottle of Château Yquem and spoke for four hours without a break on politics, history, literature and art. Dumas later gave his own description for a French newspaper exuberant to the verge of caricature of driving through the vast demesne of Holland Park full of lowing herds and countless deer, to the massive portals of the ancient Castle; of being received by a vast retinue of gorgeously attired flunkeys; of Lord Holland's greeting him in a vaulted chamber strewn with State papers. Anthony Panizzi, an exile from Italy (who gained a safe London anchorage as librarian in the British Museum), was another visitor who found sympathy and welcome at Holland House for his schemes to help his liberal compatriots. Finally a gifted young artist, George Frederick Watts, added a new element of distinction. He had stayed with Lord and Lady Holland in Florence, and impressed them as a genius. They had become his patrons and Watts stayed at Holland House during the period of its restoration. He touched up the painted panels in the Gilt Room which dated back to the seventeenth century and were attributed to the German-born decorator Francis

Cleyn; and added figures of his own to plaques on the overmantel, also painting two ceilings for the staircase from the new Inner Hall. Portraits occupied him too: a full-length portrait of Lady Holland (the 'full shortness' as she described it, referring to her small size); Panizzi with dark mutton-chop whiskers, quill in hand; little Marie Fox, the Hollands' adopted daughter, who later became Princess Lichtenstein and wrote her own account of Holland House; the beautiful Countess Castiglione and other likenesses of conspicuous merit. The story of Watts's association with Little Holland House belongs to another chapter.

The renovations were completed by 1858 to everyone's satisfaction, admired by the six to seven thousand guests who came to the afternoon parties which were a final spurt of entertainment. Yet the expense had been great, the property was now mortgaged and after Lord Holland's death in 1859, the entertainments gradually grew fewer, while the cost of keeping up not only Holland House but other properties at home and abroad became ever more formidable. In 1874 an arrangement was made with Lord Ilchester by which he became owner of the house and its contents and assumed responsibility for its liabilities, Lady Holland remaining in occupation during her lifetime. She died in 1889, Lord Ilchester in 1905, though his widow continued in possession of the house for more than 30 years—until 1935. Even before the Second World War the sadness of dissolution lay about the mansion, while around it the quickening pace of development had wrought its change.

Development began in the 1840s when Holland House itself was being refurbished. Addison Road on the west goes back to this time, taking its name of course from the great man of letters. It was adorned, says Leigh Hunt, 'with a modern chapel in good ancient style and the backs of the houses on the eastern side make sequestered acquaintance with the trees of Holland Park'. Leigh Hunt was mildly offended at the presence of a 'Cato Cottage' (a name suggested by Addison's tragedy), not to speak of 'Homer Villa'. On the east the present Holland Walk was the footpath assigned to public use by Lord Holland in 1848. Melbury Road and its region represents the development of the 1870s on the site of the old farmhouse, Little Holland House and its grounds. The 1920s brought their changes. The statue of the third Lord Holland, designed by the joint efforts of Watts and Sir Edgar Boehm and erected near the High Street, was removed to make way for the block of flats, Melbury Court, in 1926 and placed in the north park facing the house. Ilchester Place (1928) made a new approach to the grounds opposite the Conservatory, while the tall block of flats near it, Oakwood Court, rises near what were once the 'Moats' or series of fishponds, made into a lake in 1812, though this disappeared with the building activities of the 1870s. Lord Camelford's duel with Captain Best, fought there in 1804 and commemorated by Lord Holland with a Roman altar and Latin inscription, is indeed a distant memory.

If Holland House had not been so much damaged in the Second World War it would, like other great houses whose domestic day is over, have made an excellent museum. Its associations would have been more vivid if one could in fact visit those famous rooms, the Library for instance, that 'venerable chamber' of which Macaulay wrote, 'in which all the antique gravity of a college library was so singularly blended with all that female grace and wit could devise to embellish a drawing-room'. It is an effort of the imagination to picture the setting in which 'the last debate was discussed in one corner and the last comedy of Scribe in another; while Wilkie gazed with modest admiration at Sir Joshua's Baretti; while Mackintosh turned over Thomas Aquinas to verify a quotation; while Talleyrand related his conversations with Barras at the Luxembourg or his ride with Lannes over the field of Austerlitz'. In the spring of 1940 most of the valuable contents were removed, the portraits, busts and miniatures which in themselves formed a family history and a record of taste. It is satisfactory that in consequence nothing of real importance was lost in the war period. The manuscripts on which Lord Ilchester drew for his admirably full and detailed *The Home of the Hollands* and *Chronicles of Holland House* were removed to safety at Melbury. It was a curious experience to take a last peep into the ruinous interior in 1957, while the London County Council was applying itself to the difficult problem of preserving what could be preserved and demolishing what had to be sacrificed. Victorian wallpaper hung in sad festoons, makeshifts of timbering shoring up the brick walls were laid bare. One or two interesting discoveries were made: the window that once gave a view into what had been the Chapel, the traces of seventeenth-century structure in the Orangery, a box (balanced on an iron girder which had done duty as a beam) which had been the storage place of a forgotten set of Meissen china. This unfortunately crashed to the ground, to the ruin of its contents.

Yet something of the exterior effect remains in the restored south front, the modern brickwork which buttresses it is not unpleasing in effect, and the grounds of Holland Park, as the whole property is now known, have an air of well-tended seclusion that seems to defy change. A peacock displays its proud tail, the box that outlines the bright flower beds is neatly trimmed, the Dutch Garden laid out in 1812 by Buonaiuti, the Hollands' librarian, which Lord Holland described as having 'a fountain with old marble columns in the middle, and black borders and green figures and all sorts of gimcracks', has been restored. There is at least the illusion of a rural estate, in which the public can take its pleasure—and refreshment in which was once the garden ballroom. As a setting for the concerts that are a periodic event and the open-air exhibitions of sculpture that are held from time to time, the grounds of Holland Park are everything that could be wished. A plan of the house outlined in gravel gives conveniently to the casual visitor an idea of its former extent. It is possible still to sit where Rogers took his ease in the alcove once the fireplace of the old harness-room and perhaps share the feeling of the early nineteenth-century poet who wrote:

> How happily sheltered is he who reposes
> In this haunt of the Poet, o'ershadowed with roses
> While the sun is rejoicing unclouded on high
> And summer's full majesty reigns in the sky!

or of Lord Holland himself who penned the verse:

> Here Rogers sat and here for ever dwell
> With me those pleasures that he sang so well.

CHAPTER ELEVEN

The Palace and Its Gardens

Kensington Palace, which until 1899 was in the parish of St Margaret's, Westminster, but was then officially designated part of Kensington, was the next important building after Holland House to be built in the seventeenth-century countryside. A house standing on the site was bought by Sir Heneage Finch from his younger brother in 1661. Finch, a lawyer and politician, was then M.P. for Oxford University, subsequently rising to eminence as Lord Chancellor and becoming Earl of Nottingham in 1681. He reconstructed the building which was then known as Nottingham House and it was this property which William III bought for £18,000 in 1689, from the second earl. The King, then in the first year of his reign, chose Kensington as a healthy district, good for his asthma, and first inspected Holland House with a view to taking it, though perhaps he was deterred by the draughtiness of which James I had complained on his one visit to 'Cope Castle'. At all events his choice fell on Nottingham House which he immediately proceeded to rebuild and enlarge, the work being entrusted to Sir Christopher Wren. The result was in curious contrast with the Jacobean ornateness of Holland House. Wren was in his soberest architectural mood and may well have been influenced and guided by William III's Dutch leaning towards plainness and simplicity. Modest indeed are the domestic-looking red-brick 'pavilions', enclosing the three courts, the Clock Court with its west gateway and clock tower of c. 1690, the Princesses Court and the Prince of Wales Court (1723-6). The south front, c. 1690-5, is severely lacking in ornament or variety except for the row of vases over the three central bays. Some minor part of Nottingham House was unobstrusively merged into the north side of the Clock Court. Additions and alterations in the early eighteenth century, after Wren's time, in no way altered the general plainness of appearance. It had, observed Leigh Hunt, 'a sort of homely fireside character', it was a 'place to drink tea', though another nineteenth-century writer described it as 'a heterogeneous mass of dull apartments, halls and galleries, presenting externally no single feature of architectural beauty'.

The interior too as conceived by Wren was plain, and this simplicity is especially notable in Queen Mary's Gallery, c. 1690, modified only by the gilt mirror frames of carved drapery and scrollwork by Gerard Johnson and Robert Streeter (c. 1689–91) over each of the two fireplaces. The Presence Chamber has its note of ornament in the overmantel by Grinling Gibbons, c. 1695, and the King's Gallery a curious overmantel in the shape of a wind-dial by Robert Norden in a carved surround. The Queen's Staircase, with balusters of turned wood, c. 1690, is in keeping with the general domestic plainness of the whole design, though the King's Grand Staircase, 1695 and altered 1723, has a more fanciful grace of ironwork. The buildings north of the Clock Court by William Kent and others added in the reign of George I were more ornate in interior design, Kent's ceilings giving a decided liveliness of effect. His ceiling for the Presence Chamber was an early adaptation of the Pompeian style. The ornate ceiling added to the King's Gallery, with panels of scenes from the *Odyssey*, made a somewhat overpowering contrast with earlier austerity, not to entire contemporary approval. George Vertue gives the following account of Kent's interior decoration: 'At Kingsington the new Appartments built and adorned with paintings by Mr Kent are five rooms following each other at the head of the great staircase'. In the third room, he notes, are 'Niches of Marble and pedestals with statues gilt with burnished gold which makes a terrible glaring show and truly Gothic, according to the weakness of the conception of the Surveyors and Controllers of the King's Works, or their private piques. In the next Room being the largest in the middle of the Ceiling one large long Oval wherein is represented Jupiter coming to Danae, not in a Cloud of gold (but of Snow) the other parts of this Ceiling are Ornaments; the next and fifth room the Ceiling in Imitation of the Antient Roman Subterranean Ornaments—poor Stuff. All these paintings are so far short of the like works done here in England before by Verrio, Cook, Streeter, Laguerre, Thornhill, Ricci, Pellegrini, etc., in Noblemen's Houses in Town and Country.'

The works of art the Palace originally contained have since been removed to Hampton Court and Windsor. It is strange to recall that Holbein's portrait drawings of the court of Henry VIII, now at the

29 *Kensington Palace: Queen Victoria's bedroom*

30 *Kensington Palace. From an engraving by J. Kip (1724)*

31 *The Crystal Palace on its original site near Princes Gate*

32 *The Hardware Section at the 1851 Exhibition*

Royal Library, Windsor, lay forgotten in a bureau at Kensington Palace until found by accident by Queen Caroline early in the reign of George II. Some paintings, however, still remain and in the Cupola Room, 1717, forty feet high, with a painted vault by Kent, there is the notable relief by Rysbrack, the 'Roman Marriage'.

Apart from its architecture, the history of Kensington Palace is sad and solemn. Anxious and preoccupied with European politics, war with Louis XIV and rebellion or possible rebellion, William III can scarcely be thought to have enjoyed life in Kensington, from which indeed his foreign campaigning kept him away for long intervals. It was not his intention to live in seclusion, and an advantage of the palace was that it stood on the edge of the chain of royal parks that communicated with Whitehall. He constructed an avenue (of which the Row is part) through Hyde Park and St James's Park, as a convenient line of communication, and this was lit by a chain of lanterns at night. It was left to his devoted wife in his frequent absence to see to the decoration and to create formal gardens in the Dutch style. When he was present, the receptions for the nobility and gentry were no doubt as Macaulay describes them—when he speaks generally of the kings born on the continent—'. . . a matter of form . . . at least as solemn a ceremony as a funeral'. Leigh Hunt attempts to enliven the scene by imagining the presence of Swift and Sir William Temple, of Matthew Prior and William Congreve, whose comedies it seems did not offend the serious principles of the Queen, though the mere fact that they might have been there does not dispel the atmosphere of dullness. Even Leigh Hunt's light and vivacious description of imagined meetings acquires a touch of grimness when he pictures the melancholy little king and the visiting Tsar, Peter the Great, as sitting down together for an evening of deep potation. William pleasantly appears in a well-known anecdote, as being summoned to the tea-table by Lord Buckhurst, aged four; obeying the command in docile fashion and pulling the child in his toy cart along the stately gallery: although pathetically vivid is the exhaustion which followed the effort, and the fact that 'for some minutes he was incapable of uttering a word, breathing with the utmost difficulty'. Nor was the drawing-room the gayer for the presence of Mary's sister Anne, who made 'all the professions imaginable, to which the queen remained as insensible as a statue'. Sad stories of the deaths of kings and queens succeed one another in the history of the palace, beginning with the death of Queen Mary from smallpox in December 1694. Her illness made the king aware of an affection for her which the preoccupations of state had caused him to forget. He stifled his persistent cough for fear of disturbing her, so that she wondered where he was, not hearing that familiar sound. So grief-stricken was he on the day of her death that he fainted three times. More closely attached in grief to the palace than before, he insisted on being taken there to die, in 1702 after his fall from a horse at Hampton Court.

Anne and her husband, Prince George of Denmark, now occupied Kensington Palace or at least divided their time between it and St James's. It was Anne who planted Queen Anne's Mount, in a style of gardening which Addison approved in the *Spectator*. For her the Orangery or garden banqueting-room was built to the design of Sir Christopher Wren in 1704, a hundred yards to the north of the palace, a handsome building, which in spite of simply consisting of one long compartment with a circular interior chamber at each end has externally a baroque liveliness of design that distinguishes it from the main building. It was the scene of fêtes attended by the Augustan world of fashion, though the receptions of Queen Anne, however brilliant the visitors, were not less oppressive than those of her predecessors. Swift describes her as sitting with her fan in her mouth, in a circle of guests, scarcely saying a word, while she awaited the call to dinner. Once more death was the Palace's most dramatic occasion. Prince George, on whom it was settled, died there in 1708 and Anne's close friend the Duchess of Marlborough records her lament 'weeping and clapping her hands, swaying herself backward and forward clasping her hands together with other marks of passion'. She was at Kensington in 1714, when her lady-in-waiting, Mrs Danvers, found her in the Presence Chamber, staring vacantly 'with death in her look'. The Jacobite lords hurried to the deathbed of James II's daughter, hoping for some word that might lead to Stuart restoration—though no such word was uttered.

Anne's successor, George I, favoured the palace as a residence and made that attempt to give it a more ornate and splendid interior character which is largely represented by the decorations of William Kent. His paintings on the walls of the grand staircase well illustrate the fact that he was no Veronese and indeed make one wonder at the self-confidence with which he covered large areas with pretentious figure groups. The Cupola Room which he decorated is, however, sufficiently grand, with its gilt statues, its row of heads of Roman poets (from the collection of Charles I), its ceiling imitating a panelled dome, with the Star of the Garter as its central feature.

Here stands that amazing clock made in 1730 for Augusta, Princess of Wales, the 'Temple of the Four Great Monarchies' (the Greece of Alexander, Persia, Assyria and Augustan Rome), with reliefs in silver by Roubiliac, that already seem prophetic of Victorian tinsel. George II also lived in the palace with his Queen, Caroline of Anspach. Lord Hervey, who might be described as a Hanoverian Saint Simon, the enemy and butt of Alexander Pope, has maliciously described the dullness of the court to which he was vice-chamberlain. Taste at the Palace is amusingly exemplified by Hervey's account of how the Queen in the King's absence 'had taken several very bad pictures out of the great drawing-room at Kensington and put very good ones in their places', with the result that the King ordered all to be put back as before. Hervey's plea that at least the Van Dycks should be allowed to remain produced the celebrated royal fulmination, 'My Lord I have a great respect for your taste in what you understand, but in pictures I beg leave to follow my own: I suppose you assisted the Queen with your fine advice when she was pulling my house to pieces and spoiling all my furniture; thank God at least she has left the walls standing! As for the Van Dycks I do not care whether they are changed or no: but for the picture with the dirty frame over the door and the three nasty little children, I will have taken away and the old ones restored. I will have it done to-morrow before I go to London or else I know it will not be done at all.' Deferentially sarcastic, Hervey asked, 'Would your Majesty have the gigantic fat Venus restored too?' inciting the reply, 'Yes, my Lord, I am not so nice as your Lordship. I like my fat Venus much better than anything you have given me instead of her.' Various indiscreet remarks concerning fat Venuses trembled on Hervey's lips. The pictures were still not changed the next day, though the King for the moment seemed to have forgotten them in other complaints, snubbing the Queen who was drinking chocolate 'for being always stuffing', the Princess Caroline 'for being grown fat' and the Duke of Cumberland for standing awkwardly, Lord Hervey for not knowing what relation the Prince of Sulzbach was to the Elector Palatine: and then taking the Queen 'to walk and be resnubbed in the garden': though shortly after the royal decree was reluctantly obeyed. Leigh Hunt in his *The Old Court Suburb* has made his spirited additions to the picture of the testy little monarch, his long-enduring wife, and Frederick, Prince of Wales, whom both disliked. The story has it that George II was playing cards when he was informed of Frederick's death. 'Dead is he! Why, they told me he was better' was his only comment and he then returned to his game. Once more the palace witnessed royal demise. George II died there in 1760 at the age of 77, falling on the floor just after he had taken his morning cup of chocolate.

George III perhaps shared the dislike of his father, Frederick, for the place in which the latter had been compelled to live and to be frequently addressed as 'puppy' and 'scoundrel'. He preferred St James's Palace and Buckingham House. Kensington Palace now became the lodging, as it long remained, of various minor members of the royal family. The strangely mournful atmosphere it had early acquired still continued to hang about it. The 'patient and unmurmuring endurance' of the Princess Sophia, the blind daughter of George III, aroused the compassion of Miss Amelia Murray, who visited her in the palace apartments. The unfortunate Caroline of Brunswick-Wolfenbüttel, detested by her husband the Prince of Wales and separated from him within a year after their marriage, took refuge at Kensington and lived there from 1810 to 1814 keeping an unofficial court of her own and exciting disapproval by behaviour which now seems democratic rather than the wild eccentricity it appeared to ladies of the time. She shocked them by bolting out of one of the smaller gates of the gardens and wandering 'all over Bayswater and along the Paddington Canal' on her own. Lady Brownlow was surprised and disapproving when Caroline, walking in Kensington Gardens, 'sat down on a bench occupied by two old persons' and chatted to them with the utmost freedom : equally by her showy dress on formal occasions, 'her gowns ornamented with gold or silver spangles, and her satin boots also ornamented with them'. It was, however, reluctantly conceded that while her company was very mixed it included some good people and some clever. Sydney Smith, deserting Holland House for once, appeared at her table, though Lady Brownlow thought he looked out of place there.

The more inspiring memories of the Palace are Victorian. Augustus Frederick, George III's sixth son, who occupied apartments in the south wing until his death in 1843, President of the Society of Arts and of the Royal Society, a lover of books, learning and liberal ideas, certainly raised an intellectual tone which had previously been far from high. Yet the most vivid period of Kensington Palace is that of Queen Victoria's youth there. Edward Duke of Kent and his wife, Victoria of Saxe-Coburg, occupied the south-eastern apartments of the Palace and there Victoria was born in 1819 and christened 'Alexandrina Victoria' in George I's Cupola Room. As in Holland House the imprint of Victorian memory dims the prior history of the Palace. Victoria played here with her toys as a child. 'My earliest recollections,' wrote the Queen in 1872, 'are connected with Kensington Palace where I can remember crawling on a yellow carpet spread out for that purpose—and being told that if I cried and was naughty my "Uncle Sussex" would hear me and punish me for which reason I always screamed when I saw him'. She delighted to be driven in Kensington Gardens in her goat or donkey cart. On the memorable morning at 2 a.m., 20 June 1837, she was aroused from sleep by the Archbishop of Canterbury and the Chamberlain, Lord Conyngham, to receive the news that she was Queen. The first Council meeting, where, coached by Lord Melbourne, she made so great an impression by her 'prefect calmness and self-possession' and, at the same time, 'a modesty and propriety particularly interesting and ingratiating' (as the critical Greville recorded), was held in June 1837 in what is at present the entrance hall of the London Museum.

The rooms which retain their Victorian decoration and furniture or have been restored to something of their Victorian appearance, with the help of the objects collected by the late Queen Mary, are full of period fantasy and charm. The Nursery, with its Winterhalter and Landseer's painting of a pet royal dachshund, the Erard piano on which the Prince Consort played, the toys and dolls with which the Queen played as a child, is full of memories and the connoisseur of Victorian design will not fail to notice the five-legged easy chair, the flowers under glass and the glass paperweights with views of Osborne and Balmoral. Victoria's Bedroom, where she received the news of her accession, is marvellously Victorian with its ornamental fender, embroidered screens, steel engravings and model of the Albert Memorial in a glass case. The portrait of the Queen in old age (1899), by H. von Angeli, hung in the King's Privy Chamber, seems to look sadly at cheerful relics of the past.

Like every monarch after George II, the Queen on her accession went to Buckingham Palace. Kensington Palace remained a series of apartments for members of the royal family. 'Uncle Sussex', whom the child Victoria had been frequently warned not to disturb by noisy pastimes, was there until his death in 1843, when by his own wish he was buried in the Kensal Green cemetery. His second wife, whom Victoria made Duchess of Inverness in 1840, granting her, that is, the titular style of her husband who was also Earl of Inverness, lived on at the Palace until her death in 1873, when she too was buried in the vault beneath a massive stone slab at Kensal Green. Victoria's mother, the Duchess of Kent, lived there also until her death in 1861 : other residents were the Duke and Duchess of Teck, whose children, the late Queen Mary and her brother the Earl of Athlone, were both born in the Palace, and Queen Victoria's daughter, the Princess Louise, Duchess of Argyll, who lived there after her return in 1880 from Canada where her husband was Governor-General, Princess Louise who died at the Palace in 1939, aged 92, after more than half a century of residence in what had previously been the Duke of Sussex's apartments, was an amateur artist of some note, who had lessons in sculpture from Sir Edgar Boehm, the Queen's Sculptor-in-Ordinary, and produced that statue of the Queen as a young woman which looks across the Broad Walk towards the Round Pond.

The State Apartments remained in disuse until the end of the nineteenth century. They seemed to W. J. Loftie, whose account of the Palace is given in his book on Kensington in 1888, 'incredibly gloomy and ghostly', stripped of pictures and furniture, but Queen Victoria finally had some restoration done and the State rooms were opened to the public, as a memorial of her Diamond Jubilee, in 1899. At the present time the effect is cheerful enough and the bare walls which once shocked the visitor are adequately covered, if not with great pictures at least with several of interest. Eighteenth-century views of the Thames and Whitehall, of the school of Samuel Scott, are an agreeable feature of the King's Gallery; the series of full-length portraits by Sir Godfrey Kneller in the Queen's Gallery is enlivened by his 'Chinese Convert'. Benjamin West's scenes from ancient history are sad affairs, but his 'Death of Wolfe' merits notice as his attempt to bring historical painting up-to-date. Allan Ramsay's portrait of George III, Benjamin Robert Haydon's 'The Mock Election' bought from the painter by George IV are also to be noted. The London Museum is now housed in part of the residential quarters of Victoria, Duchess of Kent, thus comprising the room where Queen Victoria was born and that (the museum's entrance hall) where she held her first Council. Though the London Museum returns to its place of origin (the first collection of exhibits made with the encouragement of King George V and Queen Mary having been held in the State Apartments in 1911), it is now cramped in these quarters and obviously requires the larger premises now projected. The visitor can hardly form an adequate idea of the wonderful survey of London life and social history which the museum presented until 1939 at Lancaster House and would be able to present again if given space, although it gives agreeable samples from its collections, including a remarkable display of Victorian objects of use and ornament.

Kensington Gardens were originally the park or estate which went with Nottingham House and its area has remained substantially the same since Heneage Finch sold the property to William III. Its boundary with Hyde Park was never altered from that defined by the sunk fence or 'ha-ha' and the historian of Kensington, Loftie, lays great stress on this, in order to dispel the impression given by earlier writers that Queen Anne and the early Hanoverians helped themselves freely to sections of Hyde Park. Thus the antiquarian Bowack, writing in 1705, remarked that 'Her Majesty has been pleased lately to plant near thirty acres more . . .', in which he was accurate enough, but Faulkner and others jumped to the wrong conclusion. The 30 acres were a part of the Palace's own grounds but converted from parkland into a planned area of garden. The absurd assumption grew up that the eastern boundary of the Gardens in Queen Anne's time was pretty well that of the Broad Walk. What happened in fact was that Queen Anne added to the small area formally laid out in the time of her predecessors, with the help of the royal gardener, Henry Wise. The Consort of George II, Queen Caroline, employed Wise's successor, Charles Bridgman, who gave to the gardens, c. 1725–30, the distinctive features of the Broad Walk: the octagonal basin known as the Round Pond; the radiating avenues that lead the eye towards Hyde Park; and the lake formed in the course of the little stream, the West Bourne—the Serpentine. In the plans of John Rocque and Joshua Rhodes (1766–72), the effect is more formal than it has since become. The bastions on the eastern side in Rocque's plan take on the look of a fortification. It is questionable whether aesthetically—as an element in an ensemble of palace and garden—the Broad Walk was ever a good idea. Its liberal width of 50 feet interposes a barrier, the gardens to the west seem huddled round the Palace. On the other hand, it early suggested public use as a promenade and the public character of the eastern extent. The gardens laid out by Bridgman were open to the public in the time of George II on Saturdays when King and Court went to Richmond, though formal dress was required, and the 'public' consisted of the fashionable and would-be fashionable world which was attracted to the vicinity of the Palace. When the Court was no longer centred there, the gardens were opened in spring and summer, and by the time of William IV, all the year round, 'to all respectably dressed persons from sunrise to sunset'. Such respectable persons then would be privileged to see the future Queen Victoria, riding on her donkey or in her goat carriage, and even to receive the 'How do you do' or 'Good morning, sir', or 'madam' with which she courteously addressed strangers in the walks.

Kensington Gardens have always had and still retain an entertaining and genial character, in contrast with the, on the whole sombre and reclusive, history of the Palace itself. Retrospectively one can see the Broad Walk as a panorama of fashion from the hooped skirts of the eighteenth century to the informalities of the present day. Leigh Hunt makes an impressive list of famous men and women who might have been strolling there in 1791 and while such lists become superfluous, seeing that famous men and women, like others, have never ceased, probably, to stroll in Kensington Gardens on occasion, there are certainly actual encounters or recollections which can affect one's attitude to the place. Mme Récamier appears vividly in the Gardens as seen by Lady Brownlow in 1802, 'à l'antique, a muslin gown clinging to her form like the folds of drapery on a statue, . . . a large veil thrown over her head'. Chateaubriand, it is pleasant to think, finished *Atala* and composed *René* in Kensington Gardens. Literary associations indeed of all kinds they have in plenty. There is Addison to approve in the *Spectator* the work of Wise and Loudon 'in the upper garden at Kensington which was at first nothing but a gravel-pit. It must have been a fine genius for gardening that could have thought of forming such an unsightly hollow into so beautiful an area and to have hit the eye with so uncommon and agreeable a scene as that which it is now wrought into'. Addison's editor, Thomas Tickell, gives us in 1722 the verses, famous for their subject rather than their poetic quality, which make such a remarkable contrast between Kensington and London:

> Here while the town in damps and darkness lies
> They breathe in sunshine and see azure skies;
> Each walk with robes of various dyes bespread,
> Seems from afar a moving tulip-bed,
> Where rich brocades and glossy damasks glow
> And chintz, the rival of the showery bow.

So rural did Kensington Gardens appear that Sheridan in 1777 satirically represents the 'Woman of Fashion' as complaining of the trees that

> ... the spread of their leaves such a shelter affords
> To those noisy impertinent creatures called birds
> Whose ridiculous chirruping ruins the scene,
> Brings the country before me and gives me the spleen.

A variety of poets has been interested in Kensington Gardens. Crabbe gave austere approval at the beginning of the nineteenth century. They had, he noted in his diary, 'a very peculiar effect; not exhilarating, I think, yet alive and pleasant'. Some half-century later, Matthew Arnold mused in one of the 'lone, open glades', aware both of the 'black-crown'd, red-boled pine-trees', the nursemaids in their poke bonnets and the children under their care. His 'Lines written in Kensington Gardens' play on the contrast between the quietude of the scene and 'the huge world which roars hard by'. 'Love and the Spring and Kensington Gardens', cries Arthur Symons in 1892, 'Hey for the heart's delight!' Sir James Barrie provided the Gardens with a whimsical spirit in his Peter Pan, to whom Sir George James Frampton has given material shape in his famous statue. The statuary and ornamental stone of the Gardens is a curious miscellany. The duplicate of G. F. Watt's Rhodes Memorial is very impressive at the eastern end of the vista from the Round Pond, with its vigorous angular forms. The bleak obelisk to the memory of the African explorer Speke, however, is striking only in its oddity and in being where it is. An amiable but undistinguished statue of Dr Jenner stands at the north end of the Long Water (the Serpentine in its Kensington Gardens aspect). The southern aspect of the Gardens on Kensington Road is dominated by the Albert Memorial, which needs separate reconsideration. Sir John Rennie's bridge over the Serpentine between the Gardens and Hyde Park has something of the grandeur that attached to the old Waterloo Bridge, while the 'Alcove' designed by Wren, removed to the vicinity of Marlborough Gate from a position in the gardens to the south of the Palace which it had in Queen Anne's time, recalls us to Augustan elegance.

As a promenade and a playground, Kensington Gardens are unchanging. Though its great elms have been pulled down as unsafe, the Broad Walk still invites the stroller and a row of saplings gives hope for the future to the lover of trees. The Round Pond is the same magnet for children as at any time in the last hundred years, and they watch with the same interest as their grandfathers or great grandfathers the progress of their model yachts over its surface. Kite-flying adds its oriental touch to the scene at the week-end. The trees and fountains at the head of the Long Water give an almost Parisian ensemble.

To the west of the Palace, that famous private thoroughfare, Kensington Palace Gardens nearly parallels the Broad Walk, the two together confining the Palace and grounds, north and south, within a long narrow rectangle. Kensington Palace Gardens—Palace Green at its southern end—was entirely a Victorian and Edwardian creation, laid out in 1843 and mainly built in the 1850s, by that time no opposition being raised to the private development of the original royal estate, by a road of mansions. The Green, anciently called the Moor, was the site of the Palace's kitchen gardens and minor buildings of some historic interest. What would have been the oldest building in Kensington, 'King Henry VIII's Conduit', supposed to have supplied water to the royal residence at Chelsea, and described at some length by Faulkner, was demolished in 1871 and its appearance can only be gauged from Faulkner's engraving. Likewise a thing of the past is the Water Tower supplying the Palace, designed by Vanbrugh. Yet the open ground remaining before the Clock Court façade and entrance-way still suggests the parade ground it was in Hanoverian times and one can imagine the troops stiffly going through their paces in the uniforms of Dettingen. As one goes northward from Palace Green into Kensington Palace Gardens, mansions on the eastern side occupy the part of the Palace's former grounds known as the Wilderness and a rough field still separates their rear premises from the north-western paths of Kensington Gardens towards Orme Square Gate.

As an avenue, now that the Broad Walk has lost its elms, Kensington Palace Gardens is a splendid and unrivalled spectacle, its plane trees forming a great arch of foliage, continuous along its length from the Bayswater Road and Notting Hill Gate to the Kensington High Street end. The gates at the northern end with their painted coat-of-arms form a suitably impressive approach (on the opposite side of the road, the tiny two-storied building survives, which marks the boundary between Kensington and Bayswater). The luxurious mansions originally built for the wealthiest of Victorians show a certain continuity of style, though their Italianate character is varied by decorative whim. The cupolas of No 24 suggest the gorgeous east, though on its façade a species of Gothic vaulting appears; while again

The Palace and Its Gardens

at No 3 a balustrade of flamboyant Gothic breaks free from restraint. Suitably, considering their size and dignity of position, the mansions accommodate a number of embassies, the rising sun of Japan glitters over the porch of No 23, the embassy of the U.S.S.R. is at No 13, the residence of the French ambassador is at No 11; here also, Norway, Nepal, Syria, the Lebanon, the Philippines, Laos are represented. Architecturally, the Palace Green section has a peculiar interest in Nos 1 and 2. No 1, the work of William Morris's collaborator, Philip Webb, for the Howard family, is a striking curiosity in its combination of pointed arches and Queen Anne windows, the Pre-Raphaelite element being prominent in the features of interior decoration, by Webb, Morris, Walter Crane and Burne-Jones. No 2, the house which Thackeray occupied from 1861 until his death there in 1863, is also of note as being his own design. Kensington Palace had its hold upon his imagination as a novelist and perhaps suggested what he considered to be the first effort to revive the Queen Anne style, though so obstinate a thing is period character that his house in every detail proclaims itself Victorian. Leigh Hunt remarks on the 'white and pretty lodge' at the entrance of 'the new road leading to Bayswater', though on the mansions with which in his time Kensington Palace Gardens was gradually filling he looked with some disfavour.

CHAPTER TWELVE

The Old Court Suburb

The royal interest in Kensington and the building of the Palace no doubt encouraged the building of private houses and the creation of the 'Old Court Suburb', as Kensington was long described. The appearance of so metropolitan a feature as a 'square' in the rural surroundings of the borough at the end of the seventeenth century suggests that a fashionable development was already foreseen, though Kensington Square, under its original title of King's Square, a little antedates the purchase of Nottingham House by William III. In his *Records of Kensington Square* (which the present writer has been privileged to read in manuscript), a study not only charming in style but the result of intimate research, Lord Ponsonby of Shulbrede indicates its comparatively humble beginning. It was first known simply as 'the Square' and is so referred to in 1681, though by 1687 it was King's Square. In that year, Thomas Young, probably one of Sir Christopher Wren's workmen, who prospered as a builder, purchased a plot of land 'neere King's Square in ye parish of Kensington' and in the same year, as an existing title-deed shows, was occupying one of the houses. Like the neighbouring King Street (now Derry Street) and James Street (now Ansdell Street) it seems to have been named after James II and like these streets (whose little cottages W. Luker Junior drew very nicely in the 1880s—though they are long demolished) consisted originally of a number of small and modest buildings. Their tenants included Thomas Young, who built new houses in the square c. 1687–90, and such of his fellow-workmen as a carpenter, bricklayer and painter, while there were various, obviously small, shops—grocer, shoemaker, butcher, baker, etc. arranged in only a rough quadrilateral. The arrival of the Court and the reconstruction of Nottingham House as Kensington Palace stimulated the completion of the square on a more ambitious scale. Bowack in 1705 remarks that 'for beauty of buildings and worthy inhabitants it exceeds several noted squares of London'. 'Persons of quality', to use Faulkner's phrase, replaced the craftsmen and yeomen as residents and until the reign of George III, Kensington Square remained a town unit, a social centre, set down in the middle of open country.

Lord Ponsonby has some delightful speculations, as well as revealing facts, about the past tenancy of the square. 'I longed to know more about Mrs Collumbine and Theophilus Aubauzit but only their striking names have been handed down to posterity,' he remarks. He notes the curious changes in its character suggested by the names of householders—for instance the 'recurrence towards the end of the eighteenth century of French names such as Defeau, Duplesse, Dechamp, Auterac, Chauvet, Delafons, etc.'. No doubt they were émigrés. It may be recalled that the old Kensington House, not far away (on the site of Kensington Court, facing the gates of Palace Green), was occupied by French emigrant Jesuit priests who conducted a French college there. Richard Lalor Sheil, quoted by Leigh Hunt in *The Old Court Suburb*, describes his visit to 'the large old-fashioned house with many remains of decayed splendour'. 'The moment I entered my ears were filled with the shrill vociferations of some hundreds of little emigrants, who were engaged in their various amusements and babbled, screamed, laughed and shouted in all the velocity of their rapid and joyous language.' The supposed earlier residence in the square of Hortense Mancini, Cardinal Mazarin's niece, the wild beauty who won Charles II's favour, would seem, however, by Lord Ponsonby's investigations, to have been an error propagated by Faulkner and others following him. It was 'Mrs Claudine de Bragelone, one of the Duchess of Mazarin's women' who lodged in the square and not the Duchess herself. Mme de Bragelone —or Bragelongne—died 'at Mr Margaret's house' there in 1692.

Visions of the reckless Duchess, attended by her philosophic admirer St Evremond, head over heels in debt and gambling away all she possessed, must be confined to Chelsea, where in the old Paradise Row she certainly did live. At the same time in the last decade of the seventeenth century Kensington Square was assuming aristocratic dignity. It could boast of an earl, a baronet, a bishop. Sir Robert Hamilton, Bart (to be distinguished from a contemporary of the same name), was a Stuart supporter, made a baronet by Charles II, consigned to the Tower as a suspect by William III in 1689, but soon after released. He came to the square with his wife in 1693.

Sir Hele Hooke, captain in the volunteer corps of which William III was honorary colonel, was living there in 1696. Whether the young Earl of Gainsborough was living in the square in 1697 may be considered doubtful, but Charles Talbot, 12th Earl and only Duke of Shrewsbury, was certainly there in 1699. It was this changeable politician (called by Swift nevertheless the 'favourite of the nation') who played so large a part in bringing over William III, yet kept up a Jacobite connection. He retired from public life for a while in consequence, but returned to office under Queen Anne and at her death came out in favour of the Hanoverian succession. A well-known story tells how on her death-bed in Kensington Palace, the Queen pressed the Lord Treasurer's wand into his hands with the words 'For God's sake use it for the good of my people.' John Hough, Bishop of Worcester, who defied James II and was made a bishop by William III, and Sir Richard Blackmore, William III's physician, were other residents to whom the square was convenient in its neighbourhood to the Palace, while Dutch envoys for the same reason resided there in the time of Queen Anne and the first Georges. Holland, it may be noted, still retains its connection with Kensington—the Embassy is in the borough, the Ambassador's residence at Palace Green.

In the early eighteenth century the square was very distinguished. It had a reflected literary glow, for though associated more particularly with Chelsea, Addison may have lodged there for a while prior to his marriage and Richard Steele was certainly living there in 1708. Thomas Herring, Archbishop of Canterbury, had a house in the south-east corner, what is now the two houses which delightfully survive there. The Marquis of Powis and the Earl of Clanricarde are among early Georgian notabilities. The removal of the Court from Kensington Palace, however, inevitably made it less fashionable. Dr Mathias Mawson, Bishop of Ely, continued placidly in residence at the south-west corner of the square until the year of his death (1770), but meanwhile it may be supposed the social constituents were changing. After the French Revolution it seems to have filled up with French refugees and in 1792 harboured an illustrious and more or less fugitive French visitor in Talleyrand, who is said to have stayed in Archbishop Herring's house, and was within easy reach of his friends at Holland House.

Yet, like other parts of Kensington, Kensington Square attains a peak of interest in the Victorian age. The Court circle had gone, the economist, the philosopher, the historian, the artist arrived.

The eminent political economist William Nassau Senior lived at No 33; John Stuart Mill at No 18. It was here that occurred that famous literary calamity, the inadvertent burning by a housemaid of Carlyle's manuscript of the *French Revolution*, entrusted to Mill to read. One gazes with a certain awe at the fireplace in which these distinguished ashes were probably found. Caroline Fox in 1840 described Mill's 'little garden' (little by Holland House standards), his 'charming library', his 'exquisitely chiselled features', his voice—'refinement itself'. At No 14 the historian John Richard Green finished his *Short History of the English People* and wrote his *The Making of England*. Thackeray was virtually a resident, for he lived in neighbouring Young Street (called after the builder of the square). In the twentieth century the huge store, Barker's, has grown round but spared the bow-fronted red-brick house in which *Vanity Fair* was written, though delivery vans come and go in the yard where once its garden was. In *Esmond*, also written in Young Street, in 1852, he has given a celebrated evocation of the seventeenth-century square and the Jacobite intrigue centring round Lady Castlewood's house, 'over against the Greyhound' (rebuilt, and still in that form existing, public house): while his daughter Lady Ritchie, it may be noted here, who charmingly described Old Kensington, lived on the opposite side of Young Street next to the Greyhound.

Of 13 Young Street Thackeray wrote to his mother: 'There's a good study for me downstairs and a dining-room and a drawing-room and a little court or garden and a little greenhouse: and Kensington Gardens at the gate and omnibuses every two minutes. What can mortal want more?' His daughter Anne gives further detail: 'My father used to write in his study at the back of the house in Young Street. The vine shaded his two windows, which looked out upon the bit of garden, and the medlar tree and the Spanish jessamine of which the yellow flowers scented our old brick walls. . . . The top schoolroom was over my father's bedroom and the bedroom was over the study where he used to write. I liked the top schoolroom the best of all the rooms in the dear old house, the sky was in it and the evening bells used to ring into it across the garden . . . and the floor sloped so that if you put down a ball it would roll in a leisurely way right across the room of its own accord. And then there was a mystery—a small trapdoor between the windows which we could never open. Where did the trapdoor lead to? It was the gateway of paradise, of many paradises to us.' The visitors were a constant source of interest and wonder to the little girl: 'One of the most notable persons who ever came into our old bow-windowed drawing-room in Young Street is a guest never to be forgotten by me, Charlotte Brontë, a tiny, delicate little person whose small hand nevertheless grasped a mighty lever which set all the literary world of that day vibrating ... a serious little lady, pale with fair straight hair and steady eyes. She may be a little over thirty, she is dressed in a little barége dress with a pattern of faint green moss. She enters in mittens, in silence, in seriousness.' This, however, was the tense occasion when conversation languished. Mrs Brookfield's question to the shy genius 'Do you like London, Miss Brontë?' elicited only the grave reply 'Yes and No,' and constraint arrived at a point when Thackeray tiptoed out of the room and escaped to his club.

To return to the square itself, art was represented by the painter Richard Redgrave, R.A., and his brother Samuel, the writer on art, who lived at No 29 from 1838 to 1841, and later by Edward Burne-Jones (No 41, 1864-7) and his wife before they settled at the Grange, North End Road. The early friend of the Pre-Raphaelites, Vernon Lushington, lived at No 36, 1878-1903; the friend of Ruskin, Sir John Simon, sanitary reformer and pathologist, lived with his wife at No 40 from about 1863 to 1903. Albani, the famous opera singer, lived at No 21 in the 1870s. The composer Sir Hubert Parry came to No 17 in 1886 and wrote many of his compositions there. Mrs Patrick Campbell, the famous actress, lived at No 33 from 1898 to 1916.

Kensington Square was unusual among London squares from a social point of view in several respects during this period. The same families occupied the same houses for a length of time unusual in London. One might cite as a distinguished example No 17 which has had a family history of over 70 years. After Sir Hubert Parry's death in 1918, Lady Maud Parry continued to live there until she died in 1932. Her eldest daughter, Dorothea, who married Arthur Ponsonby (Lord Ponsonby of Shulbrede) in 1898, came into possession of the house which still remains with the Ponsonby family. The square had also an intimate life of its own. Mrs Dorothea Barter, the daughter of Dr Arthur Roberts, who lived at No 30 for many years, has described in the *Cornhill Magazine* (October 1936) how 'Old inhabitants called on newcomers, so that everyone knew everyone else and we children played together in the square gardens and enjoyed a series of parties at each other's houses at Christmas time. ... We had our Square Magazine and our Square Garden Committee....' The dwellers met and talked on Sunday evenings, while the gardener, in his green coat with brass buttons and a high hat with a gold band, seemed also in his way to represent the unity and personality of the square. Its various circles of culture too call for note. Famous historians gathered round John Richard Green, in Mrs Humphry Ward's words 'the pretty house in Kensington Square was the centre of a small society such as England produces more rarely than France. Mr Lecky came (from, it may be noted, 39 Onslow Gardens), Sir Henry Maine, Mr Freeman, Mr Bryce, Bishop Stubbs sometimes, Mr Stopford Brooke and many more.' Similarly during Burne-Jones's occupancy, No 41 was the centre of a Pre-Raphaelite circle, Madox Brown, William Morris, William De Morgan, Ruskin, Swinburne. Among the pupils of Parry who came to No 17 were Vaughan Williams, Walford Davies, Landon Ronald; while in the house of Mrs Patrick Campbell one might meet Yeats or George Bernard Shaw.

The still vivid memories of the past and the ties of an intimate local life have bred a spirit of solidarity which has prevented the square from being completely engulfed and destroyed in modern times. 'Dear little Kensington Square,' said Sir Max Beerbohm in a broadcast of 1936, 'has been saved, by the obstinacy of some enlightened tenants, from the clutches of Mammon,' though its old singularity as a piece of town in the midst of fields has been so far reversed that it seems to be pressed and hemmed in on every side. Great have been the surrounding changes since Lady Burne-Jones wrote of it as 'undisturbed by the world with nothing but gardens between it and the narrow high street'. It is pleasantly surprising to realise that the houses on the north, west and south sides are mainly original, in spite of alterations and the irregularities of aspect thus produced. Nos 11 and 12, originally one house, have a well-preserved exterior and the porch head of No 11 with its decorative shell is a notable feature. No 17 has a fine Queen Anne staircase and below, the basement, originally a ground floor, has features which suggest that the house began as a farmhouse before the square came into being. The Convent of the Assumption occupies the site of Bishop Mawson's 'grand old brick house'. Nos 25–30, converted into a grammar school in the last century, have been reconverted to private use. No 29 is notable for its Georgian doorway. Though the east side has been rebuilt and the 'Greyhound' (No 1), as it originally was, with the stone greyhounds over the porch, is no more than a picturesque memory, Kensington Square has not lost its historic personality and one of its delightful aspects is the care with which restorations have been made and the way in which it is protected by its residents.

Other relics of old Kensington, older, that is, than Queen Victoria's reign, are few and mainly reside in street names. A look at Rocque's maps is sufficient to show how few ancient relics there could be. The High Street was a short stretch of buildings at the bend from the entrance to the Palace to the beginning of the present Campden Hill Road. It was narrow and may have had a certain picturesqueness, remaining probably pretty much the same until the middle of the nineteenth century. The daughter of Richard Redgrave, in her memoir of her father, remarks that 'The old Court suburb was very exclusive . . . the old church, the irregular line of the shops, the red-brick gateway leading to William III's palace made it resemble an old Dutch town. The turnpike and the barracks where a squadron of cavalry was always on duty guarded the entrance from Kensington to London, while the grand old trees both of Kensington Gardens and of the gardens on the other side gave it the look of being embowered in greenery.' London was still distant and getting to it an expedition which required some forethought : 'in going to town from Kensington it was often necessary to take your place in the coach the day before'. None of the old buildings in the High Street have survived. Its old taverns, the 'Red Lion' (a little way east of Young Street), the 'King of Prussia' (formerly No 55), the 'Town Hall' (engulfed by Derry and Toms), the 'King's Arms' (which made way for the Royal Palace Hotel), were demolished in the 'nineties and the early years of this century. The shops of John Barker, established in 1870, swallowed the old shops one by one, creating in more recent times the half-mile stretch of stores which included Pontings and Derry and Toms, dominantly Edwardian in character. The road widening of 1903 finally erased any resemblance to the old High Street and also caused the commercial buildings to expand behind it in that proximity to Kensington Square which its tenants have often lamented.

Church Street, until recent times, has had, at least at its northern and southern ends, a flavour of antiquity, perhaps due rather to its antique shops than its age. The eighteenth-century map shows it as a lane, wandering in rural fashion, with a few buildings near the church at one end and more at the 'gravel pits' (Notting Hill Gate) end. The busy corner opposite the church, with its present-day shops and restaurants, still has some of the Georgian buildings that appear in an eighteenth-century print; though reconstruction at Notting Hill Gate destroyed a large northern sector of the street.

In our map to the west of 'Church Lane', Campden House stood as yet alone. The position of the house (destroyed by fire in 1862) is roughly defined by Sheffield Terrace, Hornton Street, Gloucester

Walk and the western side of Church Street. It was built in 1612 by Sir Baptist Hicks, a city merchant who according to an often repeated legend won the land from Sir Walter Cope at a game of cards. A smaller version of 'Cope's Castle', it was a mansion in the Jacobean style, with turrets surmounted by cupolas, bays and large windows, an ornate porch, an open parapet and picturesque roofs with dormer windows. Its appearance can be gathered from the drawing made in 1647 by Wenceslaus Hollar (Kensington Central Library). Drawings in the Kensington Library show its dining-room with an elaborate oak mantelpiece with six Corinthian columns supporting a pediment and carved caryatids. In the course of time the exterior underwent considerable change, not for the better, to judge by the engraving in Faulkner's *History of Kensington* (1820). Turrets and cupolas, parapets and ornamental detail have gone, though this crude print may have had little correspondence with reality. It is certainly very different from W. Luker Junior's more authentic-looking wash drawing of Campden House from Gloucester Walk, as given in Loftie's *Picturesque Kensington*, though this, of course, shows the results of late-Victorian restoration.

Sir Baptist Hicks was raised to the peerage in 1628 as Lord Campden, taking that title from his estate at Chipping Campden and thus providing a name for his house and the present description of Campden Hill, with its road, square, street and terrace. Its history may be briefly recalled. Like Holland House it was occupied by the Parliamentarians during the Civil War but the Royalist third Lord Campden retained possession and Charles II visited him there after the Restoration. The Princess Anne (afterwards Queen Anne) rented the house from 1691 to 1696, living there with her precocious and delicate son, William Henry, Duke of Gloucester, who died in 1700 at the age of eleven. 'Little Campden House', also known as 'the Elms', was built in the grounds on the western side, for the accommodation of her suite; this too is now demolished.

In 1719 Campden House was sold to Lord Lechmere and is mentioned in the celebrated ballad pastiche attributed to Swift, 'Duke upon Duke', which describes how the noble owner backed out of a duel:

> Back in the dark, by Brompton Park
> He turned up through the Gore,
> So slunk to Campden House so high,
> All in his coach and four.

In 1735 the house was bought by Stephen Pitt, after whom the present Pitt Street is called. It then became a girls' school, whose poor food and restrictions on free movement and exercise were blamed by the traveller Arthur Young for the death of his daughter in 1797. The school ceased to exist in the 1840s, and was reconditioned as a private house by a Mr Wooley, who fitted up a theatre for amateur theatricals, performances including *The Lighthouse* in which Charles Dickens took part. Heavily insured by its owner in 1860, Campden House was burnt down in 1862, the two circumstances together giving rise to suspicion and a law case. The Metropolitan Railway, whose line runs beneath, rebuilt and sold the house, but this in 1900 was replaced by the flats of Campden House Court. Looking at their exuberance of pink and buff today, the visitor may well find the long history of the site curiously remote. 'Little Campden House' was divided into two houses, in one of which the portrait painter Sir Arthur Cope, R.A., lived from 1896 to 1926, but with the destruction of the buildings by a flying bomb in 1944 the last visible trace of the historic past disappeared.

Bullingham House is another vanished building, *c.* 1700 (demolished in 1892), and commemorated only by Bullingham Mansions which stand on the site between Church Street and Pitt Street. The northern part of the old house (originally two) has been identified with the 'Orbell's Buildings' where Sir Isaac Newton died in 1727. On the southern side of the High Street, near Wright's Lane, was Scarsdale House, built by the Earl of Scarsdale about the same time as Kensington Square. The house and grounds were swallowed by Pontings in 1893, though some part of the upper façade remains, while Scarsdale Villas recall its memory. It is a relief to find a pre-nineteenth-century building existing at the present day in the shape of Aubrey House, still tucked away in delightful seclusion and plain and comfortable dignity behind Holland Park, though minus the orchards and acres of farm land it had in the eighteenth century. Originally the 'Wells House' on this site, the nucleus of a spa with a mineral spring, it was rebuilt as a private house in the mid-eighteenth century, being variously referred to as 'the Villa at Notting Hill', 'Notting Hill House' and finally as Aubrey House. Lady Mary Coke, whose letters and journals provide an interesting local commentary, lived there from 1767 to 1788 and in the 1870s it was owned by William Alexander, of whose daughter Whistler painted the exquisite portrait 'Harmony in Grey and Green' now in the Tate Gallery. To complete the catalogue of historical disappearances mention must be made of Hale House, otherwise known as Cromwell House, which stood on the south side of Cromwell Road where Queensberry Place now is and was supposed by local tradition to have been that of Oliver Cromwell himself. The house was demolished, however, in 1853 and the association survives merely in the name of Cromwell Road.

An account of pre-Victorian Kensington must comprise the first stage of the great nineteenth-century development up to the first years of Queen Victoria's reign or roughly to about the year 1840. In this period, substantial houses, rows of cottages, streets and squares began to cluster round various focal points, Notting Hill, Campden Hill, Kensington Gore, Earl's Court and in the south, on the north side of the Fulham Road, in the district known as Little Chelsea and in the Brompton area. Architecturally, this period, which the term 'Regency' does not quite, but goes some way to, cover, provides a pleasant and still pleasantly discernible chapter of Kensington's history. The larger houses retain something of Georgian simplicity, the smaller have a trim modesty which is often delightful. In the survey of 1837 one finds the High Street has begun to take residential definition. St Mary Abbot's Terrace and Upper and Lower Phillimore Place appear to the north on either side of the southern approach to Holland House; on the other side of the road, Edwardes Square and Pembroke Square now appear. Edwardes Square, with its houses now so carefully tended and smartly painted and its little garden temple, is of present interest as an example of what may be called the rehabilitation of Kensington and for its past associations. It was built c. 1812–13 by a Frenchman, Changier, who also built Earl's Terrace —according to tradition he expected to house his compatriots after Napoleon should have successfully invaded England. The small scale of the houses, as contrasted with the extent of the square's gardens, suggested to Leigh Hunt that Changier wished to appeal to a French sense of economy. Hunt came with his wife and family from Cheyne Row to Edwardes Square in 1840 and greatly preferring Kensington to Chelsea lived at No 32 for eleven years and there wrote his entertaining 'memorials of Kensington'—The Old Court Suburb. Lady Ritchie had a vivid recollection of Leigh Hunt's appearance: 'We were walking across Kensington Square early one morning when we heard someone hurrying after us and calling my father by his name. A bright-eyed active old man with long wavy white hair and a picturesque cloak flung over one shoulder. I can see him still, as he crossed the corner of the square and followed us with a light rapid step. . . . There was a sort of eagerness and vividness about the stranger which was very impressive. You could not help watching him and his cloak which kept slipping from its place and which he caught at again and again. We wondered at his romantic, foreign looks and his gaiety and his bright eager way. Afterwards we were told that this was Leigh Hunt.'

By 1837 a row of villas had appeared on the east side of Addison Road and a series of detached houses of some state in the street (as distinct from the district), Campden Hill (also known as 'The Dukeries' in its earlier days from its titled inhabitants, now radically changed). Four houses on the south side were built in that transition style between late Georgian and early Victorian, *c*. 1820. Cam House, so named by Lord Phillimore, who acquired the lease in 1900, was originally Bedford Lodge, first occupied by the Duke and Duchess of Bedford and called Bedford Lodge, and then by the Duke of Argyll who named it Argyll Lodge. Holland Park School, with its modern expanse of glass and more than 2,000 pupils was built on the site of Cam House in 1959. Holly Lodge, of note as the home of Lord Macaulay (1856–9) was demolished in 1965 to make way for a department of Queen Elizabeth College, the former King's College of Household and Social Science. Thornwood Lodge, once numbering the Marquis of Hastings and the Earl of Glasgow among its tenants, was demolished in 1956. Bute House derived its name from the second Marquess of Bute who lived there from 1830 to 1842 and was re-built in 1914 as the King's College of Household and Social Science. Houses on the north side of Campden Hill included Moray Lodge, whose owner in the 1880s, Arthur Lewis, gave those festive and musical parties so popular in the high Bohemian circles of the time and described by George du Maurier in *Trilby*. Moray Lodge was demolished in 1955. A remnant of the old era was preserved in Thorpe Lodge, adapted for Holland Park School's use.

Streets by 1837 were linking Campden Hill and Church Street, Peel Street, Campden Street and Bedford Gardens. The little cottage houses of Campden Street have gained a new attractiveness at the present time, presenting a gay spectacle with their colour washes of pink, pale blue and white, while Peel Street is a scene of transition from the shabbines of the past to the well-kept, 'converted' cottage of today. In various parts of Kensington one still comes with delight on the simple charm of the early nineteenth century, well exemplified in Canning Place and adjoining terraces off Gloucester Road or such a little bower as Gordon Place off the High Street, a *cul-de-sac* with little front gardens full of flowers.

Kensington, east and south in the pre- and early-Victorian period, was beginning to encroach on the nursery gardens and farm land. Gloucester Road was still 'Hogmore Lane', though Gloucester Lodge, built by the Duchess of Gloucester *c*. 1805, promised its future name. George Canning lived for many years at the Lodge, which was demolished in 1853. His contemporary William Wilberforce, the advocate of Negro emancipation, lived at Gore House, Kensington Gore (1808–21). The Gore, that curiously named area, probably indicating a triangular piece of land, had had a few houses since the late eighteenth century. There was Kingston House, built *c*. 1770 by Evelyn Pierrepoint, second and last Duke of Kingston-upon-Hull, a house which survived, surprisingly until 1937. In No 2 of a row of little houses lived the demagogue John Wilkes, who 'was in the habit to the last of walking from Kensington to the city, deaf to the solicitations of hackney coachmen' (Leigh Hunt). Gore House was a separate mansion with extensive grounds—'three acres of pleasure grounds . . . and several old trees, walnut, mulberry, of thick foliage'. Here the benevolent Wilberforce could 'sit and read under their shade . . . with as much admiration of the beauties of nature . . . as if I were two hundred miles from the great city'. From 1836 to 1849 Gore House was showily romantic with the advent of Lady Blessington and Alfred Count d'Orsay. The house had been enlarged by Wilberforce and consisted of a large dining-room, a library, a drawing-room, two studies, a long gallery and ten bed- and dressing-rooms. It offered a spacious setting for the literary and fashionable gatherings over which Marguerite Blessington had previously presided at Seamore Place. These salons were a kind of last flare of the gay and reckless world of the Regency, though, against the background of the new age with its growing sobriety, its promoters have a strangely exaggerated and anachronistic character, of which their contemporaries were, sometimes mirthfully and sometimes disapprovingly, aware. The Countess, the former Miss Power from Tipperary, was 47 when she came to Gore House, a widow, her second husband, Charles John Gardiner, the first Earl of Blessington, having died in Paris, seven years earlier. Alfred Guillaume Gabriel, Count d'Orsay, post-revolutionary French aristocrat, the son of General Count d'Orsay, was at this time 35, and the Countess's devoted admirer and constant companion, although he had married in 1827 Lady Harriet Gardiner, the Earl of Blessington's daughter by his first wife.

This complexity of relationship found little favour in the eyes of, for example, the Hollands. The Count had a 'cottage orné' on Kensington Gore adjoining Gore House, but a semi-basement room in Gore House itself was fitted up for him as a studio.

Their career there was, indeed, as Michael Sadleir terms it in his book, *Blessington–D'Orsay*, a 'masquerade'. The Countess, middle-aged, good-humoured and with pretensions to literary celebrity as the author of a novel and the editor of the *Book of Beauty*, was prepared to spend with both hands the fortune her husband had left her on lavish dinner-parties and other entertainments, and the Count, in every form of extravagance, was more than an able assistant. As a 'dandy', a 'clothes wearing man' in Carlyle's definition, to whom every luxury was a right, he was an astonishingly vivid successor to Beau Brummell. In person he was, said Jane Welsh Carlyle, 'as resplendent as a diamond beetle' and with his chestnut hair, hazel eyes, glowing complexion and luxuriance of beard beneath the chin, he suggests as well as the Regency beau the more romantic hero of a novel by Bulwer Lytton or Harrison Ainsworth. Thackeray's daughter took a more favourable view of the man than the artist: 'Count d'Orsay was the most splendid person I ever remember seeing and he had a little pencil sketch in his hand, which he left behind him upon the table. It was a very feeble sketch; it seemed scarcely possible that so grand a being should not be a bolder draughtsman. He appeared to us one Sunday morning in the sunshine. I came down to breakfast, found him sitting beside my father at the table with an untasted cup of tea before him; he seemed to fill the bow-window with radiance as if he were Apollo; he leant against his chair with one elbow resting on its back, with shining studs and curls and boots. We could see his horse looking in at us over the blind. It was indeed a sight for a little girl to remember all her life. I think my father had a certain weakness for dandies, those knights of the broadcloth and the shining fronts. Magnificent apparitions used to dawn upon us in the hall, glorious beings ascended the stairs on their way to the study but this one outshone them all.' That he was also a wit has been disputed. His remark at dinner when Lady Holland successively dropped her napkin, fan, fork, spoon and wineglass, 'Put my couvert on the floor, I will finish my dinner there. It will be much more convenient to miladi,' was not perhaps a witticism of the first water, and his brilliance was mainly one of appearance, but beyond doubt glittered to great effect at the celebrated Gore House parties.

The list of guests was brilliant too, though the gentlemen were more numerous than the ladies, who were apt to look askance at the household. The Duke of Wellington was a visitor delighted by one of the Gore House pets, the talking crow which croaked, 'Up boys and at 'em.' The Count painted a view of the garden in which there appeared the Duke, Lord Brougham, Lord Douro, Sir Edwin Landseer sketching, the feminine element being provided by the two Miss Powers, Lady Blessington's nieces. The men of letters were numerous, Thomas Campbell, Thomas Moore (on one occasion singing 'When first I met thee' with 'a pathos that beggars description'), old Samuel Rogers, Walter Savage Landor, Bulwer Lytton, Thackeray, Dickens, John Forster, while the appearance of Countess Guiccioli recalled Lady Blessington's old acquaintance with her and Byron and of Prince Louis Napoleon, Count d'Orsay's imperialist leanings.

It may be surmised that the parties were not so costly as the Count's gambling at Crockfords. The fortune disappeared; in addition Heath, the publisher of the *Book of Beauty* and its successor *The Keepsake*, which Lady Blessington also edited, went bankrupt and editorship no longer provided its income. D'Orsay applied himself to his painting and drawing, his portrait drawings being the most valuable thing he did, though it was not supposed that he made enough by his art to keep him in gloves. Early in the 1840s the tradespeople began to take alarm; the whole establishment was soon to collapse under the debts incurred by both. The house was besieged by creditors and bailiffs. 'D'Orsay is still a prisoner six days a week,' wrote Elizabeth Lady Holland. 'He emerges on Sunday but like Cinderella watches midnight. The bailiffs are very vigilant.' His flight to Paris in 1849 was followed by the forced sale of the house and its contents, the behaviour of those attending causing Thackeray to describe it as 'a strange sad picture of Vanity Fair'. The presence of Lawrence's portrait in the Wallace Collection is a reminder that the then Lord Hertford bought it from Gore House (for £336). Three years after the sale of effects (so shortly followed by the death of Lady Blessington in Paris) the great chef of the Reform Club, Alexis Soyer (who lived for a time in Kensington Square), took the house and with considerable acumen turned it at the time of the Great Exhibition into an 'eating house for all nations'. It then acquired, W. P. Frith relates in his memoirs, a new and unreal splendour of décor, which he discovered to be due to the employment of the famous journalist George Augustus Sala as interior decorator. The Commissioners of the Exhibition bought Gore House in 1852 and the Albert Hall and Albert Hall Mansions now occupy the grounds where Wilberforce planned the freeing of slaves and Blessington and D'Orsay entertained the nobility, the *Edinburgh* and *Quarterly* reviewers, the poets and wits and French émigrés.

Brompton—'Broom Town'—by 1837 was yielding its heath to houses; streets and squares were pushing out from the present Brompton Road. Yeoman's Row on one side still has its little houses of *c.* 1800, though the studios of a later day and post-war building have given it a somewhat miscellaneous character. Beauchamp Place too has its flavour of the past. On the north side of Brompton Road the delightful 'Regency' row of houses and shops keeps great distinction and character with its row of plane trees and wide terraced pavement. Brompton Square, still retaining a certain seclusion, appeared in 1826 and to the same date belongs the prim, stiff little church, Holy Trinity, reticently retiring now behind the Oratory. Montpelier Square dates to about 1837, but from Pelham Crescent to Little Chelsea (with Kensington on the north and Chelsea on the south side of the Fulham Road) there was still a stretch of open country. North Kensington too, beyond the cluster of houses at Notting Hill and the gravel pits, was open farm land. A lane meandered from what is now Pembridge Road past Portobello Farm, so called to commemorate Admiral Vernon's capture of Portobello in the Panama Isthmus in 1739. The name and course of the lane survive in Portobello Road, which now presents the contrast of a post-war housing estate and a background of old-fashioned dinginess for one of the busiest of London's street markets. Here was (when Faulkner wrote in 1820) 'one of the most rural and pleasant walks in the summer in the vicinity of London, leading to the high bridge over the Paddington Canal, south of the Harrow Road which is the northern boundary of this parish'. It is strange to think that George Morland who was fond of the 'very ancient' public house at Kensal Green, 'The Plough', found in this pre-Victorian Kensington material for his paintings of the eighteenth-century rural scene. The public road to Kensal Green passed through the farmyard of Notting Barn Farm, to the west of Portobello Farm (Latimer Road). The Kensington Library has a painting attributed to Mulready of another— Notting Hill Farm, in the region where the 'Mitre Tavern', No 40 Holland Park Avenue, now stands. The 'Hippodrome' or racecourse occupied a considerable area to the south of Notting Barn Farm, and the entrance to it was opposite Notting Hill station, though it lasted only from 1837 to 1841, the ground being too heavy for racing or training. It had reverted to open country by 1844, with cornfields and meadowland to west, north and east. The grassy knoll incorporated in the racecourse for the benefit of pedestrians, from which it was possible to see in the rural distance Hampstead and Harrow-on-the-Hill, was that on which the church of St John the Evangelist now stands. To the west of the Hippodrome while it existed there were only a few kilns and cottages which marked a settlement of potters, 'The Potteries', the tradition of which remains in the name Pottery Lane. A single kiln built into the wall in Walmer Road remains. The area, with its stagnant pools, open sewers and tumbledown hovels was denounced by Charles Dickens as 'a plague spot scarcely equalled for its insalubrity by any other in London'. Part of the site of this slum of the 1840s was to be decently covered at a later date by a council estate, Henry Dickens Court, its component houses being named after Dickens characters.

On the whole, the Old Court Suburb was more country than town when Victoria came to the throne. It was then, with the great increase of both town population and wealth, that the incursion came, accelerated by the Great Exhibition of 1851, creating what we think of as the typical Kensington.

CHAPTER THIRTEEN

Kensington of the Victorians

The population figures tell their story. At the beginning of the nineteenth century Kensington had 8,600 inhabitants. There was a moderate increase to 27,000 in 1841, and a great jump from 70,000 in 1861 to 163,000 in 1881. These figures broadly speaking reflect the general expansion of London in this period, though proportionately the increase is much greater than say in Chelsea or Hampstead during the same period of time. The Great Exhibition of 1851, the Exhibition of 1862 and the establishment of museums and colleges all tended to attract the upper middle-class westwards, though the attraction of an area so well-wooded and garden-like was separate and considerable. The terraces of big private houses with stuccoed fronts and heavy, columned porches and a range of coach and stable houses at the back, though not peculiar to Kensington, are there particularly dominant and characteristic. It is a form of architecture which can be dated back to Nash's terraces round Regent's Park, though it was not, in general, employed with anything like the variety and sense of design that Nash showed. The rows of porches were monotonous, the effect was in the main pompous without being magnificent. On the other hand, the rooms were large, a fact which the present day with its narrow economies of space has learned to appreciate. Wealth and respectability, these were the two cardinal virtues which these houses represented.

Architecturally, however, Kensington is of particular interest nowadays when an anti-Victorian animus has been giving way to curiosity and scholarly study, in representing many different aspects of the aspirations of the nineteenth century. The Gothic Revival is notably exemplified. A variety of buildings testifies to the Victorian search for a style, and in the 1870s and 1880s imagination and idealism add their element of fancy to the aspect of the region. That

208

remarkable architect Norman Shaw left as definite an impress on Kensington as on Chelsea, diversifying the older stucco with red brick and 'Renaissance' detail, 'Queen Anne gone mad' in the disapproving remark of the period; to the historian of Kensington, W. J. Loftie, 'the wildest extravagances of what may be called eclectic art'. Shaw inaugurated the epoch of flats, passing through every stage of design from his exuberance to the neo-Georgian of the 1920s, well illustrated in the High Street and the modern style which startlingly intrudes its simplicity among the Victorian façades (like Wells Coates's admirable flats in Palace Gate). Socially, and in its interior settings, Kensington represented particularly well both the prosperous and the cultured Victorian middle-class. Behind those columned porches flourished the family life which George du Maurier playfully, but with an edge of satire, drew in *Punch*, though its drawing-rooms, which interior decorators have in this century so often transformed with a triumphant 'Before' and 'After' (signalised in the magazines of architecture and housekeeping), would now be hard to find in their original condition. It was also the home of great Victorians, those most in harmony with their period, writers such as Macaulay and Thackeray, such painters as Lord Leighton, John Millais and G. F. Watts, whose life there is a fascinating part of Kensington's history.

Macaulay's connection with Kensington is of particular note. As a young Member of Parliament, a brilliant contributor to the *Edinburgh Review* and a formidable partisan in the Whig interest, he paid his first visit to Holland House in 1831. It was the beginning of the long intimacy with the house and its circle, which he more impressively than anyone else has described and praised. His stay in India as member of the Supreme Council and subsequently his busy political and literary life, while for many years he lived in the Albany, did not interrupt his friendship with the Hollands and it was appropriate that in his later years he should settle near by at Holly Lodge, Campden Hill. This was in 1856, Macaulay himself being 56 and especially respected for the *History of England*, the third and fourth volumes of which had appeared the year before amid general acclaim. His nephew and biographer has described the rural seclusion of the house. The 'winding lane' in which it stood is a lane no more. The 'lawn whose unbroken slope of verdure was worthy of the county house of a Lord Lieutenant', the elms, the willow, the mulberry trees, the bowers of lilac and laburnum, to Macaulay 'a paradise of shrubs and turf' are only a memory. He divided his affection between the library, more spacious than the other rooms and enlarged by a pillared recess, and the garden, declaring that of 'all the countries through which I have been travelling none could show such a carpet of soft rich green herbage as mine'. He took to gardening himself and describes with considerable humour his war on dandelions whose 'great impudent flaring yellow faces turned up at me'. 'How I grabbed them up! How I enjoyed their destruction!' It was typical of the man and his age that he mused on the 'curious question' of whether it was Christianlike to hate a dandelion so savagely. Holly Lodge suited Macaulay so well that he rarely left it. Many were the breakfast parties of which it was the scene, where the host's prodigious memory and powers of conversation held the guests entranced even until midday. Here he wrote the fifth volume of his great fragment of history, published only after his death, for he died at Holly Lodge in 1859—in the library, dressed as usual and with a book open before him.

Thackeray, from the time he came to Young Street in 1846 until his death at the house in Palace Green in 1863, had a parallel association with Kensington. We follow him from Young Street, where he wrote *Vanity Fair, Pendennis* and *Esmond*, and received his memorable visit from his unknown admirer, Charlotte Brontë, to a larger house, No 36 Onslow Square. It was here that he wrote *The Virginians* and as its editor planned the first number of the *Cornhill Magazine*—Macaulay was reading its instalment of *Lovel the Widower* on the day of his death. There followed the short tenure of the villa he designed for himself in Palace Green. As Macaulay illuminates Holland House, so does Thackeray Kensington Palace and Kensington Square, though he too knew the Hollands. Lord Holland relates how Thackeray sang their praises, 'saying that we liked agreeable people and did not care for rank and quarterings, that our house was open to all' and that the person he addressed not knowing him said, 'Oh, yes, I hear they *even* receive Mr. Thackeray of *Punch* celebrity'.

There was indeed much of *Punch* in Kensington—or of Kensington in *Punch*. Its early editors, Shirley Brooks and Mark Lemon, the star among its early wits, Douglas Jerrold, all lived there and their concerted jibes in the 1840s at 'our own little railway—the Kensington' made that railway extension notorious as 'Mr. Punch's Line'. Often enough too the drawings of the Victorian *Punch* breathed the spirit of the prosperous Kensington middle-class.

The Exhibition of 1851 may be looked on as the pivot on which the history of Kensington turned. Only passing reference is here in place to the famous story of the Exhibition itself. An erroneous idea has grown up that the Albert Memorial marks its site, though this is not so; it occupied 19 acres somewhat to the east in Hyde Park, its main southern entrance being at Prince of Wales Gate. It is not a part of Kensington's history, geographically speaking. Yet the tremendous success of this first of international exhibitions, when more than six million people from all over the world came to admire the wonderful improvisation of iron and glass, Sir Joseph Paxton's 'Crystal Palace'—three times the length of St Paul's Cathedral, with its 14,000 exhibits, valued at £2,000,000—had most important results on the borough's development. It produced the substantial profit of £186,437 and it is an impressive fact that the 1851 Commission still exists, administering a large income. What to do with this profit was in a sense already determined by the whole trend of the Prince Consort's ideas, his idealistic schemes for the improvement of both industry and education in which he was ably assisted by the man who had played an energetic part in promoting the Exhibition itself, Henry Cole. The magnificent conception of a new 'university city', a constellation of museums and colleges, emerged. The site was available, largely unencumbered by existing buildings, and 'being recommended for the dryness of the soil and as the only ground safe for future years amidst the growth of the metropolis'. When the Gore House estate (about 21 acres) was bought in 1852 for £60,000, the first intention was to build a new National Gallery there. The Baron de Villars' adjoining estate of some 50 acres was bought for the projected Museum of Manufactures for £153,500. Private houses of suitable dignity were to be interspersed among the educational buildings, thus providing a dependable and continued source of income. South Kensington was born.

It is perhaps a national failing that the brilliant ideas initiated on British soil so seldom take a coherent architectural form. Sir Christopher Wren, unfortunately, was not alive to give grandeur to the new 'cité universitaire' and it cannot be denied that the Prince Consort's great scheme found a somewhat haphazard realisation. Everyone knew that the Crystal Palace had been one of the main assets of the Exhibition. 'With a large proportion (of visitors)' said *The Times*, 'it was the edifice itself which took the firmest hold upon their hearts. Its vastness, its simplicity and regularity of structural details . . . must have left a strong impression.' Yet it remained for the twentieth century to discern the elements of a new architecture in Paxton's building, and the indifference with which it was sold into private hands and removed to Sydenham remains notable. No one seems to have thought of consulting Paxton as to future designs, and the follow-up International Exhibition of 1862 was provided with a building not by him but by Captain Francis Fowke, R.E., official architect of the Science and Art Department. It extended from Prince Albert's Road (now Queen's Gate) on the west to the Exhibition Road, with a frontage on Cromwell Road, the main part occupying the later site of the National History Museum. Prints show an uninspired and monotonous façade, though the two glass domes, one at either end (260 feet high and 160 feet in diameter), were impressive if merely in size. It is hardly to be wondered at that, like many sequels, the Exhibition failed to capture the attention and imagination as its predecessor had done.

Meanwhile the Museum of Manufactures had begun the devious course which was eventually to lead to the Victoria and Albert Museum. It was opened in 1852 as a temporary expedient at Marlborough House, where a selection of manufactured products bought from the Great Exhibition was shown, together with other objects from the Government School of Design at Somerset House. 'The application of the fine arts to objects of utility' which they were intended to represent had long been a somewhat vaguely formulated ideal, and the Government School of Design, set up as early as 1837, was a result. Some hesitation as to the precise meaning of the word 'Design' is shown by the change of title for the exhibits at Marlborough House from Museum of Manufactures to Museum of Ornamental Art. It was a very odd-looking building at South Kensington—or Brompton—to which the Museum was transferred in 1857, known to derisive fame as the 'Brompton Boilers', though additions were soon made to the original iron structure. Long called comprehensively 'the South Kensington Museum' its exhibits represented both science and art, though under the auspices of Henry Cole, secretary of the Science and Art Department from 1857 to 1873, artistic craftsmanship became increasingly its main concern.

There is no doubt that this Victorian official was a creator of South Kensington as we know it, and the principal executive of Prince Albert's plans. His career had been consistently one of improvement and reform. As a young man, he had contributed much to the organisation of the Public Record Office and the proper care of ancient documents which he had found in deplorable confusion and neglect. He had co-operated energetically with Sir Rowland Hill in postal reform and had taken an active part in the exhibitions between 1847 and 1850 by which the Royal Society of Arts sought improvement in design and paved the way for 1851. Under the pseudonym of Felix Summerly he himself had designed children's books and pottery in which art and use were consciously brought together. Forceful, tireless, an enthusiast, he was, in effect, the dictatorial ruler of the Museum's destinies, and his bust and mosaic portrait in the Victoria and Albert Museum fittingly commemorate his association with it. That he had some of the limitations of his age and of his own type of ability was no doubt only to be expected. Like the Prince whom he served he had intelligently sensed some connection between manufacture and design which was still to be revealed, yet neither he nor anyone else yet realised that design was anything but the application of ornamental styles of the past to contemporary effort and this fact influenced both the external and internal aspect of the Museum. That the new brick buildings of the 1860s were in a 'Lombard Early Renaissance' style, making much use of terra-cotta and mosaic, may perhaps be traced to an enthusiasm conceived by Cole when on holiday in Italy; and though Captain Fowke, who designed them, may, as Dr Pevsner has suggested, have been influenced by the architect, Gottfried Semper, he was also very much influenced by Henry Cole's taste for Italian forms of design. A mosaic memorial to the Great Exhibition appears externally in the pediment of the Quadrangle buildings finished *c.* 1868 to Fowke's plan (he died 1865) and internally a frieze in glass mosaic dates to 1862, while faience tiles also played a considerable part. The old Ceramic Gallery (1868) presented a strangely fascinating spectacle of ornateness in this respect, though its tiled Corinthian columns have now been covered over. In the work of decoration, students of the National Art Training School (precursor of the Royal College of Art, and also on the Museum site) played an active part. What may be called the 'South Kensington style' that grew out of such efforts has left its traces in many parts of London of the later Victorian period and an interesting example, not far from the Museum itself, may be found in the 'Bunch of Grapes' public-house at the corner of Yeoman's Row.

Cole made a point of enlisting the famous artists of his time and the 'classicism' of Edward Poynter and Frederic Leighton has left its stamp. To the array of artists on the mosaic frieze, Poynter contributed the figures of Phidias and Apelles, and Leighton, Cimabue and Niccolo Pisano. The dining-room of the old restaurant was decorated by William Morris's firm, with panels painted by Burne-Jones, the grill-room by Poynter with allegorical panels and painted tiles. These fascinating period pieces are in strange contrast with the aseptic plainness of the new restaurant of today. Other notable works commissioned by Cole were the two frescoes executed by Leighton between c. 1870 and 1885. It had been a thought of Prince Albert that frescoes of 'The Industrial Arts of Peace' and 'The Industrial Arts of War' would be a suitable memento of the Crimean War and these were the subjects on which Leighton worked at intervals for many years.

The death of the Prince Consort in 1861 left the general feeling that Kensington was the fitting place for a memorial to him and both the Albert Memorial and the Royal Albert Hall may be looked on in this light not to speak of the memorial to the Great Exhibition (1858). Those two remarkable structures, the Royal Albert Hall and the Albert Memorial, reflect in their different ways the Victorian search for a style in architecture and the 'Battle of Styles' which opposed Gothic and Italian sources to one another, the factions being known as 'Goths' and 'Romans'. Hence we have on one side of the road the Gothic Memorial, and on the other the Roman Hall. Consistency of design, as Cole himself was disturbed to realise, was lost. A Gothic impress was laid on Kensington by no less resolute a hand than that of Sir George Gilbert Scott, the arch-restorer of cathedrals and convinced and learned mediaevalist. Scott's design for the Memorial was chosen by the Queen with the help of a Committee including the Earls of Derby and Clarendon, Sir Charles Eastlake, P.R.A., and the Lord Mayor (William Cubitt) from among the projects submitted by six architects, a Gothic shrine seeming the happiest of solutions. Taking nine years to build (1863–72) and costing £120,000, it was looked on by the architect as his greatest effort and is today as disconcerting to the eye as many critics in the past have found it. A shrine (or ciborium) 175 feet high is inappropriately large, and severed from any connection with adjacent architecture this exaggerated size is all the more apparent. Nor can it be said that the sculptors and designers employed were either Gothic in spirit or anything but commonplace. Those who would try to find a neglected great work of art in the much criticised memorial can scarcely deny these assertions. On the other hand it has an extraordinary amount of detail to browse over and symbolises art and science with a comprehensiveness both historical and, in keeping with the spirit of the Great Exhibition, international. The statue of the Prince, holding a catalogue of the Exhibition, by John Henry Foley, R.A., cast in gun-metal from the Government stores at Woolwich and 'gilt with gold of triple thickness', was the central feature round which were ranged emblems of his varied interests and studies. The four continents at the outer corners, Europe (Patrick Macdowell), Asia (J. H. Foley), Africa (William Theed), America (John Bell) allude to the international character of his work. Groups above are Agriculture (W. Calder Marshall), Manufactures (Henry Weekes), Commerce (Thomas Thornycroft), Engineering (John Lawlor). The series of 169 portrait sculptures on the podium, by H. H. Armstead and J. B. Philip, represent Poetry, Painting, Music, Architecture and Sculpture, ranging from Van Eyck to David Wilkie, Phidias to Flaxman, Cheops to Pugin, Virgil to Schiller, Palestrina to Mendelssohn. Allegorical figures of the Fine Arts are in the mosaic tympana, executed by Salviati & Co of Murano to the designs of Clayton and Bell, above columns of Ross of Mull granite. Bronze-gilt statues in the spire represent the Christian virtues, Faith, Hope, Charity and Humility; another set, the moral virtues, Fortitude, Prudence, Justice and Temperance, while eight bronzes at the angles show Astronomy, Chemistry, Geology, Geometry, Rhetoric, Medicine, Philosophy and Physiology. At the present day it is curiously possible to be absorbed in this singular compendium, impressed by the idealism of its designer and the efficiency with which so large a work was executed, without being in any way moved by it as a work of art.

It was Scott's ambition to design also that great Central Hall of Arts and Sciences which had figured prominently in Prince Albert's plans; for which the Gore House estate had been bought. The Prince's death in 1861 halted the scheme only for a time and indeed made its execution all the more desirable as another great memorial to him. 'An early Gothic treatment with a tinge of Byzantine' was the idea of Sir Gilbert Scott, who greatly coveted the commission to design the building, though to Henry Cole and others this seemed a somewhat alarming prospect. Indeed to him the whole system by which the aspect of public buildings might be determined by the caprice or personal leanings of the architect or the Commissioner of Works seemed irresponsible. Scott, however, was not the chosen architect. Captain Fowke was again employed and the favoured 'Early Renaissance' in purple brick and terra-cotta was the stylistic theme, complicated by an enthusiasm for the ancient Roman amphitheatre which Fowke and Cole, on holiday together, acquired at Nîmes and

Arles. The impressive result has been variously compared with the Colosseum at Rome and Semper's Dresden Opera House. The application of 'art' to the exterior was not forgotten and the mosaic frieze, symbolically representing the arts, commerce and manufactures, was one of the most ambitious of Victorian decorative efforts, though only a somewhat vague general impression of it can be gained from the ground. Six feet wide, about 800 feet long, it was made in sections of 50 feet, of encaustic tesserae by Messrs Minton & Co whom students of the South Kensington School of Art assisted. The designs, drawings for which are still retained at the Hall, were by a number of Academy painters, Horsley, Armitage, Yeames, Marks, Poynter, Pickersgill and the sculptor Armstead, who was extensively employed also on the Albert Memorial. The grandeur of size and of a coherent geometrical shape combined make the Albert Hall one of the most impressive of Victorian buildings. The effect of the interior, that oval vastness accommodating 8,000 people with its three tiers of boxes and its great organ, one of the largest in the world, is unfailing in its power and full of vivid memories of the many spectacular events it has known. According to Augustus Hare it had no beauty and was quite inappropriate for its use as a hall of music, though this has been its main purpose since the great concerts of the 1870s and would seem an absurd comment to the devotee of the Promenade Concerts at the present time.

Architecturally, the expansion of museums and colleges went on in the curiously haphazard way that has been noted. The Italian style of Fowke appears in the remaining Exhibition buildings of 1862 which formerly enclosed the gardens of the Royal Horticultural Society, but though he won the first award in the competition for a new extension of the British Museum, the Natural History Museum, his design was set aside in favour of that of Alfred Waterhouse, which was much to the annoyance, or at least bewilderment, of Henry Cole, who could not understand why resort should be needed to a style which no one could quite place and was sometimes called Byzantine and sometimes Norman. Stylistically this 'Romanesque' and rigidly symmetrical building (1875–81), faced with terracotta, still puzzles the eye, though its long front on the Cromwell Road gains impressiveness not only from size but from its profusion of carved animals, birds and reptiles. The search for a style produced another remarkable curiosity in the Imperial Institute (1887–93) designed by T. E. Collcutt, the outcome of the Colonial Exhibition of 1886, and afterwards a building of dual function, being in part an examination hall of London University and also a series of exhibition halls presenting the history and resources of the Dominions and Colonies, while various bodies concerned with colonial research and production were also housed there. The site is now largely occupied by the Imperial College of Science though protest against the demolition of the Institute's buildings spared the central tower (280 feet high) as an architectural landmark. The Commonwealth Institute, opened in 1962 at the southern extremity of Holland Park, abutting on Kensington High Street, took over and gave a new significance to the function of the old Institute.

The interesting novelty of museum architecture was increased by the miscellany of motifs in Sir Aston Webb's additions to the South Kensington Museum (1899–1909), its octagonal centrepiece and open lantern being a distinctive landmark but quite unlike anything else in the neighbourhood. With this building, the opening of which by King Edward VII in 1909 formally brought into use the new name requested by Queen Victoria—'Victoria and Albert Museum' (though so hardy is traditional nomenclature that even today it is still often referred to, to the authorities' despair, as the 'South Kensington Museum')—the gamut of Victorian style had indeed been run. The haphazard-seeming architectural growth, the variety sometimes entertaining and sometimes odd, does not, however, disguise the magnificent fashion in which the Prince Consort's schemes were substantially realised, and continue to operate. From the Exhibition of 1851 to the array of museums and colleges at the present time is a record of consistent expansion to which Prince Albert's equal care for science and the arts gave its impetus.

The two principal churches of Kensington represent as sharp a distinction in style as in doctrine: on the one hand the Victorian Gothic of St Mary Abbots, and on the other, the Italian Baroque of the Roman Catholic Oratory in Brompton Road. In St Mary Abbots, Sir Gilbert Scott produced a companion piece to the Albert Memorial, though in a more austere revivalist mood. The original church which dated back to the twelfth century, it is now impossible to lament, the tower, its last vestige, disappearing in the eighteenth century: though it must have been small in keeping with the needs of a country hamlet, 'built of Flint and rough Stone with little Art or Order', in the words of Bowack, who viewed its tower in 1705. The modest growth of population in the seventeenth century and the advent of the Court caused first a number of piecemeal alterations and enlargements and a more general rebuilding in 1696, to the cost of which William III and Queen Mary contributed. The parishioners were accommodated, during the rebuilding, in the chapel of Holland House. A curtained pew was reserved for the royal family and continued in use by its members at Kensington Palace down to the time when the Duchess of Kent returned thanks after the birth of Queen Victoria. This was the church described by Bishop Blomfield as the ugliest in his diocese, and to judge by extant engravings of the eighteenth century and the last photographic record of the 1860s (Kensington Public Library) it was without any distinction either of size or style, though in its box pews Wilberforce and Canning, Thackeray and Macaulay knelt at their devotions. The structure and foundations were evidently faulty, for there are frequent records of cracking and collapse which, together with 'that sense of closeness and crowding, to which the increasing population naturally tended' (Leigh Hunt), gave rise to an appeal in 1866 (in Archbishop Sinclair's words) 'some grand design worthy of old Kensington'. In size certainly the resulting building by Sir Gilbert Scott (1869–72) is a 'grand design'. He allowed for a congregation of 1,800. The spire, 278 feet high (completed in 1879), was only 14 feet lower than that of St Mary Redcliffe, Bristol, by which it was inspired. The total length is 179 feet and across the transepts from north to south 109 feet. That it lacks both externally and internally the spirit of the thirteenth- and fourteenth-century models from which is was adapted is evident enough, though the spire looks well from a distance and the inhabitants of old Kensington Square regarded it with affection before the intervening stores were built. Internally there are few details of historic interest. All the monuments of the older church were made away with in the seventeenth-century rebuilding. There remain some minor survivals of pre-Victorian date, the languid monument to the Earl of Warwick and Holland, Addison's stepson, by the Bolognese sculptor J. B. Guelphi, a panel by Grinling Gibbons (1702) from a memorial to the naturalist and friend of Sir Hans Sloane, William Courten, and a tablet and bust by Chantrey of Thomas Rennell, Vicar of Kensington, 1816–24. The pulpit, dated 1697, is that said to have been presented to the parish by William III. Most of the seventeenth-century plate is now to be seen at the Victoria and Albert Museum. The font by Scott and the stained glass by Clayton and Bell have all the cold elaboration of revival.

The student of Victorian ecclesiastical architecture, a study in which there are discoveries of curious interest to be made, has indeed much to see in Kensington. Churches were necessarily new as the borough population expanded and the fields and woods gave way to houses. St. Barnabas, Addison Road, with its prim turrets (by Lewis Vulliamy), consecrated in 1827 and T. L. Donaldson's Holy Trinity, Brompton, 1829, are early simplicities of 'Gothic', but there are 26 more churches of later date in which the Victorian style passes through various phases from the 1840s, with a growing elaboration in the later years of the century as in Butterfield's St Augustine, Queen's Gate, 1871, and Roumieu Gough's St Cuthbert, Philbeach Gardens, 1887, and seen at its best in G. F. Bodley's Holy Trinity, Prince Consort Road, 1904.

The Brompton Oratory, the church of the Congregation of the Oratory, an order of secular priests founded by St Philip Neri in Rome, 1575, is again distinct architecturally, the design by H. Gribble (with dome by G. Sherrin) conforming closely to the Italian baroque of the sixteenth century. The Italian character of the interior is heightened by the facsimile of the statue of St Peter in the nave of St Peter's Rome and the marble statues of the Apostles by the seventeenth-century sculptor, Mazzuoli, which came from Siena Cathedral. The part played by Cardinal Newman in establishing the Oratory in England in 1847 is commemorated by the statue of Newman to the west of the Oratory by Bodley and Garner, 1896. A sepulchral comment on the growth of population, not of Kensington alone but of London in general, is provided by the Brompton (West London and Westminster) Cemetery, opened in 1840, and the Kensal Green Cemetery (of which part lies in Kensington), 1832. Here indeed is ample material for solemn meditation among mausolea of strange variety and the inscriptions that lead down many paths of local memory. It is fitting that at Brompton should be buried Sir Henry Cole and Captain Fowke who collaborated to so much effect in the creation of the museum zone: and at Kensal Green, those so closely associated with Kensington as Sydney Smith, Leigh Hunt (though his grave for many years bore no stone), William Makepeace Thackeray, Shirley Brooks, the editor of Punch (who lived at 22 Brompton Square), John Leech, the painter Sir Augustus Callcott, the Duke of Sussex, son of George III, and the Princess Sophia, who died at York House in Church Street in 1848. Among examples of quaintly figurative sculpture at Brompton, one may pause before the tomb of Robert Coombes (1860), the champion sculler of Thames and Tyne, portrayed with honorific coat and badge, his overturned skiff in stone, symbolising alike his prowess and demise.

Style in the domestic buildings of Victorian Kensington has several aspects. There is the age of stucco and the porch which gives a certain uniformity and even monotony to the mansions of Cromwell Road and Exhibition Road. There are the occasional extravagances of size and elaboration, once to be observed in such freaks as Kensington House and Tower Cressy. There is the late-Victorian development of brick and 'Queen Anne', signalised by the remarkable and unpredictable efforts of Norman Shaw. Connected with this last architecturally is the growth of an artist population and its result in a series of large studio-houses reflecting often in an extraordinary fashion the individual tastes and ideas of their owners.

Kensington House, which was built by a man of wealth, Albert Grant, in 1872 remained intact for only ten years and its fearful symmetry can now only be visualised in the careful wash-drawing of W. Luker Junior, and the disapproving description of W. J. Loftie. It must indeed have been a house of fantasy, one of those strange dreams of grandeur which some Victorian minds conceived without reference to architects or any idea of art. It stood in Kensington Gore, replacing the old houses which stood on the site, the original seventeenth-century Kensington House and Colby House, built by Sir Thomas Colby in 1720. It also effected the demolition of a 'rookery', a nest of the poor who were found fresh quarters in Notting Hill. 'The new house speedily rose in all its hideous magnificence, surrounded by grounds so large that they might be called a park. Conservatories, arbours, lakes, Swiss chalets and innumerable varieties of trees, shrubs and flowers seemed to grow up as if by magic.' The grounds stretched as far as Kensington Square. Yet the new Kensington House was never lived in; financially the owner had overreached himself. Loftie recalls the small prices for which its columns of granite and Italian marble were sold, the house which had cost some £250,000 realising little more than £10,000. It was replaced in 1883 by the still existing Kensington Court in which Jackson of Oxford and John Stevenson wiped out the grandiose memory of Albert Grant's palazzo with Tudor detail in terra-cotta and an assortment of Renaissance motifs. Tower Cressy, of earlier date (1854), lasted longer—until it was destroyed by a flying bomb in 1944—and was more artistically freakish than Kensington House. It was indeed a towering structure, with splendid views from the roof, built by Thomas Page, the civil engineer who designed Westminster Bridge and constructed the Albert Embankment, in honour of the Black Prince; the Prince's emblems appeared on each stage of the exterior. It had, however, the curious effect of a Renaissance palace that had suddenly shot skyward, though a porch with pointed arch gave its reminder of the Middle Ages. The tower of the Grand Junction Waterworks, near to Tower Cressy in date and constructed by Sir John Aird, solemn and impressive landmark until its demolition in 1972, with some faint suggestion of an Italian campanile, had more to commend it in that simplicity which in general distinguishes the Victorian functional building from those of other than industrial or engineering purpose.

The break with the Kensington tradition in architecure in the 1870s and 1880s so emphatically marked by the buildings of Norman Shaw is still very evident. He was at his best in the house he designed in 1873 for the Hon. W. Lowther (Lowther Lodge), with its warm red brick, its tall chimneys, and its varied gables. Now the premises of the Royal Geographical Society, it breaks and contrasts with the solemn rotundity of the Albert Hall in unrestrained picturesqueness. The Albert Hall Mansions of 1879, which set the fashion for later Victorian flat building, remains, in comparison, a grim bulk, in spite of its gables and oriels, a self-centred piece of architecture heedless of its surroundings. Other interesting buildings by Norman Shaw are to be found among those studio-houses which deserve a chapter to themselves.

CHAPTER FOURTEEN

The Artist's Kensington

Though Kensington had no such historic association with art as that of Holbein with Chelsea and has never had so close-knit an artist society as the neighbouring borough, many painters, sculptors and graphic artists have lived there since the early nineteenth century. As a young but already famous painter, Sir David Wilkie settled in Lower Phillimore Place in 1811 and there painted his 'Distraining for Rent' and other popular works. Later he lived at Maitland House on the east side of Church Street (demolished 1904–5). He had often seen the young Victoria in her childhood days in Kensington and when summoned to paint 'The Queen's First Council' in 1837, 'my reception' he remarks, 'had a little the air of an early acquaintance'. The brothers Redgrave, as has been noted, lived in Kensington Square and Richard Redgrave, R.A. (1804–88), is further associated with the origins of South Kensington as head of the Government School of Design and one of the organisers of the Great Exhibition. The animal painter Richard Ansdell lived at Lytham House in the same neighbourhood. Samuel William Reynolds, the mezzotint engraver (1773–1835), lived at No 15 Holland Street. The landscape painter Sir Augustus Callcott (1779–1844) lived in The Mall off Church Street. William Mulready, the Irish painter (1786–1863), settled in Linden Grove, a lane adjoining what is now Linden Gardens, and it was there in the large house which for some reason, we are told, though he began with ambitious ideas for its decoration remained neglected and bare, that he designed his famous envelope for the first penny post. The painters of Kensington in his time had a life-school which he attended as an old man to make pen-and-ink studies of heads and hands. The bequest of his patron, John Sheepshanks, has provided the Victoria and Albert Museum with 15 of his works, including his painting of the Kensington Gravel Pits. John Leech poured out his drawings for *Punch* from a house in the High Street, near Wright's Lane, where he died in 1864. W. P. Frith, R.A., had a house in Pembridge Villas on a site subsequently occupied by a Lex Garage and it was there he painted his 'Derby Day' of 1858 and the 'Railway Station' of 1862 from the conveniently near Paddington.

Though some of the above-mentioned artists lived well on into the latter half of the century—Frith who reached the age of 90 died (in St John's Wood) in 1909—one can to some extent distinguish this group from the later artist settlers who represent the remarkable affluence and popularity of the late Victorian artist. Among the Pre-Raphaelites who came to Kensington are Burne-Jones (before he settled at North End), William Holman Hunt and Hunt's pupil Robert Braithwaite Martineau. A long list could be made of the successful academicians of Kensington, Sidney Cooper, Vicat Cole, Peter Graham, J. C. Hook, J. Horsley, Henry Moore, Colin Hunter, Val Prinsep, Luke Fildes, Marcus Stone. An added list would comprise those who represent the 'classicism' of the late Victorian age. In Holland Lane, from 1877 to 1891, lived Albert Moore who derived from his study of the Elgin Marbles so distinctive a type of what might be called Anglo-Greek beauty, while Lord Leighton and Sir Edward Poynter are outstandingly of Kensington both by residence and by their close connection with its museum and art teaching. While it was perhaps too dignified and 'senatorial' to be described by such a bohemian title as 'artists' quarter' the development of the region adjoining Holland House is of special note.

Little Holland House, so much associated with George Frederick Watts, comes first, as a link between the Holland history and that of the artist settlements. It had belonged to the Hollands since 1774. It was left in 1837 to Caroline Fox, Lord Holland's aunt (described in her later years by Sydney Smith as an 'aged angel') who lived there for many years with a relative, Miss Elizabeth Vernon, and delighted in it as a 'little paradise'. It needs a certain effort now to appreciate that entirely rural atmosphere which she describes, though Frederick Griggs in an admirable pen drawing conveys something of the charm of the old irregular building in its gardens, scented with laburnum, hawthorn and honeysuckle. After the death of Caroline Fox in 1844, the house was let and in 1850 taken on a 21 years' lease by Mr and Mrs. Thoby Prinsep. Prinsep was a man of wealth who had spent 35 years in India in the service of the East India Company. His wife, the former Miss Pattle, was the sister of the beautiful Lady Somers whose portrait Watts painted. Acquainted in this way with the

Prinseps, Watts introduced them to this property of his friends the Hollands; and when they established themselves there, was provided with a studio. He lived there on the same familiar yet independent footing that he had previously enjoyed in Holland House itself. 'He came to stay three days,' said Mrs Prinsep, 'he stayed thirty years' —though Watts seems to have been under the impression that a long-term arrangement was understood from the first. He became, however, one of the family, a pet name—'Signor'—was found for him and his presence added to the fame of the frequent social gatherings at Little Holland House. Caroline Fox had there entertained her brother's friends—Macaulay, Mackintosh, Coleridge, Jeremy Bentham; the Prinseps had a new literary and artistic circle: Thackeray, Richard Doyle, Tennyson, Rossetti, Burne-Jones. There was Mrs Cameron to take her photographs of celebrities on the lawn and Adelaide Sartoris to sing, with touching effect, his own poems for Tennyson, while of an evening Joachim would play his violin under the deep blue ceiling of the drawing-room. The years passed happily for Watts until in his middle-age he made his extraordinary marriage with the young Ellen Terry. For the girl of sixteen, Little Holland House and its famous painter represented in prospect the fulfilment of a dream, the other world to which the young actress aspired, 'a world full of pictures and music and gentle, artistic people with quiet voices and elegant manners'. She had been introduced to Watts by Tom Taylor, the dramatist and man of letters who was later to become editor of Punch, a friend of the Terry family. The stage seemed to her a poor place when compared with the wonderful studio where she and Kate Terry were painted as 'The Sisters'. The house was 'a paradise where only beautiful things were allowed to come'. How she admired 'Beauty', 'Dash' and 'Talent', as the three sisters, Mrs Prinsep, Lady Somers and Mrs Cameron were known. With what awe she viewed the visitors to Little Holland House; Gladstone 'like a volcano at rest'; Disraeli with his straggling black curls and garish blue tie, indifferently attending a garden party; Tennyson who was so interested in her first romance. The fact that she had never been to school, except as the Shakespearean stage might be considered so, made her reverence the more.

There was something equally dreamy and regardless of the realities of age, health and sex in the attitude of Watts himself. She represented that ideal combination of beauty and innocence which had so dangerous a fascination for great Victorians. The delicate bachelor of 47 had found a to him perfect model of whom he has left a singularly charming portrait. So it came about in 1864 that 'Miss Ellen Alice Terry, the pleasing young actress who was lately a member of the Haymarket Company', in the words of the newspaper announcement, was 'united in the bonds of Matrimony' with Mr G. F. Watts at the church of St Barnabas, Kensington. The veil of Victorian reticence hangs over that single year of marriage (of which there is no mention in the official biography of the painter). The loyalty of Ellen Terry in her reminiscences did not lift it, it became later 'like a story in a book I once read', she was content to regard it as an 'honest misunderstanding' and even from a distance of time to demur at its being called unhappy. Yet both had embraced only a dream and the marriage was an episode in which afterwards neither could quite believe. Watts meeting her unexpectedly at Brighton some time after she had left him remarked only, as if of a child, that 'she had grown'.

Yet it was not only the difference of age or the relations between them but the peculiar constitution of Little Holland House that was involved and had its effect. This correct and middle-aged Victorian paradise, forming a protective circle round 'genius', gave a cold welcome to the girl from the bohemian world of the stage. Automatically she was reduced to the position of an unruly child who must be trained in correct behaviour and follow 'a rigorous system of education and seclusion'. The talent and high spirits with which she had played Puck in *A Midsummer Night's Dream* and Arthur in *King John* were rather to be reproved than otherwise and her reported appearance after dinner in the guise of Cupid was a startling disturbance of the atmosphere in which the poems of Tennyson and the music of Joachim were reverently heard. It was a 'hornet's nest' in the words of Captain Edward Cheney (friend and business counsellor of the Holland family) from which she escaped to find refuge with the architect E. W. Godwin. There is a final curious scene in Kensington after a new Little Holland House had been built when she was staying at the house next door. They saw each other through the hedge but did not speak, though subsequently Watts wrote to her, anxious that she should not think badly of him or that the circumstances should not be given publicity.

The Little Holland House 'court' itself was not everlasting. Three years after the ill-assorted marriage, in 1867, came the first uneasy intimation that the change threatened. Watts became aware of it when he asked permission to build a sculptor's studio and found with dismay that there was no definite assurance that the Prinseps' lease would be renewed. Lady Holland's circumstances indeed were in that entanglement which led some years later to her making over the administration of the whole Holland Park property to Lord Ilchester. The agreement of 1871 forbade any building lease that would 'interfere with the beauty and enjoyment of the house' but left Lord Ilchester free to dispose of the Little Holland House portion of the estate, and this he quickly marked down for development, planning a new street, Melbury Road. Overwhelmed at first, later sadly resigned, Watts applied himself assiduously to portraiture so that he might be able to build a house of his own in the district to which he was attached. The new Little Holland House, 6 Melbury Road, in which he took up residence in 1876, was the first to be erected there. There was pathos in his request for a 'little shrub or young tree or so, "In Memoriam", something that will not be missed', which he might plant in the new garden. As in Holland House itself he had painted murals on the walls of the old Little Holland House and some part of these was detached and preserved by the care of his friend, Mrs Charles Wylie, with the aid of two workmen. It was here he worked on his great equestrian statue, for the memorial to Cecil Rhodes, 'Physical Energy', the replica of which is appropriately placed in Kensington Gardens, dividing his time in his later years and until his death in 1904 between Melbury Road and the country house he had built at Compton in Surrey 'Limnerslease' (adjacent to what is now the Watts Museum). Little Holland House still exists, though divided, and long occupied by tenants practising the arts. They could use the long and loft room with its tall studio window and its system of toplights where the artist worked on his large and philosophic canvases, the smaller studio indoors (the Victorian artists were rarely satisfied with one). The sculpture studio stood in the garden, the latter diminutive by comparison with the lawns of the old house where Watts communed with nature or benignly contemplated the Prinseps' guests as they played croquet.

It was the presence of Watts at Little Holland House that attracted another famous Victorian to the district, Frederic Leighton. He was 13 years younger than Watts, whom he first met in 1855, but their friendship continued unbroken for 40 years. In 1865 Leighton decided to leave Orme Square, Bayswater, and build his own house. He chose Holland Park Road for its nearness to his friend, among other things. It became indeed his regular practice for many years to march briskly round the corner from Holland Road into Melbury Road at nine o'clock for a morning chat with Watts. Holland Park

Road itself was then a narrow lane of small cottages and stables, which prompted Leighton to make the laughing remark 'I live in a mews'—living in a mews not having yet become the sought-after luxury of modern times. His architect was his friend, George Aitchison, though Leighton took an active part both in the design of the house and its scheme of interior decoration. Externally it was, and remains, a modest mansion of red brick, without remarkable features, except for that dominant window on the garden side that indicates the main studio. According to Aitchison every detail of construction was supervised by Leighton himself. It was ready for occupation in 1866, though the decoration of the interior was a labour of love, extending over a long period, and when complete it represented a number of aspects of its owner's tastes and interests. In the hall as it originally was, a painting by the Viennese artist Steinle recalled the student period which Leighton spent under his tuition at Frankfurt. A statuette of Icarus testing his wings, bought from the young Alfred Gilbert who was to become famous as the sculptor of 'Eros', bore witness to Leighton's sympathy with and helpfulness towards fellow artists. His discernment as an art collector appeared in the pictures in the drawing-room, by Corot, Constable, Delacroix and Daubigny (whom Leighton invited to London). His travels had their reflection in the Arabian Court, most striking feature of the house, and the many sketches by Leighton himself of Italy, Greece, Spain and Egypt that covered the walls of his studio. The Arabian Court (or 'Arab Hall') one sees today, was an exotic feature that might seem out of key with Leighton's devotion to the classical art of Europe. It is necessary to recall his frequent journeys to the Eastern Mediterranean, to Rhodes and Lindos where he acquired a taste for 'specimens of old Persian faience', to Damascus where he visited his friend, the translator of the *Arabian Nights*, Sir Richard Burton, and collected further examples of ceramics and tiles, his visit to Egypt in the year before the Suez Canal was opened to traffic, when he enjoyed an almost royal progress down the Nile. Trophies of these adventures were the intricately fretted woodwork which came from Cairo, the inscription from the Koran in Arabic characters over the door, the recesses with their display of Persian, Rhodian and Damascus ware, the blue of tiles, the shimmering gilt dome, the fountain carved from a solid block of black marble, the Damascene stained-glass windows. The general design was adapted from a Saracenic palace at Palermo, but Leighton employed friends and contemporaries to complete the scheme. Sir Edgar Boehm, the

Queen's sculptor, carved the capitals of its columns with representations of rare birds, Walter Crane contributed the mosaic frieze, and William De Morgan, the follower of William Morris, and a remarkable artist craftsman (who turned to novels in later life), spent infinite labour in matching the colour depth of Oriental tiles. The quality of his peacock blue can well be appreciated in the tiles on the staircase. As the visitor may judge, these nineteenth-century additions do not appear out of place in the wealth of ornament and even add to its fabulous effect. It remains one of the most extraordinary show-pieces that London has to offer, though as a kind of museum room it cannot make quite the same impression as on the dazzled eyes of Victorian visitors for whom it was indeed a palace of enchantment. Completed in 1877, it was the scene in the late-Victorian years of those lavish musical entertainments in which Leighton delighted. One must imagine the sparkle of black-and-white, colour and jewellery, in the evening dress of assembled Society circulating round the tinkling fountain and among the embanked flowers, and after their fill of visual wonders, listening to the violin of Joseph Joachim, who performed here as at Little Holland House. In the fashion of the time, Leighton had two studios adjoining, a large and a small, the smaller having more glass to make the most of London's winter daylight. This is the room now turned into a picture gallery, with a selection of paintings of Kensington and by Kensington artists. The large studio, which suffered from the damage and decay of wartime has been somewhat simplified in restoration, though there still survives that cast of part of the Parthenon frieze on the south wall, which testifies to Leighton's classical ideal, further exemplified in such characteristic paintings of his own as the 'Pavona' and 'Clytemnestra' preserved among other works at Leighton House. Since 1926, when the Kensington Borough Council acquired the house, it has developed a useful function as a cultural centre where exhibitions, lectures and concerts are held. The excellent exhibition of paintings and drawings of old Kensington which marked its re-opening after restoration from the bomb damage of the Second World War promised a new phase of its existence which has since been usefully extended.

In 1969 the large selection of paintings and sculpture obtained on loan from the Tate Gallery and of furniture from the Victoria and Albert Museum gave Leighton House the added interest of a gallery of Victorian art and design. It was with alarm that Holland House saw the new buildings rising in the Melbury Road region. Dismayed reference was made to the 'fantastic erections of Watts and Leighton'. Lady Holland in 1876 complained to Lady Ilchester of the 'dreadful houses' that threatened to spoil the view from the house. Lord Ilchester even offered (with something of the magnificence of an earlier day) to construct an artificial mound which would blot out the unpleasant sight, though naturally enough the expense involved prevented this project from maturing.

Yet the presence of Watts and Leighton inevitably attracted other artists, the district even acquiring the name of 'the Leighton settlement'. The Victorian academicians who enjoyed an unexampled prosperity by their subject pictures and the large sale of engravings made from them were able to indulge themselves architecturally and Norman Shaw, elected A.R.A. in 1872, was profitably employed by his colleagues of the Academy. He designed No 8 Melbury Road for Marcus Stone in 1876. Marcus Stone had already won fame by such historical subjects as his 'Edward II and his Favourite, Piers Gaveston' and was turning to those sentimental costume pieces which had still greater vogue.

For him Norman Shaw designed a house in his Queen Anne manner with tall narrow windows and first-floor oriels and of course those characteristic larger windows which denoted the studio, luxurious core of all these buildings. Shaw also designed No 11 for Luke Fildes in 1877. Luke Fildes was another artist of wealth and fame whose affecting picture of 1874, a queue of outcasts waiting for admission to the Casual Ward, was railed off at the Academy, so dense were the crowds to see it, and sold for 2,000 guineas. It was here at a later date that he painted his celebrated 'The Doctor', now in the Tate Gallery, reconstructing in his studio, the spaciousness of which amply allowed it, the humble cottage bedroom where he placed the grave frock-coated doctor watching over the sick child. No 2 Melbury Road was the studio of the sculptor Sir William Hamo Thornycroft, author of such monuments as the 'Oliver Cromwell' (Westminster) and 'General Gordon' (Trafalgar Square) and son of the sculptor Thomas Thornycroft who was also a resident of Melbury Road. Holman Hunt lived at No 18. Valentine (Val) Prinsep, the son of Watts's friends and patrons, who was encouraged to become a painter both by Watts and by Rossetti (with whom he took part in the decoration of the Oxford Union), won success both with portraits and subject pictures and lived at No 1 Holland Park Road (in a house designed by Philip Webb) until his death in 1904.

For the most part the studio houses have been converted to other use. The house of Holman Hunt, for instance, is a series of flats. For an idea of their atmosphere in the palmy days of the Victorian artist, one must search among the 'Illustrated Interviews' in the early numbers of the *Strand Magazine*, to which Eliot and Fry's photographs add a valuable documentation. There one strolls with Luke Fildes in his half-acre of garden, contiguous to that of Leighton, yet each so cloistered and quiet, or peeps into the interiors, so opulently realising the aspirations of the 1870s and 1880s. The walls, with their embossed papers of crimson and gold, covered with pictures in massive frames or with rows of painted dishes, the profusion of furniture of every description, the rich miscellany of objects in which the time delighted, can no longer be viewed in actuality. In Melbury Road one remarkable house remains in which the interior décor has its reminder to give of the aims and tastes of its original owner and designer: No 9, Tower House, on which that imaginative architect William Burges spent many years of loving effort.

Burges was a Londoner, born in 1827, who acquired a leaning towards the Gothic style as a pupil of Edward Blore, the designer of Sir Walter Scott's 'Abbotsford', and of the architect and writer on art, Sir Mathew Digby Wyatt. His main commissions were ecclesiastical and he designed the cathedrals of Cork, Brisbane and Lille, though he also restored, rebuilt and planned a complete scheme of interior decoration for Cardiff Castle and Castell Coch to the commission of the Marquis of Bute (1865–75). He was, however, a man of more complex mind and talent than the average revivalist in architecture. He was for one thing more sumptuously eclectic, being attracted by many different forms of design, Greek, Pompeian and even Japanese as well as the thirteenth-century French Gothic on which he based his churches. Nor did he see any difficulty in combining such a variety of motifs in a single scheme. On the other hand the quality of his mind may well be called mediaeval and is seen in his delight in intricately elaborate systems of symbolic meaning. To this one must add a well-developed sense of humour as well as a certain creative and personal gift which lifted his conceptions out of the frigid category of imitation and into a richly fantastic realm of his own. To build 'a model residence of the fifteenth century' in nineteenth-century Kensington, this being his declared aim, might seem an absurdity more open to Lady Holland's criticism than the houses of Leighton and Watts, had it not been carried out with so much enjoyment and imagination. It is said to have cost over £30,000 and occupied him from 1875 to 1881 (the year of his death). From the road, its round tower with its castle-like embrasures attracts the eye and arouses the curiosity. The bronze entrance door with its representation of the Four Ages of Man, and the letter-box covered by a bronze Mercury prepared the visitor for the baronial grandeur of the hall. Structurally Burges seems to have had Cardiff Castle in mind and in some features of decoration, for instance the sculptured overmantels of the rooms, adapts the additions of his own fancy which he had made at Cardiff. Of this fancy the hall already shows the nimble play. There is a Pompeian touch in the mosaic depicting Burges's white poodle, 'Pinky', its name inlaid with decorative care, while the main mosaic floor design is devoted to Theseus and the Minotaur and traces out the Cretan maze. A second bronze door (adapted from Ripon Cathedral) leads into the garden where also his ingenious mind left both classical and mediaeval mementoes. Among the trees, originally belonging to Holland Park, is a terrace with mosaic pavements and marble seats inspired by those appearing in Sir Laurence Alma-Tadema's painting 'Sappho'. It was, however, an illumination of the 'Romaunt de la Rose' in the British Museum that caused him to raise the flowerbeds by copings a foot above the level of the paths. In various rooms such motifs as Time, Love, Earth, Sea and Chaucer's House of Fame were lovingly elaborated. On the enamelled metal ceiling are the Sun and Planets, the Signs of the Zodiac, the Seasons and the Winds. Over the marble fireplace is 'the spirit of the house'—a female figure with face and hands of ivory and eyes of lapis lazuli, holding a rock crystal ball and sceptre. A frieze of painted tiles representing the 'Fairy Tales of Antiquity' was comprehensive enough to include Cinderella and Robinson Crusoe, Jack the Giant Killer and Robin Hood, Red Riding Hood and Peter Wilkins and his winged wife. The library perhaps is the most fascinating room of all. On its ceiling are paintings of the great 'Lawgivers'—Luther among them as well as Justinian and Moses. A feat of the imagination is the sculptured fireplace representing the Spirit of Grammar sending out the Parts of Speech into the World. One can think of no one but Burges who would have conceived such an idea or carried it out so brilliantly. Here are the Pronouns blowing trumpets, Queen Verb followed by her pages—the Articles—and Porters (Nouns) with their load of Adjectives; while all the letters of the alphabet are woven into the corbelling. A cupboard bookcase is painted with philosophers and literary men and on its inner panels with birds from the hand of H. Stacy Marks, R.A., one of Burges's neighbours in Melbury Road. Yet every room had its wealth—in the drawing-room its fireplace carving of the Garden of the Hesperides, its coloured windows with symbolic representations of arts, sciences, jewels, birds and heroines of antiquity; the dressing-room with its deep-blue ceiling and representation of the different levels of the sea. Two items of furnishing in the guest-room aroused particular interest when shown at the Victoria and Albert Museum's exhibition of Victorian and Edwardian Decorative Arts in 1952; the bed of carved, painted and gilt wood, inset with mirrors, roundels of rock crystal and pieces of illumination under glass, with a headpiece by Henry Halliday, R.A., of the Judgment of Paris; and the washstand, also carved, painted and gilt, its bowl of marble inset with silver fishes and a butterfly and the inscription *'Venez laver'* on the cold tap (of ornamental bronze). Not all the original movable pieces of furniture remain in the house, and during an empty period it suffered from vandalism. Though again in private occupancy it was restored in 1966 to its original condition and completed by reference to Burges's own drawings.

No 9 Melbury Road merits description at some length, for it cannot be considered otherwise than as one of the most wonderful houses in London, more interesting even than Leighton House in its expression of its builder's remarkable personality.

It was perhaps rather his friendship with Thackeray than anything else that attracted John Everett Millais to Kensington in the 'sixties. He visited Thackeray at Palace Green and heartily approved of the novelist's Queen Anne house which he thought 'beautiful'. He was one of those who went to Thackeray's funeral at Kensal Green in 1863—'a mournful scene', he described it, 'and badly managed. A crowd of women were there—from curiosity I suppose—dressed in all colours; and round the grave scarlet and blue feathers shone out prominently!' The year before he had bought No 7 Cromwell Place, which remained his town house until 1878, when he removed to the mansion he built for himself, No 2 Palace Gate. By this time he was courted as a portrait painter and famous for a long series of sentimental subject pictures and the house reflected his eminence, though without those extravagant touches in which others took pleasure. 'None of the thought-out quaintness of the Anglo-Dutch revival,' runs a description of the 1880s, 'but a great plain square house. . . . From the side towards the park the most conspicuous thing is the great studio window.' The architect Philip Hardwick

planned it from Millais' rough sketch and if the exterior was somewhat shapeless the interior was spacious in conception. The hall,
with its marble columns and floor 35 feet square, led to the wide
staircase rising in three flights to the first floor. On the landing was
the fountain, a persistent feature of the Victorian artist's house, with
its black marble sea-lion designed by Sir Edgar Boehm. 'The general
effect was that of a Genoese palazzo.' The studio on the first floor
was 40 feet long by 25 wide and 20 high. It was 'distinguished from
most of the studios lately built in London by simplicity'. 'There are
no cunningly devised corners or galleries or ingle nooks or window
seats.' The comment indicates what an important architectural feature the studio had become in these late-Victorian days. Its history
indeed has still to be written. It might begin with the skylit attic of
the struggling romantic painter in the earlier years of the nineteenth
century, growing steadily larger with the prosperity of artists in
general and assuming a distinct personality picturesque or grandiose.
Nowadays for various reasons it is obsolete—painters work where
they can or must. The floor of Millais' studio was of parquet and, in
the remark his visitors commonly made, 'What a lovely room for
a dance!' there was already an ominous presage of the frivolous
uses to which studios have since been diverted. That a mere artist
should live in this splendour was certainly surprising to many. The
caustic remark of Thomas Carlyle when he visited Palace Gate gives
its instance: 'Has paint done all this, Mr Millais?' to which he may
or may not have added, as the story goes, 'It shows how many fools
there are in the world.'

Unlike Leighton and the men of Melbury Road, Millais had no
garden, though he delighted in the lilies of the valley that grew in
the back courtyard and the vine that flourished as vines immemori-
ally had in Kensington. A walk in Kensington Gardens was his
favourite exercise in London until the time of his last illness. The
house as it is now, unaltered outside, retains within no reminder
save in its proportions of its original occupant. The staircase is still
impressive but the Boehm sea-lion has gone, the rooms have been
converted to office use, the building was eventually occupied by the
Pakistan Embassy, one of its officials seeming puzzled by a visit from
the writer and unaware of working in a house where Gladstone and
Beaconsfield, Tennyson, Newman, the Duchess of Westminster, Lily
Langtry and so many others of Victorian fame had once sat for their
portraits.

It is regrettable from a British point of view that one of the most brilliant schemes of nineteenth-century interior decoration should have been taken away not only from Kensington but from the country—the 'Peacock Room' designed by Whistler in the house in Princes Gate of the art collector and patron, facetiously termed by the artist 'the Liverpool Medici'—Francis Leyland. The story has its own curious irony. For a time Leyland was one of Whistler's devoted patrons. He bought from him the picture 'La Princesse du Pays de la Porcelaine', which, not without a trace of Rossetti's influence, so exquisitely conveys the taste and the atmosphere of a generation delighting in the ceramics and design of the Far East. That Whistler should devise an appropriate interior setting for his work seems to have been agreed, yet Leyland apparently did not reckon with an enthusiasm that would lead Whistler to paint over the Spanish leather which covered the walls with a gorgeous decorative array of peacock motifs in an adaptation of Japanese design. The work was done in the owner's absence; his anger at the 'ruin' of the old Spanish leather which he valued highly prevented him from appreciating the beauty of what Whistler had done, and was a main reason for the rupture between them, leading Whistler to paint a ferocious caricature of his ex-patron. A sad consequence of the affair was the death of the architect Thomas Jekyll who had been originally entrusted with the decoration of the dining-room and had bought the historic leather for £1,000; he went out of his mind after seeing its conversion into a pattern of blue and gold.

Leyland accepted the *fait accompli* of the Peacock Room but after his death it was bodily taken down, exhibited at the galleries of Messrs Colnaghi and Obach in 1904 and bought by the American collector Charles L. Freer, who had previously obtained possession of 'La Princesse du Pays de la Porcelaine'. Both the picture and its setting are now part of the Collection in the Freer Gallery of Art, Washington.

In other respects No 49 Princes Gate when owned by Mr and Mrs Leyland may be taken as an example of late-Victorian taste, a splendid miscellany of which Kensington furnished many examples. His dream, it was said, was that 'he might live the life of an old Venetian merchant in modern London'. He made no attempt to convert the unremarkable exterior, but to transform it within into something resembling an Italian palace and in this had the assistance of the ubiquitous Norman Shaw who introduced the unfortunate Jekyll to aid in detailed decoration. His taste, however, and that of his advisers (notably the dealer Murray Marks) was widely eclectic.

He collected (on Marks's recommendation) the 'Blue and White' oriental porcelain which the enthusiasm of both Rossetti and Whistler had given a collector's vogue: and it was this collection for which the famous dining-room was first intended to be the background. On the walls were many pictures by the Pre-Raphaelites, nine by Rossetti, seven by Burne-Jones, one by Ford Madox Brown. The house (in an article in *Harper's Magazine* for December 1890) was indeed referred to as 'a Pre-Raphaelite mansion'. The 'classicism' of the time was also represented by three pictures of ideal women in their vaguely Greek costume by Albert Moore. On the somewhat doubtful assumption that a Botticelli Madonna would harmonise perfectly with Rossetti's 'Blessed Damozel', Leyland had six pictures attributed to the Italian master and others by Signorelli, Crivelli, Lotto and Luini. Other objects and articles of furniture made an astonishing assortment, the gilt figures from a Venetian palace that had once adorned the prow of a galley, the Ming vases and those of Japanese cloisonné, Indo-Portuguese cabinets, and the work of Italian, German and French cabinet-makers interspersed with the solid comfort of easy chair and divan that belonged to 1870; while small ornaments and bibelots were in profusion. The drawing-room, which could be thrown open into a huge salon, 70 feet long, was divided for ordinary occasions by two screens designed by Norman Shaw after the style of the rood loft of the Cathedral of Bois-le-Duc. What happened to them the writer is unable to say, but at least the visitor to the Victoria and Albert Museum can see the source of their inspiration in the Bois-le-Duc- screen, acquired through Murray Marks. As so often one must regret that the interior of a Kensington mansion in the Victorian heyday can only be seen in the imagination. The same applies to the classical décor of No 52 Princes Gate devised by Frederic Leighton and his architect Aitchison together with the minor artist and official at South Kensington, Thomas Armstrong, for Mr Eustace Smith, M.P., with its dado in ivory, ebony and mother-of-pearl, its Leightonian frieze and its picture of classical maidens let into the walls. Or again to the Pre-Raphaelite interior of No 1 Palace Green on which William Morris and Burne-Jones worked together. The Victorian interior has largely disappeared before we have had a chance to re-examine it.

The Artist's Kensington

CHAPTER FIFTEEN

Growth and Change

The museums remain one of the most important and interesting aspects of modern Kensington and while it would be out of place here to speak in detail of their contents, it is necessary to remark on the way in which they have developed in recent times. They are not mausolea, lifeless and static, but growing organisms with an expanding function in education and research. Not everyone perhaps realises that the Victoria and Albert Museum houses a National Art Library, the largest of its kind in the world, containing some 250,000 books, pamphlets, periodicals and original documents, and that this is constantly at the service of students. Or that the Circulation Department carries out the old distributing function first initiated by the Victorian School of Design on a greatly extended scale, sending out loan exhibitions of pictures, prints, textiles, porcelain, silver, glass, etc. to museums, art galleries, art schools and training colleges all over the country; that it comprises also the National Loan Collection of Lantern Slides representing examples of architecture, sculpture, painting and decoration from all over the world, freely at the service of lecturers on art. It is an impressive thought that in the Department of Engraving, Illustration and Design alone there are over 500,000 items, of which many thousands have been added in the last 25 years. It is still, to some extent perhaps with an embarrassment of riches, a 'multiple' museum, not exclusively a gallery of design in various useful or ornamental forms and only in fragmentary fashion the new National Gallery of pictures that was first envisaged. On the other hand, whether they should logically be there or not, the visitor will not complain at the presence of a superb collection of the national school of water-colour, a collection of post-classical sculpture such as can nowhere else be seen in London, a magnificent array of works by John Constable. As masterpieces of

Renaissance art, the seven cartoons by Raphael, deposited on loan with the consent of Queen Victoria in 1865, should no doubt have their proper place in the National Gallery in Trafalgar Square though they are now well shown in the large space of the concert-room. Here indeed is one of the modern improvements that have been made in the Museum. It is possible to recall when these great works were hung in an upper balcony so narrow that it was hard to see them. Even within living memory they were still treated as designs for tapestry of awkward dimensions rather than as the unique product of a masterhand. Their present placing is only one aspect of the great transformation of recent years, since the end of the Second World War, which has involved the creation of 'primary collections', showing in historical sequence the various styles and periods of European art. This has been accompanied by a new treatment of design and layout and lighting which has been successful in eliminating the lingering stuffiness of an earlier conception of museums. A wholesale simplification, a deliberate lightening of background colour, has given a new value to the objects shown. Nor can one speak of the Victoria and Albert Museum in recent years without reference to its many memorable special exhibitions. Here in 1945 was that exhibition of Royal Effigies from Westminster Abbey which gave the public for the first time a close view of the Abbey's sculptural masterpieces. In the same year was held that famous exhibition of works by Picasso and Matisse which caused so much controversy; in 1946 'Britain Can Make It', with its brilliant display setting for modern industrial design; in 1952 the 'Victorian and Edwardian Decorative Arts', the first serious attempt to do justice to the individual designers of the period, appropriately including tiles by William De Morgan from Leighton House and furniture from William Burges's Tower House. These can be singled out from a long list of exhibitions as events by which the Museum has contributed to give fresh information and outlook on art.

Since its post-war reorganisation (1948), the Royal College of Arts, so named in 1906 (always closely associated with the Museum), has more thoroughly than ever before applied itself to the purpose for which it was intended in its previous phases of existence as the School of Design (1837) and the School of Practical Art (1852). While it still gives brilliant painters and sculptors to British art, it has come to play an increasingly important part in training the designers of manufactured articles. 'Design' previously of somewhat vague significance in the Victorian sense of 'Ornamental Art' or

'Art Workmanship' has been redefined and the scope and thorough-
ness of teaching extended by the creation of separate faculties of
Graphic, Industrial, Interior and Fashion Design. This post-war development has caused industry to absorb recruits from the College
with a new eagerness; while the commission to provide the stained-
glass windows for the nave of the new Coventry Cathedral (1956)
has been described as 'the most important undertaking attempted by
the College in its long history'.

A display of special Kensington interest at the Victoria and Albert
Museum is that of prints and water-colours showing early stages of
the Museum's appearance, notable among them the brilliant water-
colours of Anthony Carey Stannus, a little-known artist though an
exhibitor at the Royal Academy from 1862 to 1880. He painted an
excellent series of views of the buildings in 1863, including the
quaintly timbered original Refreshment Rooms, next the Oratory,
and including such characteristic features of the time as hansom
cabs, horse buses and the Italian organ-grinder and his monkey; and
a romantic view of the old staff residences with the curious dome of
the International Exhibition of 1862 rising behind. A charming
drawing by Charles E. Emery shows an interesting mixture of
temporary and new buildings in 1872 with the present Imperial
College of Science in the background, while J. C. Lanchenick informs
us as to the odd effect of the 'Brompton Boilers' in 1863. Of Kensington in general, the Museum collection has a drawing of Gore House
by moonlight made by Sir Edwin Landseer on a summer night in
1848 while he talked with Lady Blessington and Count D'Orsay;
views from Gore Lane by Peter de Wint showing respectively Holy
Trinity Church, Brompton, and St Luke's Church, Chelsea; a set of
views of Kensington Gardens and the Serpentine in the 1840s by
William Callow, and a drawing by John Wykeham Archer (1808–
64), celebrated in his day for pictures of old London, of Holland
House.

The Science Museum has developed in no less remarkable and
parallel fashion. An offshoot of the old 'Science and Art' combination, it attained its separate maturity in this century, though two
worlds wars hindered the completion of the new buildings begun
in 1913. In 1939 the Museum still occupied the East Block of 1913
and earlier temporary buildings. During the war it was occupied by
an R.A.F. Signals School and did not return to its peace-time use
until 1946, with less space than ever. It was necessary to cope not
only with this limitation but to take into account the enormous

development of science which the two wars have helped to push forward. Over a million people annually visit the reconstructed post-war collections. The Museum provides also a National Science Library, as the Victoria and Albert has its Art Library, and an analo-gous loan service. The Imperial College of Science and Technology, which incorporates the Royal College of Science, the Royal School of Mines and the City and Guilds College has at the same time enor-mously expanded and must expand still further. Since 1953 thirteen new professional chairs have been established including one of nuclear power. The Imperial College produces more engineers than any other body in Britain and applications from would-be students in this intensively scientific age far exceed the vacancies. The Geological Museum is housed in a building which dates back only to 1935. The writer recalls the small and dusky building, 28 Jermyn Street, in which the collections, originally made at the instance of the Geological Survey, had been housed since 1851; and the surprise with which one came upon it in the narrow street so largely devoted to fashionable hatters and shirt-makers. It is strange that some people think museums are dull places—here no less than in its large neighbours there is so much that is calculated to appeal to the imagination, even if one has no special knowledge or practical aim. The terrestial globe that shows the geology of the earth; the copy of the Farnese Hercules—ten tons of Portland stone; the array of beautiful precious stones; the excellent dioramas—a primeval coal forest, a reconstruction of the Thames Valley about 100,000 years ago, or an oil-field of today—are full of fascinating suggestion as well as information. In a similar spirit one may approach the Natural History Museum, where modern presentation makes the best of Waterhouse's huge and romantic galleries; here again is a marvellous commentary on life past and present, though it is necessary also to remember the work that is always in progress behind the scenes, the laboratories and workshops where the precise identification of animals, plants, fossils, rocks and minerals goes on and is turned to useful account in all sorts of ways.

The tradition that associates Kensington with exhibitions is per-petuated in the Earls Court exhibitions, though their history is in a lighter key than that of the Victorian international displays. They began in 1887 with the Wild West of Buffalo Bill Cody, and merged with the attractions of a pleasure garden in the Edwardian Age when the 'Big Wheel' added a distinctive feature to the landscape until 1907. The present Exhibition Building in ferro-concrete, by

C. Howard Crane (1937) is notable for its size, its three façades each measuring 700 feet or more, and for its functional plainness of aspect. During the Second World War it housed refugees, but reverted to its normal role in 1947 with the revived British Industries Fair. Its vast halls have since been the scene of the Motor and other shows for which it was previously noted. In close relation to it is the separate building, the Empress Hall, with its ice rink and sporting events, though this, like Olympia farther north, is just over the Kensington boundary line.

In so large a borough as well as one possessing so many literary and artistic associations, it would be surprising if one did not find a succession of writers and painters in this century, following the great Victorians though not perhaps leaving their peculiar regional impress. It may be noted that the poet and man-of-letters Andrew Lang lived at No 1 Marloes Road until his death in 1912, that the novelist E. F. Benson lived at No 25 Brompton Square, and John Galsworthy at South House in Campden Hill Road from 1897 to 1903, though more definitely of Kensington is G. K. Chesterton who was born in Sheffield Terrace, and lived at No 11 Warwick Gardens. His father was head of an hereditary business of house agents and surveyors—agents for the Phillimore Estate (the land first built on by William Phillimore who died in 1819, the name being perpetuated in Phillimore Gardens). It had already been established in Kensington for three generations, and still exists. Mrs Cecil Chesterton in her family history *The Chestertons* has described the house, No 11 Warwick Gardens, where Gilbert Keith and his brother spent their boyhood, with its flowers in dark-green window boxes and its rooms lined with bookshelves from floor to ceiling. Chesterton himself in his *Autobiography* tells with his picturesque vividness how he was impressed (as a schoolboy after Macaulay's heart) by the historical associations evoked by the district and its street names. 'All that district of Kensington was, and is, laid out like a chart to illustrate Macaulay's Essays.' 'The street opposite where we came to live bore the name of Addison : the street of our later sojourn the name of Warwick, stepson of Addison. Beyond was a road named after the house of Russell, to the south another with the name of Cromwell. Near us on our original perch in Campden Hill was the great name of Argyll. . . .' The glamour with which the streets were invested by his imagination later created its own form of local patriotism. 'I was one day wandering about the streets in part of North Kensington telling myself stories of feudal sallies and sieges in the manner of

Sir Walter Scott', when 'something irrationally arrested and pleased my eye about the look of one small block of little lighted shops and I amused myself with the supposition that these alone were to be preserved and defended, like a hamlet in the desert'. There was everything such a self-contained and defended community might be supposed to need, chemist shop, bookshop, provision merchant, a public house for drink, and for weapons an old curiosity shop bristling with swords and halberds. The local geography suggested strategic plans. 'Capturing the waterworks might really mean the military stroke of flooding the valley and with that torrent and cataract of visionary waters, the first fantastic notion of a tale called *The Napoleon of Notting Hill* rushed over my mind.' This book, which heralded a series of gaily fantastic romances and was published in 1904, adds its poetry to the region and the vividness of a phrase survives the demolition of the 1970s in Chesterton's description of 'the great grey water-tower, that strikes the stars on Campden Hill'.

'South Lodge', No 80 Campden Hill Road, is of especial interest for its association with those two notable literary personalities, Violet Hunt and Ford Madox Ford. 'South', it may be remarked, is not a point of the compass but refers to the famous astronomer Sir James South (1785–1867), who built an observatory in 1826 in the grounds of Phillimore House, which he acquired from William Robert Phillimore, its site being represented by the present Observatory Gardens, his memory being further preserved by South Villas, South House and South Lodge. Violet Hunt was the daughter of the landscape and water-colour painter Alfred William Hunt who lived at No 1 Tor Villas (the present Tor Gardens). The house, which was destroyed by a bomb in the Second World War, had, it may be added, been the home of a succession of artists, J. C. Hook the marine painter and Edward Lear having also lived there. It is sometimes wrongly assumed that Violet Hunt was related to the Pre-Raphaelite, William Holman Hunt; alternatively and also wrongly, to the Victorian water-colourist, William Henry Hunt, whose minute fruit and flowers pieces were so highly praised by Ruskin; which makes it necessary to distinguish Alfred William from either. A scholar and Fellow of Corpus Christi College, Oxford, he had won note in youth by gaining the Newdigate prize with a poem on 'Nineveh' and afterwards, though never conspicuous as a painter, had been a regular contributor to the exhibitions of the Old Water Colour Society. After his death, his wife moved to South Lodge and from her Violet Hunt acquired the house.

Ford Madox Ford was the son of the music critic and librettist Dr Franz Hueffer, who had settled in England as a young man and become one of the Rossettis' Pre-Raphaelite circle, marrying Catherine, the younger daughter of Ford Madox Brown. Ford wrote a life of Madox Brown and from this connection derived a great fund of Pre-Raphaelite anecdote and legend which probably lost nothing from his own tendency to make the most of a story. One may look here for a source of that intimate narrative which Violet Hunt gave of the life of Elizabeth Siddall in her book *The Wife of Rossetti*. Ford Madox Ford's flair as an editor which for a time made *The English Review* outstanding for its literary quality and the encouragement of new writers; his own talent as a novelist; his personality and conversation attracted gifted people around him. In her autobiographical work *The Flurried Years* Violet Hunt tells of her first meeting with Ford, who was then editing *The English Review* at No 84 Holland Park Avenue. 'The editor lived in his office and the office was a maisonette over a poulterer's and fishmonger's combined.' 'The sickly and depraved smell of chickens,' she remarks (with an always acute sensibility to impression), 'assailed me walking upstairs past the shop premises.' The office-maisonette, however, transported the visitor into that romantic other-world into which Dr Hueffer had stepped. Its legacy was present in various forms: Pre-Raphaelite engravings, portraits of the editor's aunt, Christina Rossetti, and his grandmother, Mrs Ford Madox Brown. 'The editor' wore a brown velvet coat that had belonged to Dante Gabriel Rossetti and used a Chippendale bureau at which Christina Rossetti had written her poems.

'The editor' left Holland Park Avenue to become a paying guest at South Lodge and for some years from 1908 the joint 'salon'—as it might be called—which he and Violet Hunt assembled at South Lodge enlivened this otherwise unremarkable Victorian villa by the presence of a distinguished literary circle. It included some of the most famous writers of the day, Henry James, Joseph Conrad, H. G. Wells, Arnold Bennett; though if Ford as an editor sought contributors among men of established reputation he also set himself out to make use of and encourage new talent and the visitors to South Lodge included such portents of a new age as Ezra Pound and Wyndham Lewis.

Violet Hunt remained at South Lodge until her death in 1942, by which time it was somewhat battered by the blitz. There are accounts of the mass of material which she had collected for a projected life of the raffish friend of Rossetti and Whistler, Charles

Augustus Howell, a pendant in its Pre-Raphaelite interest to her *Wife of Rossetti*, but what became of the notes, letters, diaries of which her friends spoke, it now seems impossible to say. That many of the great artists' studios have in recent times been turned to other purposes has already been recorded, though Kensington has never ceased to have its artist population, more scattered than that of Chelsea and less conspicuously Bohemian, from Onslow Square to Notting Hill; on this a glance at the exhibitors' names and addresses in the latest Royal Academy exhibition catalogue would give its commentary. One may single out a few examples from the recent past of artists who have lived in this century, noting in some cases the remaining link with the earlier Victorian day. Turning off Church Street into Holland Street in which the graciousness of its few Georgian houses, so rare in Kensington, is now in their present well-tended state so apparent, one comes on the delightful house that was once Walter Crane's and its blue plaque is a reminder that he lived until 1915; long after he executed his mosaic frieze for Leighton House. It is as an excellent designer of children's books, and a leader of the Arts and Crafts movement in pursuit of William Morris's ideals, that he will be remembered. His association with Kensington is further marked by his appointment as Principal of the Royal College of Art in 1897. Though he did not remain there long he was one of those who urged the reform of teaching and the development of industrial design which has since become, by a reversal to the original purpose of the 'National Training School', one of the main functions of the College. The portrait painters have long kept their state in Kensington. In Cromwell Place, when passing the building now occupied by the Phaidon Press, one may recall that here Sir John Lavery had his studio until his death in 1941; a studio in the grand tradition, full of the easels, the varied fabrics, the ornate chairs and couches that are the properties of his profession; with its portrait of Lady Lavery, whose beautiful features appeared on the first currency notes which her husband designed for Eire. In The Boltons until 1931 that other immensely successful Irish portrait painter Sir William Orpen had his studio. In West House, Campden Hill Road, one of Norman Shaw's artist mansions originally designed for the American painter George Henry Boughton (1837–1905), lived the Hungarian-born Philip de Laszlo, who achieved such extraordinary popular success as a society portrait-painter.

More remarkable as an artist than these was James Pryde, that romantic and isolated figure who won early celebrity by the posters he designed in the 'nineties in collaboration with Sir William Nicholson and subsequently produced at too rare intervals romantic and sombre paintings of interiors and imagined architecture. His studio, at No 3 Lansdowne House, Holland Park, was like one of his own pictures, with its great sooty window that seemed almost to create darkness rather than throw light, and its immense curtain that fell in long dusky folds. Here in his later days one might see him, a tall, distinguished figure still preserving the elegance of the 'nineties, contemplating some monochrome sketch of crumbling architecture, which long remained unfinished. It was here in the dark days of 1941 that he lay stricken by his final illness, forgotten and alone until, discovered at last by friends, he was removed to St Mary Abbot's Hospital, where he died.

Percy Wyndham Lewis, remarkable both as writer and painter, whom T. S. Eliot referred to as 'the most fascinating personality of our time', must also be counted among those who have added lustre to modern Kensington. For many years and until his death in 1957 he occupied No 27A Notting Hill Studios. Though the war years were spent elsewhere, his return there in 1945 marked the beginning of a belated interest in his paintings and drawings which culminated in the Tate Gallery exhibition of 1956; and the renewal of his literary output, his trilogy *The Human Age*, broadcast in 1955, being one of its products. A vein of humour appears in one of his minor post-war works in which he describes various trials and difficulties of the time in 'Rotting Hill'.

Of Kensington in general the growth has been as irregular as elsewhere in London. The High Street, broad as it becomes, is still a miscellany. The word certainly applies to the small huddle of buildings at the beginning of the High Street which imperfectly represents—architecturally speaking and as viewed from the outside —the important functions of Town Hall and Public Library. The 'Tudor' style of 1852 (Library) and the more or less 'Italian' style of 1878 (Town Hall) tease the eye in proximity to the Gothic of St Mary Abbot's and in contrast with the grandiose but also much varied constellation of stores which extends for half a mile on the opposite side of the road.

The big stores likewise at various heights and in various styles show in their exteriors the gradual process of growth since 1870, when John Barker first opened his two small shops, in the late-Victorian front of Pontings, the still-Edwardian main building of Barkers, by Sir Reginald Blomfield, 1912–13, the more recent showiness of Derry and Toms (1933) now Biba, and the additions to Barker's in 1937, completed in 1957 and giving impressive dominance to a long façade. It has been the custom among the lovers of time past and of historic Kensington to deplore this wedge of commerce in the former aristocratic seclusion of the district and the gallant stand of Kensington Square against the usurpers of space has already been recorded. Yet the western move, which has brought large stores from their previous sites in Central London, is seen by others not as something to deplore but as the beginning of a new era. The attractive prospect opens up of the High Street as a new Bond Street, more emphatically than before constituting a sumptuous thoroughfare of trade and fashion. It would, it is said, give a needed coherence to the borough and with the thought of this expansion goes discussion of a possible 'Festival of Kensington', bringing its host of visitors. For its full effect this prospective expansion would ideally need some scheme of architectural grandeur or unity, though many practical problems would face a new John Nash or Baron Haussmann, unknown in the time of George IV or Napoleon III.

Whichever way one walks in present-day Kensington, one finds past and present either in contrast or interesting combination. It has its lively market quarter as well as its areas of dignified seclusion. One turns from the busy corner where Pembridge Road meets Notting Hill into the quiet beginning of the long Portobello Road past a terrace of two-storey cottages, placidly and even charmingly Victorian, to find at a week-end the liveliest of street markets in progress. Here is the contrast of the picturesque as represented by the old buildings on one side of the street, the gay stalls and motley crowd with the modern and impersonal sobriety of the Portobello Housing Estate opposite them. The market displays the overflow of the antique shops which flourish in Church Street and other parts of Kensington. Though not exclusively so, 'antique' largely signifies Victorian objects of 'art and virtu', partly no doubt because they have again come into fashion and perhaps also because there are more of them available than objects of other times. The landscapes of accomplished amateur water-colourists of the past, oil paintings of obscure vintage, drawings of streets and even public houses executed with 'primitive' sharpness of detail; pinchbeck replicas of heavy Victorian jewellery; extraordinary vases of milky hue, decorated with romantic paintings of cavaliers and ladies; clocks set in rustic frameworks of bronze, with Landseeresque sculptures of stags, dogs and rearing horses; here is all the 'popular art' of the last century, in all that extravagant pomp which has a peculiar fascination for many people today. The crowds of visitors are no less interesting; it would seem as if every nation and race has converged on this open-air bazaar in the Portobello Road; crew-cropped Americans with camera slung over shoulder, Indian women in robes of crimson and gold, French, Spanish, Chinese, Japanese, West Indian ... as well as Londoners and other English folk including young men with a variety of beard and young women with a variety of clothes who, if they are not art students, look the part. This brightly coloured throng moves at a leisurely pace the length of this antique fair, which merges by degrees with the stalls of fruiterers and the shops of butchers and grocers. One can still see, now and then, that rare sight in modern London, an artist in a doorway, sufficiently stirred by the old-fashioned plentifulness of incident in form and colour to note it in his sketch-book.

To study the northward expansion of Kensington and its varied phases of planning one may investigate the course of Ladbroke Grove. The 'Kensington Park' area, laid out about 1850 by the architect and topographical draughtsman Thomas Allom on the site of the old racecourse, still has a pleasant feature in its many gardens. So many 'Gardens' are there in Kensington that the word, originally popularised in the borough by the number of its market-gardens and nurseries, sometimes implies hardly more than street. In the Kensington Park region, however, they are prolific and extensive. Ladbroke Square is interesting for the seven acres of trees and lawn which make one side of the square seem very remote from the other. Going northwards to the industrial Harrow Road one enters the zone of the 1870s and Ladbroke Grove takes on some of the middle-class grimness of that period. To the west, however, if one turns along Barlby Road and walks round St Charles's Square, one enters a region which, surprisingly, was open country even in this century. One may compare the little between-wars brick houses of Barlby Road, which have a cottagey look, with the post-war flats of St Charles's Square, while large new blocks of flats begin to dwarf their surroundings. It is a curious townscape, with its patches of hopeful planning, diversified by the red-brick buildings of the college founded by Cardinal Manning, with railway sidings and the gas-holders of the Western Gas Works for backcloth and surrounding reminders of the past in the shape of crumbling and war-worn little houses of the 1870s which in decay have added a new intensity to their original ugliness. Yet once again nature helps out and the tree-lined streets and flourishing back gardens of this 'St Quintin Park Estate', as the whole area is known, are a reminder of its ex-rural character.

The interest of such an excursion lies in the discovery of a 'farthest north' and the last inroad on open country rather than in some previously unknown and exceptional beauty. Beating the bounds to the south and wandering along the Fulham Road between South Kensington and the Brompton Cemetery, in the district once equivocally known as 'Little Chelsea', one finds another aspect of development. There is little to remind us of either the wild heath or the nurseries of the past, and the old pleasantly named lanes that traversed the district have exchanged their titles for others of more impressive or aristocratic sound : Walnut Tree Walk becoming Redcliffe Gardens, Thistle Grove—Drayton Gardens, Honey Lane—Ifield Road. One remembers an earlier lament. 'Now,' wrote Crofton Croker, the author of *A Walk from London to Fulham*, in 1860, 'is Brompton all built or being built over, which makes the precise locality of crescents and rows puzzling to old gentlemen. Its health is gone and its grove represented by a few dead trunks and some unhealthy-looking trees which stand by the roadside, their branches lopped and their growth restrained by order of the district surveyor.' Within the last quarter of a century, buildings that formed part of an eighteenth-century farm stood at the south-west corner of Drayton Gardens (the old 'Thistle Grove'), though these made way for a cinema and car park. In this century, however, the aspect of the district has not substantially changed : except in that process of renovation and adaptation so notable generally in Kensington.

This appears delightfully in the remaining early-nineteenth-century by-ways behind the wild medley of the Fulham Road. Their simplicity and small size lend themselves to an easy transformation to modern ideas of attractiveness. Very quaint and bright now is Selwood Place with its paved yards, window boxes and painted balconies; its charm is repeated in Selwood Terrace, while Elm Place, with its touches of fresh white paint, its clipped hedges and creepers, looks enchanting. The later Victorian streets present a more difficult problem—the façades of Evelyn Gardens are obstinate to modernisation. A modern front in Redcliffe Gardens seems a singular intrusion.

Kensington and Chelsea Today

Though, broadly speaking Kensington and Chelsea retain much of their individual character, the increasing momentum of change from the 1950s to the 1970s has made its inroads as in the rest of inner London. Large-scale developments entailing the destruction of old properties, the requirements of commercial building, tourism and motor traffic all ate into housing space. Hotels and restaurants came into being with remarkable speed; the hotels including the Carlton Tower in Sloane Street (1963), the Royal Garden Hotel at Kensington High Street (1964), the cylindrical Park Tower at Knightsbridge (1972), such a prodigy as the Penta Hotel in the Cromwell Road, 270 feet high, designed by Richard Seifert who has been prominent in making a number of such alterations to the London skyline and even a Hilton (of unusually subdued design) at the end of Holland Park Avenue. The demands of the motorway are instanced in the ambitious Westway flyover which left a trail of ruined Victorian streets in North Kensington as well as the question of what to do with the sterile acres beneath it. The deterioration of the Colville area properties and the exploitation of poor tenants was a dark episode of the 1960s.

High costs and the various problems connected with housing have no doubt contributed to the decline of a resident population during this period. The combined population of the two boroughs in 1961 amounted to 218,528; in 1971 to 184,392, a decline of 34,136. That the shortage of housing continued to be a main preoccupation of the time in spite of the erection of the tower blocks of council flats that now hedge the royal borough, was a sign of the pressure caused by the various forms of expansion. Conservation had a practical as well as aesthetic and historical reason. But the latter give a vigorous commentary on the credits and debits of modern change, affecting both public buildings and private houses.

The harmony of eighteenth-century architectural style and the late Victorian as represented by the work of Norman Shaw and Charles Robert Ashbee still has its pleasure to give on Cheyne Walk and Chelsea Embankment. Though no longer a private house, No 17 Chelsea Embankment, Norman Shaw's celebrated Old Swan House (1876) retains all its exterior elegance of design. On the other hand to be regretted is the disappearance of the Magpye and Stump House, 37 Cheyne Walk (1895) designed by Ashbee, a parallel in its graceful verticality of bay with Shaw's style. The house, built on the site of the fifteenth-century Magpye and Stump, burnt down in 1886, was demolished in 1968. Equally a matter for regret is the disappearance of The White House from neighbouring Tite Street. Designed by Edward William Godwin for Whistler (1877) it was of especial note both for its association with the artist and its original-ity of plan, but it was demolished in 1964.

Concern at the disappearance of architectural landmarks was meanwhile growing and had its focus towards the end of the 1950s in the proposal to demolish the Imperial Institute as well as the Royal School of Needlework and other adjoining buildings to make way for the enlarged Imperial College of Science and Technology. The com-promise solution has preserved the tall central tower of Thomas Edward Collcutt as a feature of the Kensington skyline, if inevitably incongruous with the new and functional science buildings around. Two good results are to be chronicled; a new awareness of the com-paratively recent past that led to the formation of the Victorian Society in 1958 with the promise of an intelligent care for the best of a much slighted period; and the phoenix-like emergence of the Commonwealth Institute from the ashes of its imperial forerunner.

The Commonwealth Institute, opened in 1962 at the southern tip of Holland Park and facing Kensington High Street had a clearer sense of purpose than the old building of 1893, founded by the Prince of Wales to commemorate Queen Victoria's Golden Jubilee.

The Commonwealth idea replaced the Imperial in the architectural design of Sir Robert Matthew, completed in 1962, and the themes and methods of display. An informal tent-like appearance amid the trees of the Ilchester Estate was an original feature. The interior presents a brilliant series of displays country by country in ordered sequence, the old dominions at the base, the African states in the middle gallery and above the islands in all the seven seas. The pictorialisation of facts and figures, photographs, painted backgrounds and characteristic products are skilfully contrived on the lines conceived by the Exhibition designer, James Gardner, to give each its own atmosphere. Art gallery, cinema and library add to the value of the whole remarkable conception.

A pleasant modern feature of Holland Park is the number of young men and women to be seen in camping rig and representing many nationalities, making their way to the King George VI Memorial Youth Hostel. The building designed by Sir Hugh Casson and opened in 1959 has its annex in the restored East Wing of Holland House and contrasts in its modern plainness with what survives of ornate Jacobean design. Institutional building has flourished in the last two decades. The hand-made brick and Portland stone, with flanking royal symbols of sculpture of the Central Library in Kensington designed by E. Vincent Harris and opened in 1960, is a grandiose start for the new Civic Centre to be completed by the new Town Hall, designed by Sir Basil Spence and rising on the site of the Niddry Lodge of the 1830s and its grounds.

The nature of modern architecture is by no means stereotyped as Sir Basil Spence's Knightsbridge Barracks (1967–70) has somewhat controversially shown. Many buildings have a functional character that is expressive of present-day purpose. The Royal College of Art building at Kensington Gore, opened in 1962 and the work of a consortium of designers, H. T. Cadbury-Brown, Sir Hugh Casson and Professor R. Y. Goodden, is a sober foil to its spectacular neighbour, the Albert Hall. Structural simplicity characterises the modern premises of the Chelsea College of Science and Technology and the Chelsea School of Art at Manresa Road. The newest of the borough's museums, the National Army Museum in Royal Hospital Road, opened in 1974, makes good use of brick in an exterior of dignified plainness. Grown larger than Sandhurst could accommodate, the collections illustrative of military history to 1914, with separate galleries of uniforms, equipment and military paintings are seen to full advantage.

Almost a new town though by now with an established profile, Notting Hill Gate comprises the lofty Campden Tower (1962), a boulevard of large stores and a link with the realm of the embassies in Kensington Palace Gardens in the Czech Centre designed by Sir Robert Matthew. A last stand of the local conservationist was made in the 1970s on behalf of the former Coronet Theatre which became the Gaumont Cinema in 1950, nostalgic memory bringing to mind the time when Sarah Bernhardt acted there.

In the two main thoroughfares, the King's Road Chelsea and the Kensington High Street, it would be possible to note many incidental changes in recent times, but these are probably best summed up in the crowds each attract, so varied in type and attire and, more than ever in the past, representative of many nationalities; the shops and entertainments that serve them adding a transient glamour to an area of London that otherwise has still a local character of its own.

Index

Index

Index

Index

Index

Ifield Road, 247
Ilchester, Earls of, 164, 167, 174, 226, 229
Ilchester Place, 174–5
Imperial College of Science and Technology, 217, 239, 249
Imperial Institute, 157, 216–17, 249
Inverness, Duchess of, 185–6
Ireton, General, 165

James I, 40
James, Henry, 81–3; memorial in All Saints, 30
Jekyll, Thomas, 234
Jennings, Henry Constantine, 131–2
Jerrold, Douglas, 210
Jervoise, Richard, 27–8
Joachim, Joseph, 224, 228
John, Augustus, 128
Johnson, Gerard, 178
Johnson, Dr Samuel, 54, 61, 62, 86–9, 130
Jones, Lady Catherine, 38
Jones, Inigo, 45, 164
Jones, William, 60, 149–50

Keene, Charles, 108–10
Kensal, 157
Kensal Green, 206
Kensal Green cemetery, 157, 185, 186, 219
Kensing Holt, 157
Kensington, origin of name, 156
Kensington Canal, 157
Kensington Church Street, 198, 222
Kensington Court, 220
Kensington Gardens, 157, 187–90, 238
Kensington Gore, 157, 203, 220, 250
Kensington High Street, 158, 198, 201, 209, 217, 223, 244, 245, 248, 249, 251
Kensington House, 193, 220
Kensington Palace, 155, 177–87
Kensington Palace Gardens, 190–91
Kensington Park, 246–7
Kensington Square, 155, 192–5, 196–7, 222

Kent, Edward, Duke of, and Duchess of, 184, 186
Kent, William, 178, 181, 182, 190
King, John, 49
King George VI Memorial Youth Hostel, 250
King Henry VIII's Conduit, 190
King's Road, 32, 36, 55, 108, 121, 146–8, 251
King's Square, 192
Kingsley, Henry, 30–31, 120
Kingston House, 203
Kip's engraving of Beaufort House, 20, 117–18
Kneller, Sir Godfrey, 126, 186
Knewstub, W. J., 94
Knightsbridge, 248
Knightsbridge Barracks, 250
Knyff, Leonard, 20

Ladbroke Grove, 246
Ladbroke Square, 246
Lanchenick, J. C., 238
Landseer, Sir Edwin, 172, 185, 238
Lang, Andrew, 240
Lansdowne House, 244
Laszlo, Philip de, 243
Lavery, Sir John, 243
Lawrence, S., 126
Lawrence, Sir Thomas, 166, 205
Lawrence Chapel, All Saints, 28
Lawrence House, 35
Lawrence Street, 46, 85
Lawson, Cecil Gordon, and F. Wilfrid, 108
Lear, Edward, 241
Le Blon, Christopher, 44
Lechmere, Lord, 199
Lee, Thomas Stirling, 115, 116
Leech, John, 219, 222–3
Leete, Ralph, 43
Leighton, Lord Frederic, 213, 214, 223, 226–8, 229, 235
Leighton House, 227–8
Lemon, Mark, 210
Lennox, Lady Sarah, 167
Leoni, Giacomo, 36

Index

Index

National Army Museum, 250
National Art Library, 236
National Art Training School, 213
National Loan Collection of Lantern Slides, 236
National Science Collection, 239
Natural History Museum, 155, 216, 239
Nicholson, Sir William, 244
Niddry Lodge, 250
'Nine Elms', 54–5
Norden, Robert, 178
North Kensington, 206, 248
Northcote, James, 85
Northumberland, Duchess of, 27
Notting Barn Farm, 206
Notting Barns, 163
Notting Hill Farm, 206
Notting Hill Gate, 198, 250–51
Notting Hill Studios, 244
Nottingham, Heneage Finch, Earl of, 177
Nottingham House, 177

Oakley, Edward, 143
Oakley Street, 46, 79
Oakwood Court, 175
O'Brien, William, 168
Observatory Gardens, 241
Old Church, Chelsea, 26–31
Old Church Street, 48
'Old Swan', 55–6, 57, 119
Old Swan House, 249
Onslow Square, 210
Orange House, 97
Oratory, Brompton Road, 217, 219
Orbell's Buildings, 200
Ormond House, 47
Orpen, Sir William, 243

Page, Thomas, 220
Palace Gate, 209, 232
Palace Green, 191, 210, 235
Panizzi, Anthony, 173
Paradise Row, 37–8, 46–7, 91, 84–5, 108, 146
Park Tower hotel, 248

Parmentier, J., 126
Parry, Sir Hubert, 196, 197
Paultons Square, 148
Paxton, Sir Joseph, 211, 212
'Peacock Room' (by Whistler), 234
Peel Street, 202
Pembridge Villas, 223
Penta hotel, 248
Pepys, Samuel, 38, 44, 49, 56
Peter Pan statue, 189
Petyt House, 48
Pheasantry, The, 147
Phillimore, Lord, 202
Phillimore, William, 240
Phillimore, William Robert, 241
Phillimore Gardens, 240
Phillimore House, 241
Phillips, Sir Richard, 62
Physic Garden, 50–53, 140–43
Pickering, Evelyn, 97
Pitt, Stephen, 200
Pitt Street, 200
Polytechnic, Chelsea, 148
Ponsonby, Lord Arthur, 192, 193, 196
Pontings Store, 198, 200, 244
Poole, Henry, 116
Pope, Alexander, 39
Population, of Chelsea, 145–6; of Kensington, 208, 249
Portobello Farm, 206
Portobello Housing Estate, 245
Portobello Road, 206; street market, 245–6
Pottery Lane, 207
Poynter, Sir Edward, 213, 214, 223
Pre-Raphaelites, 93 ff, 127–8, 223
Princes Gate, 234, 235
Prinsep, Mr and Mrs Thoby, 223–4
Prinsep, Valentine, 229
Prospect Place, 85
Pryde, James, 243–4
Public Library, Chelsea, 148; Kensington, 244, 250
Punch, 210

Queen Elizabeth College, 202
'Queen's Elm', 54

Index

Index